Indian Business Groups

Strategy and Performance

Ram Kumar Kakani
Santosh Sangem
Madhvi Sethi

FOUNDATION
BOOKS

FOUNDATION
BOOKS

Foundation Books is an imprint of Cambridge University Press, India.

Cambridge House, 4381/4 Ansari Road, Daryaganj, New Delhi 110 002

www.cambridgeindia.org

First published 2015

Printed in India at AnVi Composers, New Delhi - 110063

ISBN 978-93-84463-37-3 Hardback

Table of Contents

List of Tables and Figures

Tables

Figures

Preface

This book focuses on product diversification strategies of business groups and the dynamics of its underlying relation to shareholder value. Product diversification as a business strategy has a long checkered history. From being amongst the most preferred strategies for driving growth from the early twentieth century to its fall from grace in developed countries to its revival attempts in the early twenty-first century, product diversification has been at the center of numerous debates, especially in the developed world. At the time that conglomerates in market-based developed economies were adopting the focus strategy, business groups in developing countries and other developed economies (especially in continental Europe) were increasing the extent of diversity of their business activities. While a number of them have proven to be adept in successfully handling this strategy, there are a large number of failures as well along the road to product diversification.

The major challenges faced by these diversified business groups include financial difficulties brought about by wasteful use of resources, professionalization of management, and managing promoter family dynamics. Liberalization and the process of opening up of developing economies has played an important role in generating opportunities for value creation across industries. Further, the last two decades have witnessed the growth of the 'new economy' with traditional sectors gradually losing their dominance in business activity.

A new set of challenges have once again been thrown up before such diversified business groups following the global credit crunch that began in the US in 2007, bringing into question their performance and the appropriateness of the diversification strategy. The rapidly changing dynamics of world markets and the technology of serving them make it imperative for top management of business groups to be highly adaptable in their approach to corporate strategy and selection of portfolio of businesses and their composition within a group.

Extant studies on value creation by diversified business groups tend to take a macro/institutional approach with diversified business groups seen as alleviating the problems created by deficient institutional structures. However, a corollary of these studies is that diversified business groups would decline in importance and possibly lead to value destruction as these institutional deficiencies are remedied across economies that have undertaken the process of reforms and economic liberalization. Both anecdotal evidence and recent academic studies suggest that the reverse outcome has occurred in developing economies, i.e., far from declining in importance, business groups have increased their dominance over business activity.

Intrigued by the continued presence and growing importance of business groups, we decided to explore the underlying dynamics of their strategy, or more precisely the decision to diversify across multiple product/service lines and the impact of the same on value creation in the Indian context. The Indian context is unique in that during the post-liberalization era of the 1990s, most business groups faced serious financial difficulties with some even struggling for survival and ultimately losing their erstwhile dominant presence. The 2000s has witnessed a revival of some of these business groups whereas many others are still searching for the appropriate strategic response to the new economic and institutional environment.

In this book, we explore the dynamics of product diversification strategy of Indian business groups through a combination of both empirical analysis and the case study approach. Overall, we cover a long period of more than 25 years of business group activity in the Indian context. We attempt to relate the performance of Indian business groups to their diversification strategy placed against the context of institutional change in the Indian economy. While we do observe that unrelated product diversification had a negative impact on value creation until the 1990s, we also note that the negative impact of such diversification on value creation had begun reducing since the late 1990s. The case studies of select business groups help us bring out more clearly the underlying factors that have been influential in the success or otherwise of the unrelated diversification strategy of Indian business groups. The combination of these underlying factors and the new institutional features of the Indian economy bring out some hitherto unexplored perspectives with their implications for management of unrelated diversified enterprises.

Acknowledgements

We gladly take this opportunity to thank all the people who have helped us through the process of producing this piece of work chiefly at IIM Calcutta, including Professor Neelakantan Ramachandran and Professor Vanga Nagi Reddy, and remain grateful to the financial support from the Aditya Birla Centre for Management Research of London Business School and the continuing support from XLRI Jamshedpur.

We would like to extend our thankfulness to Professor Tarun Khanna of Harvard Business School and Professor K. R. S. Murthy of IIM Bangalore (retired Director) for their guidance during this work. Special thanks go to Professor Sushil Khanna for sharing his data on mergers and acquisitions in the Indian corporate sector and for his detailed suggestions. Our heartfelt gratefulness towards Professor Mritunjoy Mohanty and Professor Anup Sinha and all other members of faculty at IIM Calcutta for their care and support.

We also owe our thankfulness towards our colleagues, Sajja Srinivas Rao, Sridev Ramaswamy, Biswatosh Saha, B. V. Phani, Chandrashekar Krishna Kumar, Diptesh Ghosh, Abdul Sakib Mandal, and Sanjay Basu for their assistance, criticisms, and useful insights, and also towards the doctoral students of IIM Calcutta with whom we share plenty of fond memories. We gladly acknowledge the support and encouragement of friends Syed Shabbirul Haque, Noolu Srinivas Krishna, D. R. Rao, Kukatlapalli Shaniya Khanam, Shashidhar Srinivas, Polireddy Bhaskar Subramanya Srinivas, Subodh Das, and Tooshima Sarkar.

Finally, we thank our family members for their endurance and support – our parents, sisters and brothers, our spouses, and our in-laws for their affection, understanding, and patience.

1

Introduction to Business Groups and their Strategies

Strategic management is the process through which managers ensure the long-term adaptation of their organization to their environment (Chakravarthy, 1986). Corporate strategy is the conduct by a business organization of the composition of its cluster of tangible and intangible assets. Of the various corporate strategies that firms follow, diversification arguably ranks as among the most important. *Diversification*[1] is a movement by an organization (either a firm or business group) into a wider field of products/services/activities/geographies[2] to reach out to a larger body of customers. Product diversification has a broad spectrum ranging from limited endeavors into closely related activities at one extreme, to engagement in completely unrelated activities at the other extreme (Ansoff, 1971).

1.1 Diversification and business groups

Business groups are a group of firms often initiated by family/trust and bound together by equity cross-ownership and common board membership.

Business groups are formally independent firms that are interconnected on account of single common administrative and financial control, owned and controlled by either families or trusts or foundations. These business networks are usually owned through investment firms with cross-holdings among affiliates.

1 Diversification throughout the book refers to product diversification and not geographical (or international) diversification (unless specifically stated).

2 Throughout the book, the term '*product*' would also mean '*service*'. Thus, '*product markets*' would implicitly also mean '*service markets*' as well.

Industrial activity in most countries of the world continues to be dominated by these business houses.[3] They often diversify across different product lines with many divisions under them, similar to U.S. conglomerates[4] such as General Electric Co.[5] popularly known as GE. The Dangote Group[6] from Africa, started by Aliko Dangote, is another illustration of a conglomerate with diverse interests ranging from trading commodities to manufacturing cement. In India, for instance, the A. V. Thomas group[7] controls a host of firms predominantly in the businesses of plantations and consumer products, whereas the Tata group firms controlled by the House of Tatas[8] operate in diverse product portfolio encompassing steel to software to salt.

Business houses may exhibit insignificant individual differences yet differ in systematic ways when aggregated according to suitable criteria. A business group's long-term performance would primarily be an outcome of its overall strategy, a critical element of which is the business group diversification strategy. It comprises decisions to efficiently utilize, add, retain or divest the group's existing portfolio of resources (or assets). Some of the main issues faced by a business group's strategists are: (a) choice of product and service portfolio to create economic value and (b) the mode and timing of additions and divestments in resources (or assets).

Organizational performance and organizational effectiveness are two of the many categories under which the aspects of performance of diversification strategies have been discussed. Usually, financial metrics are used to measure an organization's performance. The dimensions of such measures could be wide-ranging from an organization's shareholder value to its accounting profitability or economic profitability. Numerous scholars (e.g., Alberts and McTaggart, 1984; Myers, 1984) have frequently advocated the need to integrate perspectives from financial theory with strategic management. This book is an attempt in that direction with the focus of this work being business groups in India.

---

[3] Throughout the book, 'business group' and 'business house' mean the same.

[4] A large organization in multiple lines of business wherein there is no coherence or inherent relation between them.

[5] Please see http://www.ge.com/ for more detail (accessed in September 2013).

[6] Please see http://www.dangote-group.com/ for more detail (accessed in September 2013).

[7] Please see http://www.avtnatural.com for more detail (accessed in September 2013).

[8] Please see http://www.tata.com/ for more detail (accessed in September 2013).

1.1.1 *Governance mechanism within groups*

Business group affiliates often share a common brand identity (e.g., Tatas or Birlas[9] in India; Samsung[10] in Korea and Dangote in Africa), draw upon a common labor pool and rely on each other for financing (Fisman and Khanna, 1998). Groups, through interlocks, would allow knowledge about technological advances, market opportunities and innovative strategies, to flow among firms in the group (Keister, 1998). The common thread that often runs through group affiliates acts as a social mechanism that also reduces the likelihood of reneging of contracts (Granovetter, 1994, 1995). A case in point being the preference in the labor markets for being associated with popular business groups such as Murugappas[11] (in South India) or Adani Group[12] (in West India) or RP-Sanjiv Goenka Group[13] (in East India) or Jaypee Group[14] (in North India) as an employee compared to other types of organizations. Several of these features put groups at an advantage in dealing especially with the difficulties facing producers in emerging countries (Khanna and Palepu, 2010).

We propose that each Indian business group could be regarded as a group of firms with largely coordinated strategic decisions driven by the founding family members/promoters since:

- The managers of member firms are appointed by the business group (or, after taking the consent of the business group's senior management) to exercise control over their member firms. For instance, key decisions in Reliance Group[15], founded by Dhirubhai H Ambani, do need approval of its current group head, i.e., Mukesh Dhirubhai Ambani.
- There is a close relationship among managers of member firms; they take decisions as a single strategic unit. Moreover, the decisions are

---

[9] Please see http://www.adityabirla.com for more detail (accessed in September 2013).

[10] Please see http://www.samsung.com/hk_en/aboutsamsung/ for more detail (accessed in September 2013).

[11] Please see http://www.murugappa.com for more detail (accessed in September 2013).

[12] Please see http://www.adani.com/ for more detail (accessed in September 2013).

[13] Please see http://www.rp-sg.in/ for more detail (accessed in September 2013).

[14] Please see http://www.jalindia.com// for more detail (accessed in September 2013).

[15] Please see http://www.ril.com/html/aboutus/aboutus.html for more (accessed in September 2013).

taken in the aggregate interest of the business group as a whole.[16] For instance, though Reliance Group consists of over 100 member firms (i.e., associates and subsidiaries), most, if not all, strategic decisions of member firms reflect the aggregate interest of the business group.[17]

Moreover, we also observe member firms helping one another with financial and/or real resource transfers in times of financial distress or business hardship or otherwise. For example, when Birla Tyres, an affiliate of the BK Birla group[18] had trouble (during 1990–2010 period) – other BK Birla Group affiliates, namely, Kesoram Industries and Texmaco ensured enough support to sail through those tough times even at the cost of their falling in financial trouble. In fact, Birla Tyres is now a division of Kesoram Industries. Similarly, whenever Kingfisher Airlines, an affiliate of the UB Group[19] headed by Vijay Mallya had financial difficulties (during 2005–2010), other UB Group affiliates ensured support to sail through the tough times – before Kingfisher Airlines hit a dead end. As pointed out by Mazumdar (2008), all such events in the history of Indian business groups generally are consequences of unilateral decisions at the group level and not a product of negotiation between the managements of different affiliates of the group.

> *One of the strategic imperatives that often lies behind the structuring and restructuring of connections between group companies is actually the maintenance of control over each of them. In other words, the Indian business group is a deliberate creation of its single controlling authority and not the forging of an alliance between different such authorities.* (Mazumdar, 2008, p.5)

Therefore, for our purpose, the business groups with affiliated companies under them are not radically different from the U.S. conglomerates with many divisions under them[20] or the Japanese *keiretsus* with member firms under them. However, there exist significant differences in organizational structure between

---

16 Even when there is a clash between the interests of the business group and a member firm, usually the group's interests are given priority (see Piramal, 1996, 1997).

17 Interested readers can refer to the URL: http://www.ril.com/html/aboutus/subsidiaries_associates.html to take a peek of a sample list of associates and subsidiaries of the Reliance Group (accessed in September 2013).

18 Please see http://www.kesocorp.com for more detail (accessed in September 2013).

19 Please see http://theubgroup.com/ for more detail (accessed in September 2013).

20 Li and Li (1996), Milgrom and Roberts (1992) and Ito (1992) also make this point in the context of Japanese *keiretsu* firms.

Indian business groups and the conglomerates of the U.S. or the *keiretsus* of Japan. For instance, unlike the U.S. conglomerates, where the parent company rather than shareholders of the parent company usually have controlling stakes in a collection of lines of business, firms affiliated with Indian business groups are typically owned by a distinct set of shareholders rather than by a single parent company having controlling stakes. Another example is all the firms of Japanese *keiretsus* being linked by the same bank (holding stake) unlike present Indian business groups[21] (Fields, 1995).

There is a key difference between the Indian business group structure and that of the conglomerate structure typically found in developed, market-based economies (e.g., GE in the U.S.). The typical conglomerate structure relies on 'controlling interest', i.e., an equity stake of 51 per cent or more held directly by the parent holding company or through cross-holdings of subsidiaries as defining the entities that are part of the conglomerate. In the case of most Indian business groups, the 'parent company'/promoters combined with group companies hold significantly lower stakes. Thus, 'significant influence', a feature of associate companies[22] rather than 'control' is a key characteristic of Indian Business Groups. One may consequently suggest that this structure represents similarities with the 'kieretsu' system in which the main bank held less than controlling stakes in the kieretsu firms.[23] However, the Anti-Monopoly Law Reform of 1977 in Japan prevented the main banks from holding more than 5 per cent equity stake in non-banking firms. The identification of the 'main bank' and the 'kieretsu' in the body of research is largely dependent on the extent of funds borrowed from the main bank rather than equity stakes. While these differing ownership structures have interesting implications on corporate governance aspects; they are not the primary concern of this book and will be referred only to the extent that they have an effect on product diversification strategies.[24]

---

21 Snapping the close ties between Indian business groups and banks was an important stated objective of the bank nationalization of 1969.

22 'Associates' and the concept of 'Significant Influence' have been defined in various accounting standards such as IAS-28 (IFRS), SFAS-115 (US GAAP), and AS-23 (Indian GAAP). Significant influence is typically associated with equity stakes of 20 per cent and more.

23 Some researchers have been claimed that 'kieretsus' were a convenient fiction introduced in the 1960s Marxian debates on monopoly capitalism (Miwa & Ramseyer, 2002).

24 The institutional and historical dimensions leading to the emergence of such governance structure of Indian business groups and the implications thereof form part of a currently ongoing research project of the authors.

India has witnessed large-scale industrialization post-independence. Business groups adopted varied strategies during this expansion, some far more successfully than the others. This choice and implementation of strategies received a boost after 1985, with the arrival of the era of industrial delicensing of industries. Post-liberalization, both academicians and the press have been engaged in numerous discussions[25] regarding the success or otherwise of a particular diversification strategy for business groups vis-à-vis other strategies in the Indian scenario. Analysts have cited an organization's dominance of certain product markets or its stock market returns as evidence of a successful diversification strategy based on a wide range of arguments.[26] However, there has been no detailed long period empirical study on business groups to resolve this diversification strategy-aggregate performance puzzle in India. The implications of success/otherwise of diversification strategies vis-à-vis other strategies and their effects on profitability, growth, risk, and other financial and non-financial dimensions of business groups are also in need of examination. This book is an attempt to explore this issue and enable one to solve this puzzle.

1.2 Corporate diversification strategy

Diversification usually involves the operation of a business organization into new production (or distribution) activities. It may, therefore, involve only a small change of direction or a dramatic shift into entirely new lines of business (Saple, 2000). Diversification may be achieved by buying firms already serving the target markets or by making green field investments. Organizations diversify for various reasons, ranging from counterbalancing for technological obsolescence to employing excess productive capacity to reinvestment of earnings. For example, most East-Asian organizations diversify to create internal factor markets[27], which are more cost-effective in allocating resources

---

[25] For in-depth study please refer to *Business Today*, 1997 anniversary issue, 22 August 1997, 22 July 2000 issue, 12 February 2006 issue, 16 October 2011 issue. (also see Bagchi, 2000; Iyer, 2008; Purkayastha, 2009; and Jadhav, 2011)

[26] Refer Jadhav (2011); Karanjia (1997); Piramal. (1996, 1997); *Business Week* magazine: 14 April 1997 issue.

[27] Internal factor markets include product markets, labor markets, and financial markets. Case in point is the fact that most East-Asian organizations depend on their internal capital markets for their financing needs rather than accessing external capital markets. For example, see, Shin and Park (1999) on the Korean Chaebols.

compared to external markets (Claessens et al., 1999). On the other hand, some of the African organizations diversify to ensure that they are part of the market for 'corporate-control'. The Africa-based TGI Group[28] (with CHI and Cormart Brands) is an investment and holding company with diversified interests and investments in Nigeria, Ghana, Republic of Benin, Morocco, South Africa, and several other emerging markets.

According to Ansoff (1971), there are three main objectives behind organizational diversification – *growth*, *stability*, and *flexibility*. Diversification with *growth* is an objective designed to take advantage of favorable conditions. Diversification with *stability* as the aim acts as a hedge against unfavorable trends and foreseeable contingencies. Diversification with *flexibility* as a goal strengthens the organization against unforeseeable contingencies. Ansoff further pointed out that a strategy of diversification which is highly desirable for one of the objectives is likely to be less desirable for others. For instance, the forays by Reliance Mukesh Ambani Group into retail and (lately) sports[29] could be considered as product diversifications with the motive of *growth*. On the other hand, the software venture of the KK Birla Group[30], CFCL Technologies, could be considered as product diversification with the motive of *flexibility*. Then, again, the foray by CK Mehta Group[31] into real estate, away from their traditional focus of Fertilizers and Chemicals, may be considered as product diversification with the motive of *stability*.

Gleuck (1980) had pointed out that diversification can be used not only for growth in a particular business but also for a change of corporate direction. It has also been suggested that a business group whose growth expectation is stymied by life cycle maturities may also seek diversification into new product markets (Reed and Luffman, 1986)[32]. In such cases, the reason for branching out would be a change of direction necessary for survival rather than growth and profitability. The Welspun group[33] venture into saw pipe manufacturing

---

28 Please see http://www.tgi.co.za/ for more (accessed in September 2013).

29 Indian Premier League's (IPLs) cricket team Mumbai Indians is owned by the Reliance Mukesh Ambani group.

30 Please see http://www.chambalfertilisers.com/index.php?option = com_content&view = article&id = 27&Itemid = 137 for more (accessed in September 2013).

31 Please see http://www.mehtagroup.in/ for more (accessed in September 2013).

32 Two of the three illustrations provided earlier may be perceived from this perspective as well.

33 Please see http://www.welspun.com/ for more (accessed in September 2013).

in 1998, far away from its core business of cotton textiles, is a case in point of survival and change in direction. During the 2000s, this pipes division of Welspun group not only provided stability but also led the strong growth of the group placing them among the recognized Asian leaders in the fields of Line Pipes. Of late, Welspun group has been endeavoring an entry into the infant Solar Energy sector.

While the extent of diversification can be measured in a number of ways, it is hampered by the difficulty of precisely defining the boundaries between different products, markets, and industries. The more narrowly defined these activities are, the greater will be the apparent degree of diversification. For instance, diversification decisions of a business group measured with respect to 3-digit SIC (Standard Industrial Classification)[34] product scheme will be greater and more apparent than when measured with respect to 2-digit SIC product scheme. Similarly, diversification decisions of an entity measured with respect to 6-digit NAICS (North American Industrial Classification System)[35] product scheme will be greater and more apparent than when measured with respect to 3-digit NAICS product scheme.

Advantages of product diversification

- First, it encourages the efficient allocation of resources. A business group can choose where to invest their funds and, thus, can concentrate on the stronger markets, using its surplus in some divisions to help others grow. Some groups arrive at such decisions by making use of popular tools such as the BCG Growth-Share Matrix, a portfolio planning tool developed by the Boston Consulting

---

[34] Standard Industrial Classification (SIC) is a numerical classification made by a U.S. government body for classifying all types of industrial activity. It is an expandable four-digit classification of all manufacturing and non-manufacturing industries. The longer the number, i.e., the SIC Code, the more specific the subject. So, a bicycle manufacturer such as Avon Cycles, 2-digit SIC Code would be 37, i.e., discrete manufacturing of Transportation Equipment and its 4-digit SIC Code would be 3751, i.e., discrete manufacturing of bicycles and related spare parts. Thus, it defines an establishment by its principal activity. Economic units that use like processes to produce goods or services are grouped together. The term NAICS refers to the North American Industry Classification System. The NAICS system is a 6-digit code. It was created in 1997 to replace the older SIC Codes.

[35] See 34 ibid.

Group in the early 1970s. Another similar tradition tool is the GE/McKinsey Matrix, a nine-cell portfolio matrix developed by the McKinsey & Company in the 1970s for screening the U.S. Conglomerate *General Electric*'s (GE's) large portfolio of strategic business units (SBU).

- Second, the diversified organization can create a large internal capital market and, therefore, overcome financing constraints.
- Third, by opening up opportunities to run individual businesses, the diversified group helps to create a trained, loyal talent pool of top managers.
- Fourth, it can create significant tax advantages. For example, by carrying forward the losses to one division to offset the taxable profits of another division resulting in a lower tax outgo.
- Fifth, the diversified configuration spreads its risk across different product markets, whereas the focused organization has all its eggs in one product market basket.
- Sixth, and perhaps the most important, if used effectively, the diversified organization can make divisions fine tune their processes and systems while the headquarters can concentrate on the strategic portfolio. It can acquire new businesses and divest itself of old, unproductive ones (Ramu, 1998; Mintzberg and Quinn, 1998).

Disadvantages of product diversification

- First, the diversified organization could invest in too many businesses (which are far apart in terms of technology) and, hence, could lose their focus and become difficult to manage effectively.
- Second, they might invest too much in businesses with poor investment opportunities, bleeding out money from the group.
- Third, diversified group could practice cross-subsidization of failing business segments leading to a disincentive structure for the performance of successful divisions within group and vice versa.
- Fourth, there can be an information asymmetry between the central management and affiliate member (or divisional) managers in decentralized business groups. The information cost will be higher in conglomerates than in focused organizations.
- Fifth, and the most important, there are a lot of hidden costs due to diversification, such as those from the loss in time/resources due

to reporting and interaction between the division managers and the headquarters often leading to slow and poor decisions (Porter, 1980; Claessens et al., 1998; Ramu, 1998).

1.2.1 *Definition of diversification strategy*

For the purpose of this book, we define corporate diversification strategy as the entry or exit of an organization from lines of business activity (Ramanujam and Vardarajan, 1989). This could be by processes such as internal business development, expansion, acquisition, joint venture, strategic alliance, merger, divestment, and sell-off. This will also entail changes in its administrative structure or maintenance of status quo, systems, and other management processes. Further, following Pitts and Hopkins (1982), we use the term diversity to describe the extent to which organizations are simultaneously active in a number of distinct businesses.

1.2.2 *Types of diversification strategy*

Galbraith (1998) suggested that there are three types of product diversification, namely, *related*, *linked*, and *unrelated* diversification. While in unrelated diversification the common features are generally limited to finance and business management; in related diversification, on the other hand, additional synergies are present, such as technological know-how, marketing and distribution expertise, or facilities in production. Linked diversification, unlike related diversification, involves moving into new industries and operating at different centers of concern in those industries. The key aspect is that these industries are linked to one another by virtue of either being input providers or output consumers in the same value chain.

Related diversification

A firm following related diversification branches out into new, closely related business lines/product lines. In related diversification, there is evident potential synergy between the new and the core business based on a common facility, asset, channel, skill, and even opportunity (Mintzberg, 1998). The relationship revolves around the organization's core center. There are usually a pool of strong corporate staff and some centralized marketing, manufacturing, and research facilities.

For instance, in India, Marico Group[36] with its flagship business affiliate Marico Limited after initially starting in the coconut hair-oil products industry has been expanding into hair care, refined oil, hair care, personal care, male grooming, and so on to pursue new growth opportunities. However, each move into a new industry by Marico is made at the group's center of gravity. The new businesses are all consumer products in the global beauty and wellness space that are driven through advertising by brand managers and based on its strong distribution network in India, Bangladesh, Middle East, and other nearby African and Asian countries.

Linked diversification

This type of diversification involves moving into new industries and operating at different centers of gravity in those industries (Galbraith, 1998). However, there is a connection of some type among various businesses. Vertical integration is a form of linked diversification. A firm can integrate 'backward', i.e., it can begin producing products which were earlier procured from others, or it can opt for 'forward' integration, i.e., it starts producing new products and services, including distribution services, and moves closer to the final consumer. Usually, the reasons for vertical integration are technology, demand uncertainty, market failure, or high transaction costs and prices discrimination.

The Ambani groups' Reliance Industries Limited (RIL) followed this type of corporate development during the period of Dhirubhai Hirachand Ambani (1970-2002). Initially RIL was a producer of textiles (1970s). As such, it vertically integrated backwards to manufacture polyester-based yarn (1980s). From there, it moved downstream within the polyester industry by running polypropylene and polyethylene process plants (1990s). Simultaneously, it also started moving into the petrochemicals business. In the late 1990s, RIL had also commissioned a petroleum refinery project. However, these new businesses are in industries in which the company diversified from its upstream core. These new ventures are not operated for the benefit of the center of gravity but are stand-alone profit centers. Similarly, in the early 2000s, RIL moved towards oil and gas exploration businesses, i.e., towards the downstream core (Saha et al., 2011).

[36] Please see http://www.marico.com for more (accessed in September 2013).

Unrelated diversification

An expansion strategy which entails the spread of an investment portfolio over a wide range of unrelated products by the business group to avoid massive losses due to industry-specific idiosyncratic factors is regarded as unrelated diversification. In this case, there is departure from existing areas through entry into the same market with new products based on different technology or entry into new markets with new products. Unrelated diversifiers usually use acquisition or joint venture routes, while related companies rely more on internal development. All of the sales, advertising, distribution, and manufacturing functions are typically decentralized to the divisions.

BK Birla Group and JK Corp Group[37] are good illustrations. BK Birla Group operates in textiles, cement, wagon building, tyres, and so on; while, JK Corp is into automotive belts, dairy produce, polyester, paper, white cement, tyres, and so on. The purpose is usually to insulate the company's earnings from the uncertainty of any one industry or from the temporal business cycles in specific sector. Another purpose could be to make use of an opportunity (due to say, political or bureaucratic affiliations or even particular core competency) such as the availability of an industry license in a very profitable and highly protected industry.

In summary, several patterns of strategic change can occur in a business establishment based on its diversification strategy adopted. These involve changes to the establishments industry of origination, changes to the focus of the organization, or some combination of the two.

1.3 Business groups

1.3.1 Definition of business group

Chang and Choi (1988) define the business group as a collection of formally independent firms under a common administrative and financial control, owned and controlled by certain families.[38]

---

[37] Please see http://www.jktyre.com/aboutjktyre/other_grpcomp.aspx for more (accessed in September 2013).

[38] A lot of academic discussion about this organizational form is going on, with economists (Amsden and Hikino, 1991; Leff, 1976, 1978; Khanna and Palepu, 1998a, 1999; Whitley, 1990), sociologists (Granovetter, 1994, 1995; Hamilton, 1996) offering a range of reasons for the existence of business groups. Prominent writers have emphasized that institutions affect economic outcomes (Granovetter, 1985; Aoki, 1984, 1990; North, 1994; Williamson, 1985).

Encarnation (1989) referring to Indian 'business houses' emphasizes multiple forms of ties among group members based on family, caste, religion, language, ethnicity, and region.

Leff (1976, 1978) defines the business group as 'a multi-company firm' having two essential features. First, it draws its capital and high-level managers from sources that transcend usually a single family. The group's owner-managers typically include some members of the family within which the group's activity originated. However, what distinguishes this institution from the family concern and what gives it resources for greater scope is the fact that owner-managers from other families also participate. Candidates are people linked by relations of interpersonal trust, on the basis of similar personal, ethnic, or communal background.[39] Second, the groups usually invest and produce in several product/service markets rather than in a single product/service line. These products/services may be quite diverse, ranging from computer software to consumer durables to chemicals to consulting. These activities are sometimes selected on the basis of vertical integration. In other cases, new investments have been made in product/service markets that are unrelated, to act as a hedge or pursue a profitable opportunity. At times, they also invest in activities where the group's technical and/or managerial capabilities are applicable as inputs.

Hazari (1966) in a classic study conceptualized the business group as a single business organization and as a decision-making unit even though it constitutes a large number of individual companies.

> ... Corporate group may be defined as constituting of units which are subject to the decision-making power of a common authority... The group functions as a single organization, nevertheless, though each of the corporate units under its control is a separate legal entity. (Hazari, 1966, p.5)

For this study, we define a business group as 'a collective of formally distinct entities promoted and owned by either a family(ies), trusts or foundations set up by such family(ies), or by a body corporate(s) and that have ties to each other by virtue of common managerial and economic control, though not necessarily legal control.' For instance, the Kalyani Group[40], nurtured by Baba Kalyani, controls a host of firms predominantly in Forgings, Auto Components, Engineering Steel, and related areas. Another example is the Welspun group (previously referred

39 For example, the Tata group headed by Cyrus Mistry and the Godrej group headed by Adi Godrej.

40 Please see http://www.kalyanigroup.com/ for more (accessed in September 2013).

to in Section 1.2) promoted by two different families, namely BK Goenkas and RR Mandawewala, operating in highly diverse areas from home textiles to line pipes to renewable energy. Another example is that of the Kewalram Chanrai Group[41] founded in the year 1860 by two enterprising Indians, namely Jamatmal and Thakurdas. Today, the group is one of the largest in the continent of Africa.

1.3.2 Existence of business groups

Coase (1937) and Williamson (1975) suggest that organizations exist because they can mediate economic transactions between their members at lower costs than the market mechanism.[42] This can happen in institutional contexts wherein business groups acquire prominence because they can contribute to more efficient allocation by utilizing their generic non-marketable or non-marketed strengths – like access to privileged internal information and in-house managerial talent; access to assets and resources either from internal sources or from external sources by leveraging on reputations gained in other activities; or being able to use their existing reputation in new product/service markets, and so on (Mazumdar, 2008). The success of Ghanshyam Das Birla[43] in nurturing the Birla Group (during the 1920s–60s, especially the pre-independence period) and the success of Dhirubhai Hirachand Ambani[44] in creating the Reliance Empire (during the 1970s–90s period, especially during the pre-liberalization period) are cases in point. Hence, in some countries, the business group will be preferred to relatively costlier markets owing to an underdeveloped financial system. It has also been suggested that product liability and certain other liabilities can be reduced or avoided in business groups (Schwartz, 1985; Bethel and Liebeskind, 1998).

A similar rationale is advanced in the market disequilibrium perspective by Lecraw and Morrison (1993). They maintain that when markets are not functioning efficiently, opportunities would exist to internalize transaction activities for exploiting inefficiencies in the economy. As a consequence, market imperfections in the existing economic conditions (in both developing and developed economies) and the ability of the business groups to internalize transactions efficiently might explain the existence of various forms of diversified business groups.

---

41 Please see http://kewalramchanrai.com/ for more (accessed in September 2013).

42 See, Mazumdar (2008) for an interesting discussion.

43 See an interesting dialogue on Ghanshyam Das Birla in his work titled 'In the Shadow of the Mahatma: a personal memoir', *Orient Longmans*, 1953.

44 For more detail, refer to URL: http://www.4to40.com/legends/print.asp?p=Dhirubhai_Ambani (accessed in September 2013).

There are also non-economic reasons in the literature for the existence of business groups explaining their existence to be based on cultural and social reasons (Richter, 1999). For example, groups are often initiated by a single family and bound together by equity cross-ownership and common board membership as a mechanism of control and not of allocation of capital. Nicodano (1998) observed that the creation of a business group is just another way to deviate from one-share-one-vote principle by owners. This way of deviating produces a larger price differential in holding (and sub-holding) companies, leaving it unaltered in operating companies. Similarly, Tricker (1984) maintained that business groups, by pyramiding ownership through a vertical array of subsidiary firms, can concentrate its ownership over a large number of different firms, at the same time enabling it to assume a scale impossible to achieve with their own limited capital.

Cross-holdings and pyramidal ownership also leads to a lower bankruptcy risk to the business group even if a few group affiliates were to fail while providing them the real options for future growth in sunrise industries. In other words, it also provides a business group the classic advantages of limited liability partnerships over general ones.[45] The ownership structure of many groups such as the Ashok Garware group with its flagship company Garware Offshore Limited and holding company Garware Marine Limited is an illustration of this (see, Saha et al., 2011).

1.3.3 Business group effects

The various effects of business groups as in the extant body of literature are summarized as follows:

- Within business groups, corporate culture consists of a set of written or unwritten rules, beliefs, norms, guidelines, philosophies, or patterns to be followed by members of the group. Business groups have relied on their unique corporate values to help them improve their brand image and grow successfully. Granovetter (1994) suggests the existence of a 'moral economy' within groups which creates an atmosphere of enhanced trust wherein business group activities are conducted. He suggests that a business group's advantage also originates from a 'principle of solidarity', which may reside in family, kinship, or ethnic ties across the group's members. For instance, the unique corporate

45 See Kakani and Joshi (2006) for an illustration of the same in the Tata group.

values of Ambanis (Reliance Group), Singhanias (JK Corp Group), Kirloskars (Kirloskar Group), and Tatas (Tata Group) added with the principle of solidarity existent in the social community to which they belong/reside is indeed a key reason behind their success.

- The coordination of investment and production decisions by the business houses has both reduced the need for and lessened the burden on government planning of modern industrial sector activities in developing countries (Fisman and Khanna, 1998).
- Family governance can create value when the external market-based governance mechanisms are underdeveloped. The benefits of superior governance may manifest themselves in several ways. For example, groups that develop a superior reputation for non-opportunistic behavior might benefit in the cross-border market for accessing foreign technology and capital (Amsden and Hikino, 1991; Guillen, 1997). Generally, the ability of groups to resolve the information and contracting problems, through family bonds or otherwise, can lead to performance benefits (Khanna and Palepu, 1998a).
- Membership in diversified groups with multiple publicly listed affiliates can be associated with conflicts of interest between controlling group and other shareholders and, hence, could also be associated with agency problems. For example, groups can misallocate capital by investing cash flow generated by profitable groups in unprofitable investments (Khanna and Palepu, 1998a; Saha et al., 2011) for personal benefits rather than shareholders' value maximization at the affiliate level. Large business groups, especially from business communities known for such behavior, are often discounted by stock markets as they are avoided by institutional investors.
- Business groups are reputed to be opaque and less transparent than non-groups and have more opportunities given their more complicated structures to engage in questionable practices to the detriment of minority shareholders (Kali and Sarkar, 2011). In other words, they may willfully escalate information asymmetries vis-à-vis other shareholders for their own benefit (Ali et al., 2007; Anderson et al., 2009).
- The relatively better ties of business groups with the political and bureaucratic apparatus in the country leads them to extracting benefits from the state besides insulating them from external interference and monitoring (Dutta, 1997; Khanna and Palepu, 1998). This is the root cause of much of the asserted rent-seeking behavior in which groups are

often believed to indulge. One form of such rent-seeking behavior is to use the political connections to shield the member firms from outside interventions and to erect barriers to competition in those areas in which groups are disproportionately active. It is fairly well known that most of the business groups in construction, infrastructure, real estate, and related businesses do have access to strong political connections and tend to have large rent-seeking behavior.[46]

- Promoter-managers of a diversified group can make sub-optimal decisions due to lack of expertise in a variety of industries leading to destruction of shareholder value of the group and its minority shareholders. The last chapter of this book has vivid illustrations of the same.
- Signs of business group instability due to badly designed succession plans and improperly demarcated professional decision-making can create risks for alliance partners and other stakeholders (Pant and Rajadhyaksha, 1996). The events and rumblings in the MP Birla Group during 2004–2013, i.e., after the demise of Priyamvada Birla is an apt illustration of this. They happen when the centralized control over a group becomes incompatible with the individualities of the members who constitute that controlling authority (Mazumdar, 2008).

The intrusion of family roles into the professional sphere, poor demarcations of responsibility, and the resultant lack of clarity about where decisions get made create problems for business groups. Also, in business groups, familial relations may override competence (Pant and Rajadhyaksha, 1996) in the decision-making process. This fact is often visible in single family-based business groups. Similar indications were visible inside the Reliance Group during 2002–2004 – after the demise of their patriarch, Dhirubhai Ambani. Evidently, the social capital inside the group worked its way toward a new

---

46 There are large illustrations of such behavior in the media. See, for example,

(a) 'Friend or Foe? Wait and Watch': http://archive.tehelka.com/story_main30.asp?filename=Ne260507Friend_or_CS.asp (accessed in May 2014);

(b) Please see http://timesofindia.indiatimes.com/news/city/hyderabad/Lanco-group-chief-joins-Congress/articleshow/36910133.cms (accessed in May 2014);

(c) Please see http://businesstoday.intoday.in/story/challenges-for-unitech-builders/1/13887.html (accessed in May 2014);

(d) Please see http://indiatoday.intoday.in/story/coal-beneficiaries-donated-to-political-parties/1/217715.html (accessed in May 2014);

(e) Please see http://www.ndtv.com/article/india/full-transcript-your-call-with-naveen-jindal-273981 (accessed in May 2014).

equilibrium resulting in the creation of two business groups, namely, Reliance Mukesh Ambani Group[47] and Reliance Anil Ambani Group.[48]

1.4 Progress of business groups and the Indian economy

1.4.1 Indian groups: Concept

Piramal and Herdeck (1985) observe that the Indian business groups have been formed on the basis of the '*managing agency system*' established by the British adventurers during the nineteenth century, also known as *European controlled agency system*. This system allowed them to control vast commercial empires with a minimum of capital. At best, the '*managing agency system*' could result in certain efficiencies by pooling administrative, marketing, and production operations. At its worst, it left shareholders of the operating company at the mercy of selfish agents who milked the companies dry. By 1970, the government had completely abolished the system. An examination of the debates during 1970–75 in the Economic & Political Weekly and other works by Indian authors suggests that the peculiar features of regulatory implementation of abolition was responsible for the adoption of the legal structure of business groups that has continued until today. Investment firms with cross-holdings in companies sprang up in place of managing agencies primarily to shelter income and to conceal ultimate ownership (Herdeck and Piramal, 1985). At present, business groups in India largely control their affiliates through corporate block holding as this serves as a cross-holding mechanism wherein affiliate members within a group hold one another's equity.[49]

Lately, with the passing of the Limited Liability Partnerships Act (LLPs) in India in 2009, we observe that most business groups in India have started holding their companies through LLPs as well.[50] For example, in 2010, Reliance Mukesh

---

[47] Please see http://www.ril.com/html/aboutus/mukesh_ambani.html for more detail (accessed in September 2013).

[48] Please see http://www.relianceadagroup.com/ada/index.html for more (accessed in September 2013).

[49] This allows the owning family of a business group with limited capital to still maintain operational and administrative control within a large number of associate firms (Encarnation, 1989; Richter, 1999; Kakani and Joshi, 2006).

[50] A Limited Liability Partnership is a hybrid of partnership firms and companies and is a separate legal entity with liability being limited to the extent of stake held by a partner. For more, please refer to http://www.llp.gov.in/ (accessed in July 2010).

Ambani Group restructured its shareholding in India's most valuable company, i.e., Reliance Industries Limited, by transferring their stake to a large number of LLPs.[51] Tax experts state that LLPs offer tax efficiency over other forms of holding ownership.[52] Though internal family conflicts, due to increasing ramifications, have forced many groups to divide their assets among family members in recent years, the concept of business groups still continues and prospers.

1.4.2 *Features of Indian groups*

The organizational structure of a business house is commonly one where the promoter holds the top managerial position in most affiliate firms or employs family, friends, or founding members in such positions, the group being controlled by interpersonal relations (Gadgil, 1951). Affiliates of Indian business groups are legally separate entities, have their own shareholders, and publish their own financial statements[53]; however, there is no group bank concept as is the case in Japanese *keiretsus*.[54] Nonetheless, there is coordination of action among group members, partially orchestrated by common board members and through the involvement of the family or founding (trust) member(s) in each group (see Khanna and Palepu, 1998b; Saha et al., 2011).

Mazumdar (2008) rightly points out that participation of a multiplicity of closely linked families in providing capital and administration has not been an essential feature of Indian groups. While groups of Indian business families did cooperate during the pre-independence era, the primary objective of doing so was to challenge the British dominance of capitalist enterprise at the time. Most business groups in India and other emerging markets are dominated by a single

---

51 The names of some of the LLPs are: Bhuvanesh Enterprises LLP; Ajitesh Enterprises LLP; Badri Commercials LLP and such. For more detail please refer to http://www.ril.com/html/investor/shareownership.html (accessed in May 2014).

52 Tax experts say that (a) LLPs do not attract minimum alternate tax (MAT); (b) Tax rate on income is fixed at 30 per cent for LLPs, 3 per cent lower than limited companies; and (c) Indian companies are liable to pay 15 per cent dividend distribution tax which works out to 16.6 per cent including surcharge and education cess. In respect of distribution of after tax profits, LLPs do not attract distribution tax. For more, please refer to *The Economic Times*, 26 August 2010).

53 This is unlike business groups in Europe (especially Scandinavia), where the holding company is listed on stock exchanges and the affiliates are normally not listed.

54 Specifically, after the bank nationalization of 1969, the 'group bank' system to the extent it previously prevailed was completely wiped out.

family that has typically been associated with the group for decades (Dutta, 1997). This family involvement creates a system of social norms that reduces intra-group transaction costs by encouraging information dissemination among group associates, reducing the possibility of contractual disputes and providing a low-cost mechanism for resolution of disputes (Khanna and Palepu, 1998a). This is unlike many groups in the East-Asian countries such as Indonesia (e.g., the Salim Group[55]). Pant and Rajadhyaksha (1996) point out some peculiarities of Indian groups vis-à-vis groups in other countries. They observe that Indian business groups are usually family-based ones. These family-based business groups have certain cultural idiosyncrasies in certain areas, e.g., inheritance norms and differential treatment of male and female successors.

1.4.3 Transition in the Indian economy

- **Pre-1985 era**

  During the pre-1985 era, most Indian groups tended to prefer conglomeration and growth. One explanation often offered for the conglomerate form in numerous Indian business houses during this era is the existence of the erstwhile Indian Monopolies and Restrictive Trade Practices (MRTP) Act of 1969. The MRTP act and the regulated licensing procedures often restrained expansion in a single localized line of business for a business group due to the the potential possibility of monopoly situations (Chopra, 1985). This led to many business groups taking up licenses in almost all sectors.

  Various government policies influenced the diversification decision by the business groups. The licensing policy dictated the timing, size, and location of the new entrants and the expansion of existing capacity. Most Indian groups remained unfocussed due to the distribution of industrial operations under the government policies (see also, Saple, 2000). This was supported by lack of competitive pressures in the protected Indian domestic markets. This usually led to a safety-first approach in the form of conglomerate growth by Indian business houses (Dutta, 1997). So till 1985, business houses could think of diversifying or expanding in only those

---

55 Please see http://www.mahabharatmotors.com/salim.htm for more detail (accessed in September 2013).

sectors (or industries) in which they had a license and their strategic decision-making was limited to that extent.

- **1985–91 era**
  With the industrial reforms during 1985–1991, many of the regulations governing business group expansion (in the same sector) and new entry (in a new sector) were relaxed. Industrial licensing was abolished for most sectors (such as cement) except those related to strategic and security concerns.[56] Government approval was no longer required for new investment, mergers, or takeovers by a business house. Opening up of the industrial sector and the consequent increase in competition (Mookherjee, 1995) meant that business groups had to reassess their portfolio of activities. There was a sudden increase in the restructuring of the business group's portfolio, through expansion, splits, and mergers. Most of the restructuring activities of the post-1985 era could be described as '*strategic*' rather than government '*policy*' driven (see also, Kelkar and Rao, 1996; World Bank, 2000) as in the past.

- **Post-1991 era**
  Several positive developments had occurred on the institutional governance front since India's 1991 foreign exchange crisis:[57]
  (a) The erstwhile Controller of Capital Issues (CCI) was abolished and Securities and Exchange Board of India (SEBI) was created as a regulatory body with the explicit mandate of improving the functioning of capital markets.
  (b) The incentives of the state-run financial institutions to monitor were improved (Joshi and Little, 1997). They began to be weaned off their historically privileged access to low-cost funds. The resulting need to access public capital markets made them more conscious of the bad loans on their balance sheets. Deregulation of interest rates and the gradual elimination of consortium requirements increased competition in the financial sector.
  (c) Private sector mutual funds were allowed to compete with the state monopoly, Unit Trust of India (UTI).

---

56 Economic Survey reports for the year 1985–91, Government of India.

57 Economic Survey reports published by the Government of India every year list the changes made in detail.

(d) A takeover code was introduced in late 1994, making firms with low promoters holding and firms misusing minority shareholders money vulnerable to takeovers.[58]

(e) Restrictions on the entry of foreign investors were eliminated and regulations on their investments were substantially clarified. Salient features included the removal of floors and ceilings on investments.[59]

(f) With the implementation of the new industrial policy, most sectors were liberalized (except defense-related industries).

(g) Indian *Rupee* was made convertible to a limited extent.

(h) Many import restrictions and quotas were gone, tariff barriers were also brought down, and export industries were given more sops.

India has also seen the removal of the MRTP Act and opening up of its economy leading to an improvement in the state of its institutions governing markets post-liberalization. The decrease in import barriers/tariffs apart from the de-licensing of industries also led to an increase in the level of competition faced by business groups (World Bank, 2000).

1.4.4 Diversification issues of groups

Due to increasing industrial deregulation, business groups decided to have a re-look at their diversification strategies, restructure their portfolios, and be more competitive. If till 1985, business groups' diversification strategies were more driven by the then existing license raj, with the advent of gradual de-licensing of most sectors, they now had to decide about their diversification issues and strategies.

Some of the strategic issues facing the business groups were as follows:

- To what extent should their portfolio of industries/products be diversified?
- On what basis should they allocate resources in the portfolios' constituents?
- Should diversification be into related or unrelated areas?

---

[58] However, they were also provided an opportunity to increase their own stake at significantly lower prices compared to the market prices.

[59] Nevertheless, there was a ceiling on investment in a single firm by a foreign institutional investor of up to 5 per cent of voting rights of the firm.

These strategic questions become particularly important in case where a business house had pursued a strategy of unrelated diversification in the past (based on the licenses it had obtained). As the economy became more competitive, the importance of optimizing performance of a business group increased not only for its growth but also for its survival.

1.5 Background, motivation, and research problem

Most of the empirical literature on corporate diversification and performance has focused on firm-level analysis. Comparatively, there has been very little work on business group-level research. Probably keeping this in mind, Khanna and Palepu (2000) concluded their Journal of Finance paper as follows:[60]

> Our primary focus has been the performance of individual firms in a group. While we provide some preliminary analysis of group performance, an interesting topic for future research is to more fully explore the cross-sectional variation of the performance of Indian business groups as a function of group characteristics.

The above statement and the issues deliberated below provided us the background and motivation for this research work:

1. *Limited research in a developing country:*

Despite the large amount of literature that has analyzed the relation between corporate characteristics and accounting numbers, a need for serious research in developing countries such as India exists. Existing research has been largely based on the developed economy context, primarily the U.S. – the theories that have thereof resulted, need to be studied for their applicability in other countries. Moreover, India is a good representative for a diverse emerging economy; and the industrial scenario in India has been and is dominated by business houses.

---

60 Khanna, Tarun and Krishna Palepu. 2000. 'Is group affiliation profitable in emerging markets? An analysis of diversified Indian business groups.' *Journal of Finance* [formerly, Harvard Business School Working Paper 96-1051].

2. *Little research in the area of corporate diversification strategies of business groups and their effect on group performance:*

Khanna and Rivkin (1999) state that in India there are more than 300 business groups with 3.5 firms average per group. Their results also show that group membership makes a significant contribution to the explanatory power of variation in affiliates' performance. Indian business houses have adopted various diversification strategies, some successful and some unsuccessful. Unfortunately, research on the relationship between business group diversification and performance has been conspicuously absent. There was no systematic empirical research in India on the impact of corporate diversification strategy on financial performance of business groups. As a consequence, very little is known about diversification in a business group or the effects of diversification on business unit profitability and growth.

3. *Limited 'long time frame' research exploring economic performance of business groups:*[61]

Economic cycles and temporal factors do affect short-run studies. There has been no research (to our knowledge) in India on business groups that have taken care of the same with a longer time frame.

4. *Diversification strategy studies of business groups' in India need to be well-documented:*[62]

Studies done to date on the linkages between aggregate group performance and diversification strategy have been preliminary and lack generalizability. Examination of the financial performance of the business houses would be interesting because the performance differential may have been generated by the diversification strategies of the business houses. Detailed comparison of the performance components and other financial and non-financial variables might indicate the reasons behind the existence of any performance differential due to diversification and other group characteristics (such as, ownership, leverage, and size).

---

[61] In fact, we have not come across any specific empirical literature looking at aggregate business group performances vis-à-vis their diversification strategies and group characteristics.

[62] Except for the work done by Khanna and Palepu (2000), we have not come across any other study.

5. *Effect of policy changes on aggregate group-level financial performance and on group-level corporate strategies:*

Owing to gradual de-licensing and deregulation, there have been a lot of policy changes (including increase in competition) which might influence the aggregate shareholder value of a business group and its constituents in addition to their corporate strategies (such as, geographical and product diversification strategies). So, it will be interesting to examine the effects of these on the performance of business houses.

Based on the above discussions, the objective of our work is to examine the issues relating to diversification and performance of Indian business groups and evolve plausible explanations for the following questions, which the head of any business group typically faces:

- Is success/failure a random phenomenon independent of the diversification strategy adopted by the business group?
- What product diversification strategies should we follow in our businesses to create shareholder value?
- Are diversified business groups better performers than specialized groups?

Based on the above, the focus of this book is on examining *'the relationship between financial performance and diversification strategy of large business houses in India.'*

1.5.1 *Studying the effects of transition in the Indian economy*

The book also extends research on emerging economies by examining groups' characteristics and their performance in the context of major policy changes. It is unlikely that the effects of liberalization strategies will be fully understood unless the microeconomic responses by business groups to these policy changes are better analyzed. To study these micro-responses, India offers interesting advantages for two reasons: (a) significant economic changes have taken place in India. These changes resulted in significant deregulation of product and financial markets leading to increase in the level of domestic and international competition; and (b) large diversified business groups have continued to dominate the private sector in India. Hence, our work will also span the pre-liberalization period to post-liberalization period to identify the precise business group characteristics that had become more (or less) important due to changes in the industrial competitive policy, reduction in trade barriers, and the resulting globalization of trade in India.

1.5.2 Advantages of using Indian data

India has a number of characteristics that make it particularly well suited for such a research work. Most business group affiliates are listed, stocks of a large number of group affiliates are publicly actively traded, and unlike in many other countries (Strachan, 1976; Goto, 1982), firms are members of only one group. Further, the existence of large number of business groups in India, their data availability, and their clear demarcation facilitates empirical analysis. Moreover, (a) *accounting statements in India* are prepared according to well-established accounting standards that are at least similar in quality to those followed in many advanced economies such as Denmark and Germany (see CIFAR, 1995; Easterly and Ross, 1997); and (b) *stock markets in India* are quite large and have a history of over hundred years. These factors also increase our confidence in the reliability of the data. In this book, we shall primarily focus on the listed affiliates of Indian business groups on account of the unavailability of continuous data for all unlisted affiliates. However, we did collect financial and ownership data of unlisted affiliates of 15 randomly chosen business groups for 2000–01, 2004–05, and 2008–09.[63] With the exception of one business group, listed affiliates accounted for over 90 per cent of the revenues and profits of the group. Hence, the sample of affiliates for each business group may be considered as representative of the strategies and performance of the concerned group.

1.6 Organization of the work

In Chapter 2, we will briefly review the literature on and practices of business groups in other countries. In Chapter 3, a detailed review of the academic literature on diversification measures, and financial performance measures is presented. In Chapter 4, we develop our conceptual framework and the metrics used in this study. We also present a summary of our research questions in this chapter. In Chapter 5, we present the specific hypotheses borne out by our research questions and the details of the econometric methodology to be adopted. We also present the results of our econometric analysis for the period 1987–99. In Chapter 6, we perform an in-depth case-study analysis of select business groups for the period 1987–2013. This

[63] The groups were – Ashima, Garware, Ghia, Hamco, JM, Kalyani, Nava Bharat, Raunaq, Satyam Computers (Rajus), Tata, Torrent, Thackersey, TVS, Williamson Magor, and WS Industries.

also helps us develop a more nuanced understanding of the performance of business groups in the institutional context underlying the rapid liberalization of the 2000s. Finally, in Chapter 7, we present a summarized discussion on our findings and the implications of the same for business group strategic decision-making.

2

Business Groups across the Globe

Business groups dominate most economies. They are ubiquitous in emerging economies, where they control a substantial proportion of a country's productive assets and account for the largest and the most visible of the country's firms (Amsden and Hikino, 1991; Granovetter, 1994; Khanna and Rivkin, 1999; Mazumdar, 2008). Around the world, some of the largest firms in many countries are controlled by business groups (largely, family-based), such as Dangote (Nigeria), Fiat (Italy), Ford (U.S.), Hutchison Whampoa (Hong Kong), Maersk (Denmark), News Corp (Australia), Overseas Chinese Banking Corp (Singapore), and Samsung (South Korea). Further, many business groups have a long history. For instance, the Jardine Matheson group (Hong Kong/Singapore), the Wallenberg group (Sweden), and the Bolloré group (France) were established more than 150 years ago. However, like all other types of organizations, business groups have specific characteristics that differ from one country to another. In this chapter, we discuss the same in a few large countries across the globe. The discussion in this chapter highlights the central role of the controlling family/families at the top of a business group in designing corporate structures such that agency-related problems are minimized.

2.1 Japanese *keiretsus*

The key component of the Japanese environment is the existence of well-diversified business groups called *keiretsu* or industrial group. It is a distinctive feature of Japan's economy attracting considerable attention. This institution coordinates the activities of member firms and finances much of their investment activity. The complex relationship among firms within these groups is characterized by cross-ownership of equity, close ties with the groups' main banks, and product market ties with the other firms in the groups (Aoki, 1984). Much of the financing comes from the large city banks that form the core of each of the large groups: they are both creditors and shareholders of group firms (Hoshi et al., 1991). It is for this reason that Japanese firms are known to operate in an environment that appears to mitigate information problems in the capital market.

During the pre-war period, Japan had extremely large, diversified conglomerates (*zaibatsu*), controlled by wealthy families and dominating the Japanese economy (Hadley, 1970; Yafeh, 1995). As for the post-war period, there exists a number of controversial group affiliation definitions commonly used in the literature.[1] This is because *keiretsu* members are related to each other through a variety of ties, especially informal and unwritten including cross-shareholding and exchange of personnel. Japanese *keiretsus* are also organizations in which individual managers have considerable autonomy in their firms but coordinate their activities through the President Council and a common Main Bank (Hoshi and Kashyap, 2001). However, this might go to such an extreme that Japanese *keiretsus* have often been criticized as being 'headless bodies' because there is no dominant shareholder who bears responsibility for the actions of the group members and also values the private benefits derived from their control (Masulis, Pham, Zein, 2009).

Japanese system itself evolved out of a restrictive regulatory environment. It is widely believed that capital was scarce at least through the mid-1970s. This was exacerbated by government regulations that imposed interest-rate ceilings and limited the ability of firms to raise money abroad. In this environment of capital rationing, it was important for firms to form close relationships to banks, which were at the time the only source of capital. Thus, the firms that were able to form close ties to a bank were less liquidity constrained, although the economy as a whole may have been liquidity constrained (Hoshi et al., 1991). The literature distinguishes among horizontal, bank-centered corporate groups (*keiretsu*), and vertical, manufacturer-centered *keiretsu*. Horizontal *keiretsus* are centered on one of the six major city banks and are extensively diversified across a range of industries. In contrast, vertical *keiretsus* consist of manufacturing firms like Toyota or Hitachi and multiple tiers of suppliers, and are characteristically concentrated in one industry.

Risk sharing is an important function of the Japanese *keiretsu* corporate groups (Aoki, 1988; Nakatani, 1984). The traditional findings are that the *keiretsu* firms

1 See Weinstein and Yafeh (1995) for a detailed discussion.

tend to have not only lower operating profitability but also lower variance. The results support the idea that there is insurance within the group, though this insurance comes with a cost in terms of lower average profits. Lincoln (1996) argues that underperforming firms in Japan recover faster if they are members of one of the large six bank-centered groups. His work also shows evidence on risk sharing under the auspices of the main bank within the big six groups. In contrast, there have been few recent studies that challenge the traditional idea of insurance provided by *keiretsu* (Beason, 1998; Kang and Stulz, 2000). A noted feature of Japanese and Korean business groups is the dispatch of senior management to assist affiliates in specific projects such as business turnaround, new venture start-up, or foreign market entry (Gerlach, 1992; Guillen, 2000).

We provide below a short write up on one of the most popular Japanese *keiretsu*, namely, the Mitsubishi Group.

2.1.1 Mitsubishi group

Mitsubishi Group was established by Yataro Iwasaki in 1870 with shipping as its core business. Its initial diversification was mostly into related fields such as coal-mining (fuel for ships), shipyard (for repairing ships), and marine insurance. The managerial resources and technological capabilities gained through these ventures were utilized to get into many unrelated businesses such as automobiles, food, and chemicals. To fund all these ventures and ensure easy flow of funds, a bank, namely Mitsubishi Bank, was founded in 1919. Table 2.1 shows the key group affiliates of the group:

Table 2.1: Mitsubishi group and its major group companies

Bank	Major industries	Major group affiliates
Mitsubishi Bank (until 1996)	Banking & Securities, Chemicals, Commerce, Construction, Consulting & Research, Elderly Care, Electrical	Asahi Glass, The Bank of Tokyo-Mitsubishi UFJ, JX Holdings, Kirin Holdings, Meiji Yasuda Life Insurance, Mitsubishi Aluminum, Mitsubishi
Bank of Tokyo-Mitsubishi (1996–2005)	Machinery, Environments, Fibers Foods, Hotel, Foundations, Information, Communication & IT, Insurance, Machinery, Metal Products, Mining	Chemical, Mitsubishi Corporation, Mitsubishi Electric, Mitsubishi Estate, Mitsubishi Fuso Truck & Bus, Mitsubishi Gas Chemical, Mitsubishi Heavy Industries, Mitsubishi Kakoki, Mitsubishi Logistics,

(Continued)

Table 2.1 (Continued)

Bank of Tokyo-Mitsubishi UFJ (2006–) **Mitsubishi Trust and Banking**	Nonferrous Metals, Organizations, Precision Machinery, Pulp & Paper, Real Estate, Resources & Energy, Rubber Products, Ceramics & Glass, Steel Products, Temporary Work Services, Transport Equipment, Travel & Recreation, Warehousing & Transport	Mitsubishi Materials, Mitsubishi Motors, Mitsubishi Paper Mills, Mitsubishi Plastics, Mitsubishi Rayon, Mitsubishi Research Institute, Mitsubishi Steel Mfg, Mitsubishi UFJ Securities Holdings, Mitsubishi UFJ Trust and Banking, Nikon Nippon Yusen Kabushiki Kaisha, P.S. Mitsubishi Construction, and Tokio Marine & Nichido Fire Insurance

Source: URL www.mitsubishi.com (accessed on 14 September 2013)

The Mitsubishi group adheres to a set of principles known as 'Mitsubishi principles'. It is articulated by the fourth president of the Mitsubishi organization, Koyata Iwasaki, in the 1930s: (a) *Shoki Hoko*: Strive to enrich society, both materially and spiritually, while backing preservation of environment; (b) *Shoji Komei*: Maintain transparency and openness, conducting business with integrity & fairness; and (c) *Ritsugyo Boeki*: Expand business, based on an all-encompassing global perspective.

In the recent times, Mitsubishi Corporation, a group affiliate of the Mitsubishi Group, has become one of the world's largest general trading companies with operations in over 80 countries worldwide. In 2013, the group had over 600 group companies with one of the most popular among them being Mitsubishi Motors, the car manufacturer.

2.2 Korean *chaebols*

Many Korean firms belong to conglomerate business groups known as '*Chaebols*'. The *Chaebol* firms operate in a variety of different industries, are bound together by a nexus of explicit and implicit contracts, and maintain substantial business ties with other firms in the group (Bae et al., 2000). It is also widely believed that important corporate governance systems, including incentive-compensation contracts and legal systems to protect outside investors, are not well-established in *chaebols*. The larger *chaebols* in Korea are much more directly linked to state agencies and are dependent on their priorities than the business groups in other countries. Hence, the *chaebols*' growth patterns reflect the preferences of and opportunities provided by politicians and planners (Jones and Sakong, 1980: 269–285). The resulting agency problem is largely attributable to the *chaebols'* inherently weak governance structure. The typical *chaebol* firm does not have an outside director on the board and equity ownership by professional management is negligible. In addition, member firms within the same *chaebol* are connected by an extensive arrangement of reciprocal shareholding agreements.

One notable feature of the *chaebol* is that ownership is heavily concentrated with an individual who has almost complete control over all firms within the group. Such an ownership structure tends to provide the owner-managers of a *chaebol* with strong incentives to diversify their wealth and human capital (Amihud and Lev, 1981) and to take excessive risks to expand the *chaebol* into large different industries. Large institutional shareholders are always viewed as passive, due to the regulations on the exercise of their voting rights, and tender offers and other hostile acquisitions are rare in Korea (Bae et al., 2000). Since the owner-managers of a *chaebol* have substantial discretionary power over all important strategic decision-making, they can easily expropriate other investors in the firm by investing the firm's resources to maximize their welfare.[2] This type of agency problem is likely to be more pronounced given that poor investor protection and the lack of corporate governance mechanisms insulate owner-managers from external influences and leave them free from discipline.

Chaebol business groups served as a technology catch-up mechanism for firms during Korea's rapid growth in the 1960s–80s (Amsden, 1989). However, by the 1990s when many Korean firms had approached the technological frontier, business groups increasingly lapsed into expropriation devices for their family majority owners (Chang, 2006; Lee, Peng, & Lee, 2008). Many experts blamed *chaebols* for the East Asian financial crisis in the late 1990s. As a partial response to this financial crisis, multilateral financial institutions spearheaded a move for dismantling of business groups in South Korea. Also, there has been much pressure on the largest Korean *chaebols* to stop intra-group financial activity and to shed what are described as 'non-core assets' (Khanna and Yafeh, 2000). However, the results have been muted. However, there is some evidence that internal capital markets in the Korean *chaebol* conglomerates create value (Chang and Hong, 1999), although this view is challenged by Shin and Park (1999).

---

2 Vast literature exists in this direction. See Barclay and Holderness (1989); Barclay et al. (1993); Shleifer and Vishny (1997); La Porta et al. (1999); Wolfenzon (1999); and Johnson et al. (2000).

We provide a short comparative note on two *Chaebols* going through different levels of success, namely Hyundai and Samsung.

2.2.1 *Hyundai group and Samsung group*

Hyundai Group is a South Korean conglomerate founded by Chung Ju-yung. The first company in the group was founded in 1947 as a construction company. With government assistance, Chung and his family members rapidly expanded into various industries, eventually becoming South Korea's biggest *chaebol*. The company was forced to spin off many of its better known businesses after the 1997 Asian financial crisis and the death of its founder in 2001, including Hyundai Automotive Group, Hyundai Department Store Group, and Hyundai Heavy Industries Group. Lately, the group has now dwarfed itself and focuses on elevators, container services, and tourism. Hyundai Motor Company, a division of the Hyundai Kia Automotive Group, is the world's fourth largest automaker by units sold, operates the world's largest integrated automobile manufacturing facility, and is the world's fastest growing automaker – nonetheless the extent of management control by Hyundai Group is not clear from the existing literature.

On the other hand, the Samsung Group is South Korea's largest *chaebol* and the world's largest conglomerate by revenue with annual revenue of over US$270 billion in 2012. The Samsung Group is composed of numerous international affiliated businesses, most of them united under the Samsung brand including Samsung Electronics (the world's largest electronics and information technology firm by sales), Samsung Heavy Industries (the world's second largest shipbuilder), Samsung Engineering, Cheil Worldwide, Samsung C&T, Samsung Techwin, Samsung Securities, Samsung Life Insurance, and Samsung Everland (South Korea's first theme park) among others. Samsung group has a powerful influence on South Korea's economic development, and in 2012 it was estimated to contribute over 18% to the nation's GDP.

In 1938, Lee Byung-chull, son of a landowning family, founded Samsung Sanghoe, a small trading company with 40 employees in Taegu, Korea with just 30,000 won. The company prospered and Lee moved its head office to Seoul in 1947. After the Korean war in 1954, Lee founded Cheil Mojik and built the plant in Chimsan-dong, Daegu. It was the largest woolen mill ever in the country and this move took Samsung into the big league. Samsung diversified into many areas and Lee sought to establish Samsung as an industry leader in a wide range of enterprises and the company started moving into businesses such as insurance, securities, and retail. In the late 1960s, Samsung Group began the electronics industry. South Korean President Park Chung-Hee's regime during the 1960s and 1970s proved to be a big boon for Samsung. Since then Park focused his economic development strategy on a handful of large domestic conglomerates, protecting them from competition and assisting them financially. Samsung was one of these companies and Park banned several foreign companies from selling consumer electronics in South Korea to protect Samsung from foreign competition.

In the late 1980s and early 1990s, Samsung Electronics invested heavily in research and development, investments that were pivotal in pushing the company to the forefront of the global electronics industry. The 1990s saw Samsung acquire a number of businesses abroad. It also began to lead the way in certain electronic components. In 1993, Lee Kun-hee successor to Lee Byung-chull, downsized the company, and merged other operations to concentrate on three industries: electronics, engineering, and chemicals. In 1996, the Samsung Group re-acquired the Sungkyunkwan University foundation. Compared to other major Korean companies, Samsung survived the Asian financial crisis of 1997–98 relatively unharmed. In 2005, Samsung Electronics overtook Sony as one of the world's most popular consumer electronics brands. In 2012, Samsung Group accounted for 24 per cent of South Korea's exports, and in many domestic industries, Samsung is the sole monopoly dominating a single market. No wonder that the Group has a powerful influence on the country's economic development, politics, media and culture.

2.3 Chinese business groups

China is a transition economy having a different reform trajectory from its counterparts either in Eastern Europe or in some other emerging economies in transition (Peng, 2003; Peng & Heath, 1996). Chinese business groups have played critical roles, have received tremendous government support, and have been utilized as a tool to facilitate reform in China's ongoing institutional transition period (Gupta & Wang, 2004). Keister's (2000) book on Chinese business groups traces their origin from the post-reform period. Keister identifies three distinctive stages in the history of business groups in China. The first period was 1985 and 1986 when the Chinese government started to experiment with the establishment of business groups.

The second stage was the period from 1987 to 1989 when groups began to emerge both voluntarily and with the state's assistance. It was in 1987 that the state ministries first issued a formal policy document regarding the establishment and development of business groups to provide incentives for the state-owned enterprises to participate in the formation of business groups (Keister, 2000, p.67). The third period started in 1990 when business groups began to form readily both within and outside the state sector. This stage has seen the most rapid emergence of business groups in all industries and geographical areas.

Business groups in China have developed their own unique structures. The groups are large, multi-industry entities having strong ties with the state though not with any particular families (Keister, 1998), and in that sense, they are known as collective entities. It is of particular interest to note that business groups in state-owned sectors are not only the product of policy inducement, as found in Korea's emerging economy (Chang & Hong, 2000), but also the instrument used by the Chinese government to facilitate institutional transition and ownership reform (Ma & Lu, 2005; Yiu et al., 2005). Lee and Woo (2002) compare the main features and origins of the Chinese business groups with that of the Korean *chaebols*. They found that business groups in China tend to have more state shares, are more heavily indebted, are less profitable and accumulate capital more slowly than non-group firms, i.e., unaffiliated firms.

Peng (2006) and Jian (2007) demonstrate the prevalence of connected transactions within Chinese business groups. Yu (2009) points out that in China, hundreds of listed firms are restructured from existing enterprises through a 'carve-out', under which part of a business group is carved-out and set up as a to-be-listed firm, and the original business group remains the parent firm. Due to this unique ownership structure, connected transactions are almost a daily routine for the majority of listed firms in the country. We provide below a short write up on a Chinese group, namely the Haier Group.

2.3.1 *Haier group*

In the 1920s, a refrigerator factory was built in Qingdao to cater to the local (Chinese) market. After the 1949 establishment of the People's Republic of China, Haier was then taken over and turned into a state-owned enterprise. By the 1980s, the factory had debt of over CNY ¥1.4 million and suffered from dilapidated infrastructure, poor management, and lack of quality controls, resulting from the planned economic system and relevant bureaucratic policies. In desperation, the Qingdao government turned to a young assistant city-manager, Zhang Ruimin, responsible for a number of city-owned appliance companies. Zhang was appointed as the managing director of the factory in 1984. The new team launched refrigerators but found large quality issues in its products.

With China opening up to world markets, foreign corporations began searching for partnerships in China. At this time, Germany's Liebherr, a worldwide leader in premium refrigeration, entered into a joint venture contract offering technology to its Chinese counterpart. The installation of German equipment was accompanied by a new and rigorous commitment to quality. Combined with Zhang's disciplined management techniques, which broke from the tradition of the iron rice bowl in Chinese state-owned enterprises, the company began to turn around. With the success of Qingdao's refrigerator company, the municipal government asked it to take over some of the city's other ailing appliance makers. In 1988, the company assumed control of Qingdao Electroplating, making microwaves, and in 1991 took over Qingdao Air Conditioner Plant and Qingdao Freezer. Having diversified its product line beyond refrigerators, the company adopted a new brand name in 1991, 'Haier'. Steadily, the company set out to establish itself as the country's leading brand, focusing upon reliability and product quality and by quietly acquiring its rivals.

Its place in the domestic market was secure, and Haier moved onto the international stage with the goal of building a global brand name. The company opened a production facility in Indonesia in 1996 and in the Philippines and Malaysia in 1997. Haier continued its expansion into other international markets as well by settling up manufacturing facilities in the U.S., Europe, and Pakistan. Production facilities were even constructed in Jordan in 2003, greatly strengthening its position in the Middle East market. In Africa, Haier has plants in five countries: Tunisia, Nigeria, Egypt, Algeria, and South Africa.

Although under partial public ownership, Haier is still technically a 'collective' company, meaning that it is supposed to be owned by its employees. However, its actual ownership situation is opaque. Interference from state officials is a risk for state-controlled-enterprises like Haier. As a government entity, Haier Group was also officially barred from entering the stock exchange early on. However, the group needed funds for its expansion and, therefore, sought loopholes. In 1993, it listed a subsidiary Qingdao Haier Refrigerator Co. on the Shanghai Stock Exchange, raising CNY ¥370 million. In 2005, the group entered the Hong Kong Stock Exchange using a backdoor listing by acquiring a controlling stake in a publicly listed joint venture Haier-CCT Holdings Limited. In 2011, in just over 28 years of its formation, Haier was ranked as the largest Home Appliances and White Goods brand in the world with near 8 per cent market share and its refrigerators have been ranked as number one worldwide.

2.4 Taiwanese and Hong Kong business groups

There are a variety of forms of business groups existing, that are competitive in world markets, and these vary in certain basic characteristics because of the institutionalized socio-cultural and economic environment in which they have become established (Granovetter, 1995). Business groups in Taiwan tend to be small, loosely integrated entities characterized by didactic managerial style as opposed to the authoritarian style common in Korean and Japanese groups (Fields, 1995). The didactic style being explained by Taiwanese business networks traditional Confucian beliefs. Korea has many large, vertically integrated business groups, whereas business groups in Taiwan are smaller and horizontally integrated in the production of intermediate inputs (Feenstra et al., 1993). Noble (1998) traces the growth of Taiwanese Business Groups to the support they received from the Taiwan's Chinese Nationalist government (also called KMT) as part of their plan to control the commanding heights of the economy and allocated market entry rights to trusted elite entrepreneurs from prominent Taiwanese families who formed major business groups. An example of the same is the Formosa Plastics Group, a Taiwanese conglomerate.

2.4.1 Formosa plastics group

In 1954, the Formosa Plastics Group was founded by Wang Yung-Ching. In 1957, its plant produced 4 MT per day of Poly Vinyl Chloride (PVC) resin, the smallest PVC plant in the world at that time. It is currently chaired by Lee Chih-Tsuen. With over 50 years of development, the Formosa Plastics Group is now the largest private enterprise in Taiwan with diverse interests, including oil refining, petrochemicals, downstream intermediaries, fibers, plastics, textiles, carpets, electronic materials, transportation, and machinery products. The affiliate firms of the group include Formosa Chemicals and Fibre Corporation, Formosa Petrochemical Corporation, and more than 20 other investments in Taiwan, U.S., China, and Indonesia, in addition to several large educational and medical organizations. Lately, the groups' overseas expansions have been focused on the U.S. and China.

Redding (1996: 36) in a rich study on Hong Kong Business families[3] points out that overseas Chinese owned and managed companies typically respond by concentrating their efforts in one main field and, then, growing to replicating the same formula or through horizontally spreading into connected fields. Redding links this behavior to the strong needs of Chinese family to virtually dominate both strategy and operations by key individuals from the family based on their Confucianism values. An example of this comes by understanding the largest Hong Kong-based business group, namely Cheung Kong Group nurtured by its founder Li Ka-shing, the Chairman of Cheung Kong (Holdings) Limited and Hutchison Whampoa Limited.

2.4.2 Cheung Kong group

In 1950, Li Ka-shing started his own company, Cheung Kong Industries. From manufacturing plastics, Li led and developed his company into a leading real estate investment company in Hong Kong that was listed on the Hong Kong Stock Exchange in 1972. Cheung Kong continued to expand by acquiring Hutchison Whampoa in 1979 and Hongkong Electric Holdings Limited in 1985. Cheung Kong (Holdings) Limited is the flagship of the Cheung Kong Group, which has business operations in 56 countries around the world and employs more than 300,000 staff. As of 2012, in Hong Kong alone, the Group includes eight listed companies with a combined market capitalization of over US$100 billion. Hutchison Whampoa Limited is a Fortune Global 500 company. Based in Hong Kong, the Cheung Kong Group's businesses encompass such diverse areas as property development and investment, real estate agency and estate management, hotels, telecommunications and e-commerce, finance and investments, retail, ports and related services, energy, infrastructure projects and materials, media, and biotechnology.

2.5 Turkish business groups

The majority of large-scale firms in Turkey operate under a group affiliation and the business groups are mostly organized around a holding company, and are the outcome of investments by a single family or a small number of allied families (Yurtoglu, 1999). Very few Turkish companies are publicly traded and they exhibit highly concentrated and centralized ownership structures

[3] It is part of a edited book titled *Asian Business Networks* by Hamilton (1996).

(Yurtoglu, 2000). This issue helps keeping the affiliated firms as a coherent body among which resources could be shared and shifted as needed (Gonenc and Karadagli, 2004).

2.5.1 Koc group

Koc Group, founded by Vehbi Koc, with its headquarters in Istanbul, is a good example of a Turkish Business Group. Koç Holding A.Ş. is the top industrial conglomerate in Turkey, in terms of revenues, exports, and number of employees. Koc Holding has leading positions in energy, automotive, and finance sectors in Turkey, while holding strong leading positions both domestically and internationally in consumer durables. Vehbi Koç established the first firm in 1926 and collected all of the companies bearing his name under the roof of Koç Holding in 1963. He did this to centrally manage these companies and to provide optimum resource allocation. Having an annual growth rate of 23 per cent in the U.S. dollar terms over the past seven years, Koc Holding ranks among the 50 largest publicly traded companies in Europe and is part of the Fortune Global 500 list of largest companies in the world and this has made the Koç family one of Turkey's wealthiest dynasties.

2.6 Russian business groups

Russian business groups are usually horizontal financial-industrial groups (Perotti and Gelfer, 2001). Perotti and Gelfer (1999) argue that Russian Financial-Industrial Groups manage an internal capital market that may add value in the face of inefficient external capital markets in that country. Illustration of a Russian group is provided below using Gazprom.

2.6.1 Gazprom

Gazprom is a state-owned group and is the largest extractor of natural gas in the world. Gazprom was created in 1989 when the Ministry of Gas Industry of the Soviet Union transformed itself into a corporation, keeping all its assets intact. The company was later privatized in part, yet the Russian government still holds a controlling stake. Gazprom's major business lines are geological exploration, production, transportation, storage, processing and marketing of hydrocarbons as well as generation and marketing of heat and electric power. Gazprom possesses the largest gas transmission system in the world, with

158,200 kilometers of gas trunk lines. Major pipeline projects include Nord Stream and South Stream. In 2011, Gazprom produced 513 billion cubic meters (BCM) of natural gas, amounting to about 17 per cent of the worldwide gas production. In addition, it produced 32 million tons of oil and 12 million tons of gas condensate. Gazprom's activities accounted for 10 per cent of Russia's Gross Domestic Product in 2011. The company possesses subsidiaries in many different industry sectors, including finance, media, and aviation. In addition, it controls majority stakes in various companies.

2.7 Business groups in the United States

In the U.S., pyramidal groups were popular until the introduction of double-taxation of inter-corporate dividends ended their expansion in the 1930s (Morck, 2005). In the last few decades, business groups are not common in the U.S. (La Porta et al., 1999). Morck (2005) states that business groups in the U.S. were disentangled in the 1930s by the Roosevelt administration since the administration believed that business groups facilitate governance problems, agency issues, tax avoidance, market power, and dangerously concentrate political influence, while not providing the economic stability they claim to provide. It is also well established that the U.S. firms are not, on average, rewarded for being diversified (Lang and Stulz, 1994; Berger and Ofek, 1995), and, hence, the incentive for a firm to be conglomerate is low. However, there does exist literature stating that powerful business families, such as Morgan and Rockefeller, that does control the key U.S. businesses, especially the all-powerful banking industry.

2.8 Indonesian business groups

Indonesia and Singapore are some of the best countries to prove that business groups are connected with the political apparatus (Fisman, 2000). Large literature exists showcasing the links of Indonesia's biggest business group, Salim Groups' connections with the politically powerful, especially the Suharto regime. Fisman (2000) uses event study techniques to find a positive relation between the market value of Indonesian group affiliated firms and a measure of proximity to President Suharto and his family. It appears as though Indonesian business group affiliate firms are not much better insured than unaffiliated firms to macroeconomic shocks. A similar conclusion was also drawn in a study during the 1990s East Asian financial crisis by Chui et al. (2000).

2.8.1 *The Salim group*

The Salim Group, founded by Sudono Salim, is Indonesia's largest conglomerate with assets including Indofood Sukses Makmur, the world's largest instant noodle producer, and Bogasari, a large flour-milling operation. The Salim Group also owns major oil palm plantations and logging concessions. It has also got involved in hotels, resorts, golf courses, real estates, commercial buildings, shopping centers, and industrial estates in the last few decades. The key group affiliates of the group include: Indosiar, Indomilk, Indofood, Indomarco, Indomaret, Bintang Toedjoe, Indomobil, Indocement, Sinarmas, Indoroti, Indobakery, Astra International, Bogasari, Indogrosir, Indo Es Krim Meiji, Bank Central Asia, Djarum, and Farallo. The group has an estimate of 300–400 firms under its fold, yet only five of these are publicly listed.

2.9 Chilean business groups

Chile is one of the few countries where a group is a legal entity. Groups in Chile, as in many other South American countries, can be thought of as sharing features of conglomerates as well as LBO firms. In Chile, 'business group' has a formal definition (Majluf et al., 1998: 112): '[A Business] group is a set of companies which present such a sort of relationships and linkages in their property, management, administration, or credit responsibilities, that there is ground to believe that the economic and financial decisions of those companies are guided by or subordinated to the shared interest of the group, or that there are common financial risks in the credits obtained or in the financial instruments used.'[4] CAP Group is a good example of a Chilean Business Group.

2.9.1 *The CAP group*

The CAP Group, controlled by Roberto de Andraca and owned by Invercap SA, forms part of an extensive value chain that starts in the mining of iron ore, continues with the production of steel, and ends in steel-processing. The largest producer of iron ore and pellets on the Pacific coast of Latin America and leader in the steel and steel-processing markets in Chile, CAP SA, is a

4 Translation of Article 96, Title XV, Law 18045, Mercado de Valores. Interested readers can refer to the URL: http://www.abante.cl/files/ABT/Contenidos/Vol-1-N1/5 % 20Nureya.pdf (accessed in September 2013).

Chile-based holding company that, through its subsidiaries and affiliates, has 13 operations throughout the country. Its business is structured in three areas: CAP Mining, comprising the operations of Compania Minera del Pacifico SA (CMP), an entity active production of iron ore and pellets; CAP Steel, including the activities of Compania Siderurgica Huachipato SA (CSH), a manufacturer of steel products made with natural raw materials, and CAP Steel Solutions, operating through Novacero SA, which specializes in the production of steel pipes, tubes, and plates used in the construction, industrial, and infrastructure sectors. The company also owns such subsidiaries as PORT Investments Limited NV and Tecnocap SA, as well as it holds interests in Cintac SA, Abastecimientos CAP SA, Armacero Industrial y Comercial SA and Intasa SA. It creates value-added solutions for construction, industry, and infrastructure sectors in Chile, Peru, and Argentina.

2.10 West European business groups

Business groups and families are very popular in the West European world. Faccio and Lang (2002) studied the West European groups and found that business affiliates are more widely held in the U.K. and Ireland, whereas they have more family controlled in continental Europe. The authors find that dual class shares and pyramids enhance the control of the largest shareholders, but overall there are significant discrepancies between ownership and control in only a few countries.

2.10.1 The Ap Moller–Maersk group

The AP Moller-Maersk Group, commonly referred to as Maersk Group, is a good example of a West European business group. Mærsk started as the shipping company named Dampskibsselskabet Svendborg, founded by Captain Peter Mærsk–Møller and his son Arnold Peter Møller in Denmark. Unlike Asian business groups, one finds that the holding company is listed and widely distributed in the European context. In other words, one would find the holding company of AP Moller–Maersk A/S to be listed and traded in the stock market. Today, Maersk is a Danish business conglomerate having activities in a variety of business sectors, primarily within the transportation and energy sectors. It is the largest container ship operator and supply vessel operator in the world. Maersk Group categorizes its main business area as follows:

Table 2.2: Business lines of Mærsk group

Container shipping and related	Tankers, offshore and related	Terminal activities
Maersk Line Damco Maersk Container Industry Safmarine MCC Transport	Maersk Tankers Maersk Drilling Maersk FPSOs Maersk Supply Service Maersk LNG	APM Terminals **Oil & Gas activities** Maersk Oil **Retail & Other** Dansk Supermarket Odense Steel Shipyard Svitzer
		Technology
		Maersk Fluid Technology Maersk Maritime Technology

Source: http://www.maersk.com (accessed on 15 September 2013).

2.10.2 *The Wallenberg family*

The Wallenberg family of Sweden is another example of a European Business Group. According to various estimates, the Wallenberg group indirectly controls over one-third of GDP of Sweden (Chang, 2009). The Wallengberg group controls these enterprises through three family foundations that control the holding company, Investor, and a bank (SE-Banken). Virtually all major Swedish household names, except for Volvo, are Wallenberg companies – Saab-Scania (aircraft and trucks), Ericsson (telephone), ABB (formerly ASEA, engineering), Syngenta (formerly Astra, pharmaceuticals), Stora Enso (formerly Stora; paper and pulp), SKF (bearings), and Electrolux (household goods), and SAS (airlines), just to name the most famous ones.[5]

2.11 Business groups in Africa

In Africa, lack of vibrant factor markets (especially, *financial* and *product* factor markets) resulted in groups with strong political connections (to survive). Business families from India and other parts of the world that had an early

[5] Chang (2008). Interested readers can refer to the URL:http://citeseerx.ist.psu.edu/viewdoc/download?doi=10.1.1.153.3388&rep=rep1&type=pdf (accessed in September 2013).

entry advantage dominate many of the states and the local markets. Some of them such as Kewalram Chanrai Group, Dana Group, TGI Chi Group, and Tolaram Group are well-known names in West Africa. Similarly, Absa Shah Group and ETG Patel Group are strong names in the Eastern Africa and Southern Africa. Few local African businessmen have also established themselves in the last three decades. Two worthwhile names in the list include – Sifiso Dabengwa's telecom giant, namely MTN Group from South Africa and Aliko Dangote's diversified conglomerate, namely Dangote Group from Nigeria. Similarly, Shanduka Group was founded in 2001 as a fully African-owned investment holding company.

2.12 Summary

The discussion on business groups across the globe does point to the importance of their study given their economic size and the wide forms of groups across countries. The existence of business groups, their growth, and dominance in multiple economies also makes us believe that business groups are not short-sighted in their decisions. It also suggests that business groups do readapt to emerging environment, howsoever dynamic and uncertain it may be. Our limited review of literature on the business groups also makes us tend to agree with Morck and Yeung (2003) when they state that greater managerial ownership in family firms need not mitigate agency problems, especially when each family controls a group of publicly traded and private firms, as is the case in most countries. Such structures give rise to their own set of agency problems, as manager's act for the controlling family, but not for shareholders in general.

Our next chapter will take a step forward toward unraveling the possible ways of appreciating the business groups, especially their corporate strategies and performance. Thus, we move toward reviewing the existing literature on measures of the same and the historical linkages between diversification strategies and performance.

3

Product Diversification and Performance

Measurement and Historical Relationship

Product diversification is one of the oldest strategies that has been adopted by a number of the worlds' largest corporations at some time or the other. In this chapter, we explore the extant literature on measures of product diversification and financial performance of firms. We also review the extant empirical literature on the application of the same in firm-level studies and business group studies. While we discuss the range of measures of product diversification and financial performance, respectively, in Sections 3.1 and 3.2, Section 3.3 briefly reviews the empirical work done outside India, both at the firm level and the business group level. Extensive research has been done focusing in the past on the firm-level diversification-performance linkages in the developed countries. Some of these theories and explanations on firm-level literature are applicable to business group-level studies. Hence, we discuss the existing literature from this perspective and apply a few of these concepts of firm-level theories on business groups in Section 3.4. The institutional and other contextual factors affecting both diversification and performance of an organization are taken up in Section 3.5. In Section 3.6, we examine the business group literature in the Indian context.

3.1 Measures of diversification strategy

The existing literature on product diversification is perhaps one of the largest bodies of work in business strategy (Chen et al., 1998). Measurement has always been an important issue in product diversification studies. Product diversification was first studied by economists interested in the relationship between product diversification and monopoly (or market) power (Gort, 1962; Arnould, 1969).

Primarily, there are two types of measures to differentiate between product diversification categories – continuous and categorical measures. Business diversity is generally captured through the use of ratios to measure the degree of activity in a single business or a group of businesses (Wrigley, 1970; Rumelt, 1974).

3.1.1 *Review of continuous measures*

Some researchers have used multiple continuous diversification measures. Jacquemin and Berry's (1979) entropy measure best exemplifies such an approach. Hitherto other studies start with multiple measures but subsequently transform them into categorical measures, typically using the median or a point of discontinuity along the continuous measure as cutoff points. A continuous measure will be often preferable to a categorical breakdown (Montgomery, 1982). The use of continuous variables (by way of degrees of relatedness) would eliminate the need to use a cutoff point and may provide more meaningful information on general tendencies. Studies by Cynthia Montgomery (1982) and Krishna Palepu (1985) are illustrative of these approaches. The other key advantage of continuous measures is the fact that they can be used in multivariate regression analyses in which degrees of freedom may be a problem.

3.1.2 *North American Industrial Classification System (NAICS) or Standard Industrial Classification (SIC) based continuous measures*

The modern North American Industry Classification System (NAICS) and, its earlier version, the Standard Industrial Classification (SIC)[1] systems are numerical systems developed by the U.S.-led North American Free Trade Agreement (NAFTA) and the U.S. government body, respectively, for classifying all types of economic activity. The classification is based on the primary activity of an establishment. Both the systems stress that classification as far as possible, should conform to the actual structure of industry as it is

---

1 Introduced in 1997, the North American Industry Classification System (NAICS) is a replacement for the United States' 1987 Standard Industrial Classification (SIC) system. It is an outcome of the collaboration between the governments of Canada, Mexico, and the U.S. The NAICS is broadly compatible with the SIC. There exist websites on the Internet where the SIC is matched to NAICS classification. Please refer to URL: http://www.census.gov/epcd/naics02/S87TON02.HTM (accessed in September 2013).

found to exist (Griliches, 1992). So, the technological proximity of industries will be reflected in the NAICS (and SIC) classification, and, as Griliches (1992) rightly argued, this is what the NAICS (and SIC) stands for (in supporting the validity of this proxy). As of date, empirically, a better proxy is not readily available.

The sophistication of product count measures based on NAICS (or SIC) codes ranges from the simple counts of the number of NAICS (or SIC) codes in which an organization participates, to weighted average measures that judge the importance of each NAICS (or SIC) involvement to the particular organization. For their explicit consideration of different levels of firm involvement, weighted NAICS (or SIC)-based measures are superior to non-weighted measures when describing entity-level diversification. Empirical research by Montgomery (1982) and Chatterjee and Blocher (1992) also found that the high degree of correspondence between continuous and categorical measures could also be made out as a '*plus factor*' for SIC-based diversification measurement process. The most frequently used diversification measures based on SIC in the literature are: (a) Palepu's total diversification (DT) and unrelated diversification (DU) entropy measures; and (2) Montgomery's 2- and 3-digit SIC product count measures. We provide below a description of the popular continuous measures of product diversification in the literature – tailored for business groups:

- **Herfindahl index:** Albert Hirschman (Hirschman, 1945) created what has come to be widely known as the Herfindahl Index, a quantitative index to measure the extent of diversification. Herfindahl index applied to product diversification is calculated as the sum of the squares of each industry's sales as a proportion of total group sales. Sales in an industry are the sum of sales in that industry for all affiliate firms (of the business group) in that industry.
- **Berry's index on corporate diversification:** Among others, Berry (1975) also pointed out that diversification is to be gauged not only by the number of industries in which a business group is active, but also by the distribution of the business group's productive activity among those industries. Berry, defined a more complete index of diversification as under:

  $$D = 1 - \Sigma_{i\text{-}1 \text{ to } n} (P_i)^2$$

  Where P_i is the ratio of the business group's output in i-th industry to the business group's total output in n industries. An illustration is provided in Section 3.1.6.

- **Palepu's ENTROPY MEASURE and Montgomery's ENTROPY INDEX:** These two entropy measures are calculated as the sum of the entropy indices of related and unrelated diversification following Palepu (1985) and Montgomery (1982), respectively. The index of related diversification is based on the various affiliates within the business group that operate within the same 3-digit SIC equivalent industry and is calculated as a function of all such instances within the group operating in various 3-digit SIC equivalent industries. Similarly, the index of unrelated diversification is a function of the business group operating in different 2-digit SIC equivalent industries. In other words, each index is a weighted average of the ratio of sales within a particular 2-digit and 3-digit SIC industry category to total business group sales in that 2- and 3-digit SIC industry categories, respectively. The weights given by the mathematical formulas are illustrated in Appendix A.2. An illustration is provided in Section 3.1.6.

3.1.3 National Industrial Classification (NIC) based continuous measures

The National Industrial Classification (NIC) system is a numerical classification made by an Indian government body for classifying all types of industrial activities in India. It is an expandable 3-digit classification of all manufacturing and non-manufacturing industries based on the Annual Survey of Industries (NIC) 1987 scheme. Saple (2000) classified Indian firms' diversification on a 2-digit NIC product count measure based on their number of lines of business.

However, count measures have a serious shortcoming. For example, a business group with 99 per cent of its output accounted for a single 2-digit product is barely diversified regardless of the number of other 2-digit industries it represents by the remaining 1 per cent. A firm with its productive activity equally divided among 2-digit industries is likely to be 'more diversified'; even if no more than three 2-digit products are involved. So, instead of a product count measure, it would be better if the measures are calculated on a weighted average basis, to take care of the significance of each NIC association to the particular organization, individual weights being based on either sales or assets in those industries. This point was made on similar SIC-based count measures by researchers Berry (1975) and Montgomery (1982).

3.1.4 *Non-continuous measures: Rumelt's classification*

The generic strategies can be analyzed using Rumelt's corporate strategy categorization design (1974). Rumelt used the degree of relatedness among businesses in a diversified firm to classify highly diversified firms into a number of categories. This categorization scheme is the most accepted in the literature (Montgomery and Singh, 1984; Barton and Gordon, 1988). In assigning firms to a category of diversification strategy, Rumelt used three ratios (Montgomery and Singh, 1984):

- Specialization ratio: The extent of a firm's revenue that can be ascribed to its largest single business.
- Related ratio: The proportion of a firm's revenue that can be attributed to its largest group of related businesses.
- Vertical ratio: The proportion of a firm's revenues that arise from all by-products, intermediate products, and end products of a vertically integrated sequence of processing activities.

There are a total of nine categories based on the above three ratios. Specific category classification, information, and cutoff points are given in Appendix A.1. An illustration is also provided in Section 3.1.6. The reasons for the wide acceptance of Rumelt's taxonomy are:

- The financial characteristics of the diversification groups he made were systematically and significantly different in his study.
- Although the categorization of the firm is subjective, studies by Christenen and Montgomery (1981); and Bettis (1981) provide extensive support for the reliability of the measure.
- Past studies have extensively used Rumelt's measure (see Ramanujam and Varadarajan, 1989; Datta et al., 1991). So researchers use this measure to make their studies comparable with the existing literature.
- Rumelt's approach also recognizes similarities in sales, marketing, distribution, production, and technology.
- Each firm is thoroughly evaluated from a managerial perspective and classified according to its unique history and patterns of relatedness.

Chatterjee and Blocher's (1992) results demonstrated the predictive ability of Rumelt's measures with specific performance criteria. The results also suggested good discriminating power of continuous measures to discriminate between Rumelt's measures.

3.1.5 Other non-continuous measures

Some of the important non-continuous categorization schemes used in the literature are:

- Lins and Servaes categorization scheme: Lins and Servaes (1999) classified firms as single segment if at least 90 per cent of their total sales are derived from one 2-digit SIC segment. Establishments are classified as multi-segment if they operate in more than one 2-digit SIC code industries and none of their 2-digit SIC codes (or segments) accounts for more than 90 per cent of the total firm sales. Claessens et al. (1998, 1999) and Fauver et al. (1998) have also used this classification scheme in their empirical work. The classification scheme does not fully take into account the firm's productive activity range among the industries and is too broad in nature.
- Concentric measure: The concentric index measures 'relatedness' of industries (Montgomery and Wernerfelt, 1988; Wernerfelt and Montgomery, 1988). Concentric measure is a weighted average of each industry's sale as a per cent of total group sales, following Caves et al. (1980). The weight includes the contribution of group sales of all affiliate firms in the business group and also accounts for whether or not the firms are in the same 2-digit SIC equivalent industry.

Other non-continuous measures are primarily dependent on the SIC system. While these measures are largely based on similarities of manufacturing and/or technology-based aspects, they ignore similarities in areas such as marketing and distribution. The most referred and used non-continuous measure in the diversification literature is the Rumelt's categorization scheme.[2] Montgomery's (1982) work on product diversification measures found that Rumelt's classification looked logical and straightforward in the classification process. Breaks between categories appeared to fall in natural places, and differentiations between linkage patterns (say, constrained Vs linked) were often obvious.

3.1.6 Illustration on computing product diversification measures

We illustrate below the computed product diversification measures using the discussion in the previous section and formulas discussed in Section 3.1.2,

---

2 Few researchers viewed the Rumelt's cutoff point of 70 per cent for a *Single Business* category as too high and they used 60 per cent (Pitts, 1974) and 40 per cent (Simmonds, 1990) as the cutoff points.

Appendix A.1, and Appendix A.2 for four business groups having varied product exposure:

Table 3.1: Product diversification measures: An example

A. Business Group A						
Industry Segment with 2-digit SIC Code	22	28	29	31	32	34
Share of the Group in Industry Segment	100%	0%	0%	0%	0%	0%

Categorical Measure

Rumelt's Diversification Category	Single Business

Continuous Measure

No. of Lines of Business	1
Berry's Corporate Diversification Index	0.000
Montgomery's Unrelated Diversification Index	0.000

B. Business Group B						
Industry Segment with 2-digit SIC Code	22	28	29	31	32	34
Share of the Group in Industry Segment	1%	99%	0%	0%	0%	0%

Categorical Measure

Rumelt's Diversification Category	Single Business

Continuous Measure

No. of Lines of Business	2
Berry's Corporate Diversification Index	0.020
Montgomery's Unrelated Diversification Index	0.020

C. Business Group C						
Industry Segment with 2-digit SIC Code	22	28	29	31	32	34
Share of the Group in Industry Segment	50%	50%	0%	0%	0%	0%

(Continued)

Table 3.1 (Continued)

Categorical Measure

Rumelt's Diversification Category	Unrelated Portfolio

Continuous Measure

No. of Lines of Business	2
Berry's Corporate Diversification Index	0.500
Montgomery's Unrelated Diversification Index	0.500

D. Business Group D						
Industry Segment with 2-digit SIC Code	22	28	29	31	32	34
Share of the Group in Industry Segment	10%	10%		30%	20%	10%

Categorical Measure

Rumelt's Diversification Category	Multi-business

Continuous Measure

No. of Lines of Business	6
Berry's Corporate Diversification Index	0.800
Montgomery's Unrelated Diversification Index	0.800

Note: The Rumelt's classification arrived above is a simplified example – in reality one would take into account the level and degree of specialization, relatedness, and vertical nature of business, if any – among the different businesses of the organization.

3.1.7 *Analysis of diversification measures*

Most of the simple count-based measures discussed above have been used in India by the earlier works.[3] Perhaps, they might have been constrained

[3] The various measures used in India are: a 2-digit SIC-based product count measure (Purkayastha, 2010); a modified measure of Palepu's (1985) 2-digit SIC-based entropy index (Khanna and Palepu, 2000); Herfindahl index; concentric measure (Khanna and Palepu, 2000); 2-digit NIC-based product count measure (Saple, 2000); Berry's entropy measure based on NIC classification (Saple, 2000) and a modified Rumelt's classification system based on NIC (Kakani and Reddy, 1996).

in the availability of product-wise (reliable) data to make use of the sophisticated measures.

Using analysis of variance, cluster analysis, and discriminant analysis, Hall et al. (1994) investigated: (a) whether continuous measures (entropy and product count) differentiate between diversification categories; and (b) whether continuous and categorical measures predicted similar product diversity performance relationships. They concluded that the techniques were associated (see also, Chatterjee and Blocher, 1992).

In summary, a variety of measures have been developed, though as Pitts and Hopkins (1982) stressed, the choice of measure should be guided by the research question at hand. Also, employment of multiple measures would establish the robustness of the findings to the choice of measure (Ramanujam and Varadarajan, 1989), making the study more acceptable. Hence, our work will have multiple measures of diversification. As a non-continuous measure, we will use Rumelt's categorization design; and as a continuous measure, the study will use both Palepu's and Montgomery's 2-digit- and 3-digit-based SIC measures.

3.2 Measures of performance

Venkatraman and Ramanujam (1986) proposed a two-dimensional classification scheme highlighting 10 different measurement approaches for business performance. One dimension deals with financial versus broader operational criteria, while the other dimension focuses on primary versus secondary data sources. The scheme then produces four '*within-cell*' approaches and six '*across-cell*' approaches. The within-cell approaches are: (a) financial data/secondary sources, (b) financial data/primary sources, (c) operational data/secondary sources, and (d) operational data/primary sources. The across-cell approaches included: (a) financial data/primary and secondary sources, (b) business performance/secondary sources, and (c) financial data/secondary sources and operational data/primary sources.

Of these, the financial data/secondary sources have been the most used approach to analyze the diversification–performance linkage. Across firms and industries, it is difficult to compare any data having operational criteria as a basis. Business performance approach also cannot be easily practiced, as reliable data on measures such as '*gains in product market share*' are not easily available in India. The various complementary performance measures used in the literature are both capital market-based and financial-statement based. The measures used extensively in the literature are –

- Return on equity
- Return on invested capital (*or* total capital)
- Return on assets
- Compounded assets (*or* sales) growth
- Risk adjusted stock returns
- Abnormal stock market returns
- Tobin's Q-ratio

Appendix B gives a list of the measures used in the related literature to measure performance.

3.2.1 Financial measures

Financial theory says that business organizations (either firms or business groups) operate with the long-term goal of shareholder value maximization (Ross et al., 1999). So, the objective of any strategy is to boost shareholder value. It is assumed that most business groups would seek to maximize their shareholder wealth.[4] One of the ways by which they can do this is ensuring that their top management chooses those diversification strategies, which produce the largest possible market value for a given capital invested.

- Tobin's Q-ratio and its Surrogate Measures: The best measure of shareholder value creation in financial economics literature is the Tobin's Q-ratio (Lewellen and Badrinath, 1998). As defined by Tobin and Brainard (1968) and Tobin (1969), the Q statistic for a firm is calculated as the ratio of the market value of the outstanding financial claims on the firm to the replacement cost of the firm's assets. Under certain assumptions, Varaiya et al. (1987) proved that the market-to-book value of equity ratio and Tobin's Q-ratio are theoretically and empirically equivalent measures. Lang and Stulz (1994) and Comment and Jarrell (1995) are some of the empirical works on diversification using Tobin's Q-ratio as a performance measure.

Some of the complex measures used in the literature are:

- Excess value approach: To measure firm performance with respect to diversification, Berger and Ofek (1995), Claessens et al. (1999),

---

4 Some business groups believe in empire building and other goals (Williamson, 1985).

Lins and Servaes (1998), and Fauver et al. (1998) adopted the excess value approach. This approach defines the excess value as the natural logarithm of the ratio of the firm's actual value to its imputed value. Market capitalization, the market value of equity plus the book value of debt, is used as the measure of actual firm value. The imputed value is calculated as follows. They first compute median market-to-sales ratio for each 2-digit SIC industry using only single segment firms. They, then, multiply the firm's level of sales in each segment by its corresponding industry median market-to-sales ratio. The imputed value of the firm is obtained by summing up the multiple across all segments.

The difficulty in applying the above measure in India is that group-based and/or diversified firms dominate many industries, while some industries do not have sufficient representation for group-based and/or diversified firms. Hence, using median market-to-sales ratio of single segment firms in those industries might lead to spurious results. For example, the 2-digit SIC industry code 33, consisting of all firms in primary metal segment is dominated in India by huge private business group firms (such as Hindalco and TISCO). The single segment private firms in this industry are usually the small firms operating secondary rolling mills. So here, the calculation of imputed value and the use of excess value approach for comparison will give false results. Another example of such an industry is the service sector (2-digit SIC industry code 76) industry such as information technology (IT) software firms. During the 1985–2000 period, they were largely dominated by mostly non-diversified (and classically non-business group) firms. Though industry transformation led to a few of the business groups listing their firms[5] – nevertheless, over 80 per cent of the information technology (IT) software firms in India are singe segment private firms (and potentially resulting in a spurious result). So, we do not perceive excess value approach as a good measurement method for countries such as India. Two more market-based performance measures used in the literature at the firm-level are:

- Sharpe and Treynor measure: The Sharpe performance measure is equal to portfolio return minus risk-free rate, all divided by standard deviation. The Treynor measure is equal to portfolio return minus risk-free rate, all divided by beta. Jahera et al. (1987) used the Sharpe and Treynor performance measures in their empirical research.

[5] For example, as of year 2013, three of the four largest IT software players are business group entities, i.e., TCS (Tata Group), Wipro (Azimji Premji Group), and Mahindra Satyam (Mahindra Group). Infosys Technologies is the only exception.

- Jensen's alpha: Farjoun (1998), Hoskisson et al. (1993), and Nayyar (1992) assess firm performance relative to the stock market average by computing Jensen's alpha of firms, which measures firm performance against a portfolio with similar market risk. Jensen's alpha is the intercept term in the regression equation to estimate the systematic risk of a stock using daily stock returns.

Readers would agree that one cannot easily apply these market-based measures for aggregate business group-level analysis (unless the groups consist of only one listed firm).

3.2.2 *Non-financial (strategic) measures*

In much of the empirical literature, it is observed that the use of the traditional profitability measures to evaluate strategy was extensive. However, Chakravarthy (1986) found that traditional profitability measures for evaluating a firm's strategic performance were inadequate for discerning excellence. Chakravarthy argued that monitoring a strategy requires measures that can also capture its potential and performance in future which accounting profitability measures could not capture. Also, since historical cost-based accounting data are unable to properly capture a firm's futuristic performance, the need for a more forward-looking measure is felt. Hence, he suggested use of strategic performance variables such as 'product market share' and 'brand value'. However, the suggested variables and the other strategic performance variables in the literature are highly subjective and their ability to discriminate has not been proved. The other difficulty faced by researchers in India is in getting data, especially for business groups performing in multiple markets. This is the reason that measures like relative market position, brand value, and product market shares are often not found easily in the Indian empirical literature.

3.2.3 *Discussion on various performance measures*

Stock market measures

From the finance point of view, according to Ross et al. (1999), the stock market provides the best measure of an organization's worth: '*a firm is worth only what the market is willing to pay*'. However, Holzmann et al. (1975), and Ramanujam and Vardarajan (1989) deplored the exclusive focus on market-based measures of performance. In their opinion, stock prices suffer from the drawback of being too comprehensive, in the sense of impounding everything expected to happen in the future. Hitt and Ireland (1986) said that stock returns had potential limitations, they can be affected by some extraneous factors (e.g., economic and industry trends). Since efficiency of the capital markets has been questioned even in developed markets, such as the U.S. (Shiller, 1989), the market-based measures cannot be completely relied upon. Also, the demand and supply for a particular firm shares determines the market prices of its stock. Hence, if the floating stock is very low in the market[6], the market price of the stock cannot be relied upon as it is prone to market manipulations.

Accounting measures

Peasnell (1996) stated that accounting measures of income and book-yield bear enough resemblance to the concepts of economic profit and economic rate of return to tempt financial economists to employ them in numerous studies of performance. He showed that accounting returns are an accurate estimate of economic returns and suggested use of accounting-based measures in gauging a firm's financial performance (also see Brief and Lawson, 1992).

If there is a problem with accounting-based measures, it is that accounting measures of firm performance have traditionally ignored the problems of truthfulness in financial reporting which underpin many of the peculiar institutional features of accounting. However, accounting reports constitute the only systematically compiled, publicly available, alternative source of information about the financial affairs of business corporations, and are largely standardized and audited too. Also, accounting standards in India are comparatively better than the ones followed in other emerging markets such as Argentina. The standards are similar in quality to those followed in many advanced economies such as Denmark or Germany (see CIFAR, 1995; Easterly and Ross, 1997).

Factors determining value

Branch and Gale (1983) suggested that there are four determinants of stock price and, hence, shareholders value maximization of an organization:

6 For example, Wipro Limited has a very low free float.

(a) firm profitability; (b) firm growth; (c) risk; and (d) stock market outlook. Varaiya et al. (1987) proved that theoretically both profitability and growth determine the value of an organization. They also showed that higher growth and higher profitability firms are associated with higher firm valuations. On the other hand, firms with either poor profitability or low growth rates will be associated with poor market valuations. Profitability could be further analyzed by looking into its two constituents, profit margin, and sales turnover ratio. A business entity can increase its profitability by either increasing its margin or by increasing its efficiency level.

Several studies have pointed out that instead of searching for a single measure that most significantly determines performance; a multi-factor performance assessment should be used (Bagozzi and Philips, 1982; Keats, 1990). Their argument is based on the fact that excellence is a complex phenomenon requiring more than a single criterion for a comprehensive definition. Rappaport (1986) suggested that short-run performance measures should not be used exclusively. Based on the above discussion, multiple performance measures seem to be justified as no one measure seems to be capable of capturing multiple performance objectives. Also, the assessment of shareholder value with its components (based on several dimensions such as profitability, risk, growth, and profitability components) would give a better idea of the exact nature of factors affecting performance of a business group.

To sum up, a number of performance measures, both capital market-based and financial statement based, have been developed on the basis of various performance dimensions. Good studies employ multiple measures to establish their robustness and make it comparable with other studies. We evaluate the relationship between business group characteristics and group performance on five dimensions: shareholder value, risk, profitability, profitability magnitudes, and growth. This helped us in finding the exact factors and components driving the shareholder value maximization of a group. The dimensions and their frequently used measures in the empirical literature are given in the Table 3.2 as follows:

Table 3.2: Commonly used performance dimensions and measures in empirical studies

Shareholder Value Creation	
1. Modified Tobin's Q-ratio, 2. Market-to-Book Value Ratio	
Profitability	**Profitability Components**
1. Return on Capital Employed	1. Net Profit Margin
2. Return on Assets	2. Sales Turnover Ratio
3. Return on Net Worth	3. Gross Profit Margin
Risk	**Growth**
1. Variance of Return on Net Worth	1. Growth in Total Assets
2. Variance of Return on Capital Employed	2. Growth in Total Sales
3. Variance of Return on Assets	3. Growth in Fixed Assets

3.3 Diversification strategy and performance

Having ended the discussion on the aspects related to diversification-performance dimensions and measures, we discuss herein the research done on the relationship between both of them, both at the firm-level and at the business group level.

3.3.1 Empirical studies

Views on business groups can be divided into three streams. Scholars in the dominant stream have argued that business groups are responses to lack of intermediary institutions resulting in market imperfections and, thus, can be a source of value in emerging markets (Leff, 1978; Khanna & Palepu, 1997; Chang & Hong 2002). However, other scholars have also argued that business groups do not necessarily create value in emerging markets (Chu, 2004; Yiu et al., 2005; Lim et al., 2009). They rationalize that business groups need to invest in creating coordinating mechanisms that will facilitate monitoring of different firms across the groups. Such coordinating mechanisms entail cost and, thus, business groups may not always add value to the aggregate entities.[7] A second important stream

[7] In other words, it might benefit one or two affiliate firms within the business group – but at the cost of performance of other affiliate firms (with the group). For example, Ashok Leyland Limited (of Hinduja Group) might benefit due to the presence of Ashok Leyland Finance Limited (a finance subsidiary of the Group). Still, the Hinduja business group's overall performance need not improve due to the same.

emerges from sociology which emphasizes solidarity norms and codes of behavior as the reason for the formation of business groups (Granovetter, 2005). The third stream grounded in political economy talks of group as socially counter-productive rent seekers because of their closeness to the political system.

Firm-level studies:

The relation between diversification strategy and firm performance has been a major topic of strategic management since the seminal work of Chandler (1962). Empirical studies into diversification and firm performance had investigated cross-sectional relationships, typically among batches of more than 50 or more firms. The most prominent of all studies is the work of Rumelt (1974) which established differences in performance across strategy categories and has been extended and replicated in numerous ways. A majority of these empirical studies has found a neutral or negative relation between product diversification and firm performance. These studies have mostly used the U.S. data or data from other developed countries such as the U.K., many of them adhering to the Fortune 500 sample (Risseeuw, 1997).[8] The following box gives a brief list of the major studies and their key inferences:

Box 3.1:

- **Negative or neutral relationship:** Rhoades (1974); Rumelt (1974); Utton (1977); Galbraith and Nathanson (1978); Salter and Weinhold (1979); Bettis (1981); Nathanson and Cassano (1982); Montogomery (1985); Palepu (1985); Jahera et al. (1987); Montgomery and Wernerfelt (1988);Lang and Stulz (1994); Lloyd and Jahera (1994); Berger and Ofek (1995); Comment and Jarrell (1995); Perry (1998); Riahi-Belkaoui (2003); Chu (2004);
- **Curvilinear relationship:** Berry (1975); Christensen and Montogomery (1981); Rumelt (1982); Lecraw, (1984); Varadarajan and Ramanujam (1987); Kahloul and Hallara (2010)
- **Positive relationship:** Weston and Mansingka (1971); Michel and Shaked (1984);Chang & Hong (2000)

In a classical empirical work, Berger and Ofek (1995) estimated the value of a diversified firm's segments as if they were operated as separate firms. They

8 These firms are strictly not comparable with the business groups in the current study.

found that value loss averages were 13 to 15 per cent over the period 1986–91. This loss was not found in case of related diversification. Perry (1998) also found that related diversified firms had higher accounting- and market-based returns. Perry's findings suggested that related firms had lower levels of total risk than unrelated diversified firms. Claessens et al. (1998) used data from the East Asian countries and found a positive relation between firm performance and complementary diversification. They stated that their results are consistent with the view that external markets in less developed countries are more subject to distortions; hence, it is relatively cost-effective for firms to allocate resources internally through diversification.[9]

Riahi-Belkaoui (2003) tests the relationship between diversification strategy and earning persistence provided by Autoregressive, Integrative, and Moving Average (ARIMA) models. When higher order ARIMA models are used, this study shows the earnings persistence of the U.S. multinational firms to be positively related to size, related diversification, and vertical integration, and negatively related to unrelated diversification. Kahloul and Hallara (2010) use a longitudinal data from a sample composed of 69 large French firms quoted on the period of 1995–2005 to analyze the firm activity perimeter evolution effect on its level of risk and performance in a dynamic prospect. They notice a non-linear relationship diversification/performance. The results show a non-linear relationship among the total risk, its specific component, and the diversification.

Business group-level studies

Research on business groups in comparison to firm-level work has been scanty (Granovetter, 1994). Previous empirical studies have mostly compared the performance between business group affiliated firms with unaffiliated firms in the same economy. Chang and Choi (1988) find that the top four Korean *chaebols* outperformed other domestic firms of the economy including smaller *chaebols* and unaffiliated firms. The political network of bigger *chaebols* is pointed out as an explanation behind the results. Khanna and Palepu (1998b) find that affiliates of the most diversified groups are more profitable than focused unaffiliated firms in seven emerging markets including Argentina, Chile, India, Korea, and Taiwan. Performances of business groups have been examined in case of other developed as well as other Asian economies

---

9 See Datta et al. (1991) and Perry (1998) for an extensive survey of firm-level empirical studies on product diversification and performance relationship.

(Claessens et al., 2002c; Martin and Sayrak, 2003). Khanna and Palepu (2000) argue that even though the capital transfer is limited when firms are legally independent, the family-based business group can start new ventures in which they will hold shares along with others. Kali and Sarkar (2005) argue that interlocking directorate and propping are other two possibilities which could enhance the value of diversified business group firms.

3.4 Explanations in literature

This section looks into some of the existing theories, explanations, and factors pointed out in the literature on the nexus between diversification strategy and financial performance.

3.4.1 Internal capital markets theory

According to the internal capital markets theory, diversified institutions (including business groups and conglomerates) arise when underdeveloped capital markets permit more efficient internal management and allocation of funds than the external capital market. Williamson (1975: 145–47) indicated that the diversified firm is best understood as an alternative resource allocation mechanism. This is because the headquarter typically has access to information unavailable to external parties, which it extracts through its own internal auditing and reporting procedures.

Going by the above theory, one may posit that large diversified groups create large internal capital markets and reduce the problem of underinvestment in less developed economies. External capital markets allocate resources among single-product organizations. In the diversified multi-industry business house, by comparison, resources are allocated via an 'internal capital market': funds are distributed among profit-center divisions by the central headquarters of the group. This miniature capital market could replicate the allocative and disciplinary functions of the financial markets, shifting resources toward more profitable activities. For example, in a diversified business group with affiliates in unrelated areas, the internal capital market could shift funds to affiliates with urgent capital requirements or to members with attractive investment opportunities.

Managers inside the member firm may also be more willing to reveal information to group headquarters than to outsiders, since revealing the same information to external capital markets would also make it available to rival firms, potentially hurting the firm's competitive position. Also, the modeling approach by Gertner et al. (1994) reveals that the ownership aspect of internal capital allocation has significant consequences. It leads to increase in monitoring and better asset redeployment than institutional/bank lending; however, this comes at the cost of reducing managerial incentives and making them averse to risks as they become more vulnerable to opportunistic behavior by corporate headquarters.

Williamson (1975, 1985) claimed the need for an internal capital market as the stock market is slow, remote, and too impersonal. The existence of internal capital markets could be beneficial to the groups only when the capital markets and the existing financial system are not able to allocate capital efficiently. So, a business group will benefit immensely when the local capital markets are less developed. Groups will also benefit when projects are either *investment intensive* or *technically complex* or *long-term oriented*, i.e., there is a gestation lag and more uncertainty between investment decisions and their financial outcomes.

On the other hand, Mathur and Kenyon (1998) rightly pointed out that internal capital markets could lead to a cross-subsidization of failing business segments. Khanna and Palepu (1998) pointed out that as Indian business groups are a collection of publicly listed firms, their ability to use internal capital markets to fund on-going projects of one firm from the cash flows of the other group firms is limited. Therefore, they argued that the most important function of the group's internal capital market is to launch new ventures in which both the family and the other group affiliates might acquire ownership stakes. Probably this is done by financial subsidiaries of business groups that assume the roles of providing capital and allocating resources within the groups.

Taking it further, Castaneda (2007) suggested that the business group structure helped in the recovery of the economy of Mexico, which witnessed the collapse of the banking system and the interruption of financing flows through the domestic financial markets. Firms, when possible, started to depend more on trade credit, and the internal capital market of business groups created a financial cushion that kept the economy working. To offer a rationale for the Mexican experience, the authors presented a theoretical model where it is shown that moral hazard problems are reduced within a business group as long as affiliates in the non-tradable sector surrender control rights during periods of crisis.

3.4.2 Economies of Scope

Sumantra Ghosal (Ghosal, 1987) pointed out that the strategic importance of scope economies arises from a diversified group's ability to share investments and costs across value chains which competitors without such internal and external diversity cannot. Such sharing can take place across segments, products, and markets (Porter, 1985) and may involve joint use of different kinds of resources. A diversified firm may share physical assets such as production equipment, cash, or brand names across different businesses and markets. Cross-subsidization of markets and exploitation of a brand name is an example of sharing an intangible asset across different components of a firm's product and market portfolios.

Ghosal affirmed that a second important source of scope economies is shared external relations: with customers, suppliers, and other existing stakeholders. Hindustan Unilever has benefited considerably from its ability to market a diverse range of products through the same distribution channel to the same customers, i.e., shared external relations. In another variation, the Videocon group affiliates had expanded into new related businesses to meet the varying requirements of their existing customers. Finally, shared knowledge is the third important component of scope economies. For example, Reliance Industries believes that its strength in large project execution and resulting capabilities of creating new capacities for its products, with economies of scale gives it a competitive edge over global giants (in a range of sectors – from oil refineries to retailing to telecommunications). However, even scope economies may be costly (see Porter, 1987). As different segments or different products of a diversified company face different environmental demands, the effort to create synergies may fail or may result in compromise with the objective of external consistency. For example, the Tatas had not been successful when they tried to cash in on the 'Tata' brand name in the fast moving consumer goods segments.[10]

3.4.3 Related diversification advantages

Relatedness is the mechanism by which business groups capture synergies that can enhance the level of exchange among business units. It constitutes a major source of potential competitive advantage for the business units individually and the industrial house as a group (see Davis et al., 1992). A business group can have sustained superior performance if it is able to exploit resources (or assets) that are unavailable to its rivals (Barney, 1991; Markides and Williamson, 1996). The related diversification helps a group to exploit economies of scope by setting up mechanisms to identify important resources (or assets) available in one activity

---

[10] Perhaps, customers did not feel comfortable in associating with a perceived masculine 'brand tag' (say, Tata Automobile; Tata Engineering; Tata Constructions) with feminine products (say, Tata Shampoo or Tata Soap).

that can be used in others. Business groups would also benefit by developing internal mechanisms for transferring competencies and assets across business units.

Teece (1980, 1982), and Levy and Haber (1986) discussed the specific nature of the resources and showed that the ability to simultaneously share common assets across the organization or to transfer certain assets among processes can create a cost advantage for a diversified organization. Group specific assets that may be transferred between affiliated firms include technology, marketing capabilities, organizational knowledge, or managerial skills embodied in human capital, especially, benefits of learning-by-doing, such as, *liaisoning* with bureaucrat bodies and political leaders for regulatory approvals. Such a transfer of assets is easier and more beneficial for related and linked firms. For example, the managerial assets available to a business group at a given point in time can be transferred within a group among its various business lines (Levy, 1989). So, business houses, which effectively capitalize on relatedness, may be able to use interrelationships to overwhelm competing business houses with poorly conceived arrays of business units.

The other advantages pointed out in the literature (see Porter, 1987) for related diversification are: (a) Scale economies and exploitation of by-products can lead to a significant reduction in unit costs; and (b) A significant improvement in the product(s)/service(s) quality and appeal to customers. However, Hill and Hoskisson (1987: 334) fittingly pointed out that interdivisional coordination and resource sharing requirements, imposed by efforts to achieve relatedness, result in inflexibilities and poor responsiveness by management to market changes that adversely affect performance over focused (or single segment) business groups.

3.4.4 Coinsurance effect, diversification and risk

The idea of product diversification has often been linked with risk reduction. One potential benefit of product diversification strategy arises from combining businesses with imperfectly correlated earnings streams. This *coinsurance* effect gives diversified firms greater debt capacity than single-line businesses of similar size (Lewellen, 1971). One of the ways in which increased debt capacity creates value is by expanding tax-shields. Most empirical studies dealing with the relationship between a firm's diversification strategy and its performance have generally examined this relationship in the absence of risk considerations.

Bettis and Hall (1982) were the first to study and shed light on the nature of the linkage between risk/return performance of a firm and its diversification strategy. They found evidence of a positive risk/return relationship in unrelated diversified firms, i.e., an increase in returns comes with an increase in riskiness. The results reported by Bettis and Mahajan (1985) suggested that related diversification is no guarantee of a favorable risk/return performance, i.e., an increase in returns and a simultaneous decrease in riskiness. Furthermore, a favorable risk/return performance is extremely hard to achieve with unrelated diversification.

Montgomery and Singh (1984) found that the systematic risk of unrelated diversified firms is significantly higher than that of the market portfolio. They found that this was due to the unrelated firms lower market power and higher debt position. In contrast, Chang and Thomas (1989) maintained that risk-return configurations among diversified firms are more closely associated with structural factors associated with markets and businesses than with a particular diversification strategy chosen.

3.4.5 Market power view

Market power view theories (Hill, 1985) argue that diversified firms will 'thrive at the expense of non-diversified firms not because they are more efficient, but rather on account of their access to what is termed as conglomerate power.' This power comes by the way of their having monopoly and monopsony benefits from the market. This could be by way of increase in market concentration, by increase in the size of an economic unit and also by increase in the corresponding concentration of human and non-human resources. While, Encaqua and Jacquemin (1982) suggested that business groups do diversify for enhancing their market power, this however, must be qualified by the fact that an organization [11] with insignificant position in a number of markets will not, in sum, have this power (Gribbin, 1976).

3.4.6 Top management skills

Prahalad and Bettis (1986) are part of a school of thought that ascribes the success of some unrelated diversifiers to the superior skills of their top

[11] In India, there are many business groups that are quite diversified and exist in multiple markets, without having adequate segmental market power (or positions) in any of the markets. Take, for example, India's most diversified business group – KC Thapar group. Not many would be aware of the group's existence in such diverse range of industries.

management team. The particular skill, which they identify, is the ability of the top management team to conceptualize the management task. They argued that different competitive fields have different '*dominant logics*', i.e., different patterns of top managers to conceptualize. Some competitive fields have similar logics and may well therefore be within the grasp of a single management team to command while other competitive fields may have a different logic. In their view, it takes a very highly skilled team to conceptualize more variegated divisions and, hence, is the reason for success of some highly diversified groups. Contrarily, Mathur and Kenyon (1998) debated that it is unlikely that the top management team was picked with the above objective in mind.

3.4.7 Costs of diversified operation

Porter (1986) argued that an organization, by spreading across varied areas, creates costs, some visible and some hidden. They are due to the extra burden of diversified operations, and the distraction of top management from its areas of excellence more so for unrelated diversified. The costs for a diversified business group could be for the following reasons:

(a) As a business affiliate, every affiliate must explain its decisions to the group's top management, it should spend time and resources complying with all business group systems;
(b) It also has to live with the business groups guidelines and personnel policies, and hence has to forgo – (1) the opportunity to motivate employees with direct equity ownership[12] ; and (2) select beneficial innovative policies, i.e., firm-level innovation is sacrificed for group-level harmony in operations; and
(c) It also has to cope with the delays in strategic decisions (as communication between top management and group affiliates will involve availability of time for both the sides). These time delays may prove very costly especially when the decisions are to be taken speedily.

Scholars (Claessens et al., 1998; Mathur and Kenyon, 1998) also pointed out other costs of diversification: (a) the costs of implementing an unrelated project; and (b) the skills, efforts and expenditures needed, and the difficulties of motivating or even retaining key staff in the acquired or new business.

[12] Most affiliates of diversified Indian business groups do not motivate their employees using direct equity ownership – we observe this even in sectors such as software where employee stock options are a norm in rewarding employees.

Galbraith (1998) maintained that unrelated diversification is difficult to work (especially unrelated acquisitions), as it is very difficult to change the centers of gravity no matter where the new industry is along the industry chain. The reason is that a center of gravity shift by an organization requires dismantling of the current power structure, rejection of parts of the old culture, and establishment of new management systems.

3.4.8 Incremental process advantages of diversification

Quinn and Voyer (1994) suggested that diversification strategies provide good examples of the value of proceeding incrementally. They consciously prepare the business group to move opportunistically, by creating a '*comfort zone*' for risk taking, and developing a new ethos on the success of new divisions. Diamond (1984) pointed out that diversification can also reduce the cost of delegated monitoring. Incremental processes support both the formal aspects of diversification (price and strategic fit, for example) and the psychological and political aspects. The latter may have implications for an Indian business group. In a family-based group with an increasing number of members (due to growing family tree), this will generate some advantages apart from generating genuine, group-level psychological commitment to diversification overtime, it will keep the group members satisfied by engaging them in one division or the other. Newer members could be kept involved without disturbing others by being assigned important designations in the new divisions or business line coming up. Conceivably, we can also observe a lower cost for generating belief toward common shared values and ethos of the business group (given that they are family members).

3.4.9 Conglomerates and risk aversion

One reason for unrelated diversification is protection (Mintzberg, 1998): Large business groups tend to be risk averse – they have too much to lose – and diversification spreads the risk.[13] Secondly, as a business house grows large, it comes to dominate in its established product markets, and so must often find growth opportunities elsewhere, perhaps through more diversification. The counter argument, however, is that a diversified group may conceal bankruptcies of ailing associate firms and might sometimes support ailing affiliate members

[13] This move makes them behave in a loss-averse fashion, inhibiting them from taking an aggressive stand in the chosen businesses.

longer than necessary. Moreover, just as diversification spreads the risk, so does it also spread the adverse consequences of that risk; so a massive problem in one division can pull down the whole group.[14] Finally, there is the issue of strategic responsiveness for diversified groups' that measure their affiliate member's performance based on short-run, year-to-year, earnings yardstick (see Bower, 1970). Here, the risk to the member firms of a major innovation can be considerable and the result could be a tendency to avoid big risk bets. Hence, innovation may not thrive under the diversified configuration, affecting its long-term value.

3.4.10 Taxation benefits

Taxation plays a significant role in business decisions and might play a role in the product diversification decisions as well. It limits the extent to which firms can retain earnings without penalty (Ramu, 1998). It also creates a disincentive for the distribution of earnings by taxing dividends. Taxation laws are also known to convert the (accumulated carry forward) losses of some firms into assets for highly profitable business groups, which then acquire the right to deduct these losses from their taxable income.

3.4.11 Business houses and agency problems

Agency theory assumes the corporation to be based on a number of contracts between the owners and managers. It proposes that owners and managers pursue different goals (Fama and Jensen, 1983): Owners seek to maximize their wealth, while managers tend to maximize their own interests or payoffs (Amihud and Lev, 1981). Managers (and even owner-managers of business groups) make decisions regarding the use of corporate resources that benefit them personally at the cost of other stakeholders in the organization. An implication of this is that owner-managers can (and have in the past) embark on diversification programs for two widely discredited motives. One is 'risk diversification', and the other is 'size'. For managers of a business group, size may appear to increase their importance and status, whereas risk diversification appears to make their jobs more secure. Business group owners may feel that their importance and status varies with the number of divisions (and their sizes) they direct. In addition to

[14] Lalabhai group (during 1998–2002) is a case in point; the losses suffered by its affiliate member Arvind Mills Limited's denim division hampered the performance of its other divisions as well.

benefiting the firm's owners, diversification also benefits other stakeholders – for example, by enhancing the career opportunities and job security of coterie members of the business group (Rose & Shepard, 1997; David et al., 2010).

Agency theorists contend that sales growth may provide managers with private benefits such as high pay, power, status, and prestige. Accordingly, managers favor higher levels of sales growth than is optimal for shareholder value maximization. As weak owners are unable to sufficiently constrain managerial opportunism through governance, managers implement diversification strategies that generate higher growth that benefits managers but yield lower profits for shareholders (Kim et al., 2004). These agency issues get boosted by the empire building tendencies that many business groups tend to have (Williamson, 1975). Saha et al. (2011, p. 193–6) provides an illustration of the same using the Tata Group. So, business group owners believing in empire building might devise strategies involving low ownership stake (but high economic control) in the affiliates, without considering their overall impact on shareholder value of the group.

Claessens et al. (1998) argued that diversified groups misallocate capital by investing cash flows generated by profitable affiliates into unprofitable affiliates. Scharfstein (1998) noticed that diversified organizations appear to practice some form of sub-optimal '*socialist*' reallocation of assets/funds across divisions, say, by moving funds from high-yield profitable divisions to low-yield ones. The larger the product diversity of groups, the more will be these 'socialist' investment opportunities available, the more pronounced will be the misallocation of funds and consequent internal rent-seeking activities. The matter gets aggravated if there is lack of expertise in a variety of industries under owner–managers. La Porta et al. (1997, 1998) maintain that these conflicts associated with corporate diversification are likely to be exacerbated in emerging markets because of weak disclosure requirements, ineffective governance mechanisms, and a poorly developed market for corporate control.

3.4.12 Economics of organizations

Several prominent economists and sociologists have emphasized that institutions affect economic outcomes (Granovetter, 2005). Economists have tended to view business groups as reducing transaction costs in product, capital, and labor market – and increasing the same in the markets for 'corporate control'. Langlois (2009) discusses the economics of organization and the economics of institutions more broadly, and suggests the ways in which theoretical strands can help to organize the institutional and organizational facts about business groups. He also examines the ways in which the facts about business groups can influence how it is thought theoretically about the boundaries of the organization. The theory of the boundaries of the organization is at the core of what Williamson (1975) long ago branded as 'the New Institutional Economics' (Klein 2000). Richard Langlois (Langlois, 2009) discusses a lot of theories behind the conceptualization of his work. The box below provides an account of the studies.

Box 3.2: New Institutional Economics Approaches

- Institutional analysis: Coase (1937), Coase (1964), Demsetz (1969), Chandler (1977; 1990)
- Complementarity and similarity (Gap filling): Leibenstein 1968, Hymer (1970), Leff (1978), Langlois and Foss (1999), Chandler (1990)
- Firms, markets and institutions: Gerschenkron (1962), Rosenberg (1976), Dahmén (1970; 1988), Morck and Nakamura (2007; 2010)
- Intermediate ties, pyramids and natural states: Granovetter (1995), Lincoln and Shimotani (2010), Kock and Guillén (2001), G. Jones and Colpan (2010), Chandler (1977,1990), La Porta(1999), Morck (2010), Kohn (2009), North, Wallis, and Weingast (2009), Khanna and Yafeh (2007), Kosenko and Yafeh (2010)

A recent study on Chinese business groups brings together the performance of firms with the markets and institutions of the economy. Carney et al. (2010) addresses the institutional voids hypothesis, which suggests affiliation with a business group will improve a firm's performance in circumstances of poor-quality institutions and extensive market failures. They find support for a temporal hypothesis that affiliation with a business group improves performance, though the value of group affiliation declines over time. The authors also find support for a state '*helping hand*' hypothesis that suggests firms with high levels of state ownership initially experienced an amplified value effect from their group affiliation; and the same petered out over time.

3.5 Contextual factors, diversification, and performance

In this section, we look at the important contextual factors that are likely to affect either product diversification or performance, or both. The factors discussed are size, industry, group ownership, and financial leverage.

3.5.1 *Size of an organization*

Christensen and Montgomery (1981) and Mintzberg (1998) argued that when organizations grow large, they become inclined to diversify as they tend to dominate their traditional markets, and so must often find growth opportunities elsewhere, perhaps through more diversification. Diversification also feeds on itself. It creates a cadre of coterie members of business group's owner-managers eager to diversify, each running his or her own divisions, who push for further diversification and growth. This can occur especially when managerial discretion is sufficient to allow owner-managers to diversify the business group's activities by making acquisitions that benefit or entrench themselves at the expense of other shareholders. This implies that larger sized groups will have a higher tendency to diversify.

In India, during the 1990s, major changes have taken place in the institutional framework governing trade, moving the state from protection toward internationalization. In similar external environment, empirical work in other countries reveals that larger organizations face more opportunities and lesser difficulties in accessing international markets compared to their smaller counterparts (Roth, 1992; Smallbone and Wyer, 1995) hurting their performance. Even in India, these policy changes had a positive impact toward business groups of a larger size. In the literature, many factors are cited for such a phenomenon (Kilantaridis and Levanti, 2000), including – (a) smaller entities inability to control prices because of lack of market power; (b) their dependency upon a relatively smaller customer base; and (c) their limited access to policymakers.

3.5.2 *Influence of industry*

Porter (1980) said that the structure of the industry in which a firm operates constrains its strategies and affects its financial performance. Historically, it is widely accepted that the performance of an organization varies and depends on the different industries it operates in using the structure-conduct-performance framework (Porter, 1986; 1987). This is primarily due to the differing competitive conditions (industry concentration) in different industries in which the business organizations operate and the role of barriers to entry. Studies by Bettis and Mahajan (1985), Lecraw (1984) and Montgomery (1985) also attest to the importance of the link between industry, performance, and diversification strategy. Studies by Grant et al. (1988), Peters and Waterman (1982), and Burgelman (1983) state that far from being a causal influence on performance, strategy is really a result of poor or superior performance in core businesses, i.e., the causation runs from performance in core business to strategy making. Tanriverdi and Lee (2008) find that in the presence of network externalities, complementary related diversification strategies in production and consumption can be critical for achieving positive returns to within-industry diversification.

3.5.3 Ownership pattern and governance

Business groups (owners') stake

Strategic management researchers have long viewed ownership as an important factor in aligning managerial decision-making with the best interests of owners (Holmstrom, 1979). Nicodano (1998) pointed out that shareholders receive pecuniary benefits, such as dividends, in proportion to their ownership stake, while controlling shareholders (in our case, business groups) also enjoy private benefits that are proportional to the amount of the assets controlled. Given positive private benefits (and abstracting from pecuniary benefits), the smaller a business group's stake, the larger his rate of return from control. One way in which a business house does this is by creating subsidiary operating companies from a holding company and also by having cross investments. This practice allows groups to gain effective control of their firms with minimum amount of cash investment. Hoskisson and Hitt (1994) pointed out that, in general, diffuse ownership produces weak monitoring of managerial decisions and actions. It is likely that more diffuse the ownership, the higher the level of product diversification in the company.

Claessens et al. (1999) point out that diversification in East Asia can be attributed to a divergence between ultimate owners' (usually business groups) control rights and cash flow rights. They find that larger divergence between control and cash flow rights is associated with more diversification. DaSilva and Black (2004) provide an understanding of the associations between governance structures and diversification strategies based on a study of manufacturing companies listed on the São Paulo Stock Exchange. They find the existence of a significant positive association between the product diversification level and the independence of the chairman of the board of directors. Also, significant positive association was seen between the granting of company profit sharing and the level of product diversification since companies that choose this type of executive compensation experienced greater diversification of their product portfolio.

In contrast, Holderness and Sheehan (1991) observe that when a business group destroys value, it bears part of the costs directly through a decrease in value of its block and indirectly through damage to its reputation. A reputation for opportunistic behavior and inept management increases the cost of raising capital and contracting with third parties. This may force a business group to forgo some projects it would have otherwise undertaken. Finally, minority shareholders can also restrain groups through litigation. Based on the above discussion, we can conclude that business groups with a relatively larger stake in affiliate firms might be inclined to do significant amounts of monitoring and, hence, influence the groups' performance for the better.

The role of institutional investors: Domestic vs foreign

In the recent past, institutional owners, particularly the foreign institutional investors, are playing an increasing role in the decision-making processes of the firm, particularly by increasing their latent power in constraining choice of strategies. Chaganti and Damanpour (1991) found that the degree of institutional stockholding is positively related to the firm's performance. Douma et al. (2006) show that the previously documented positive effect of foreign ownership on the firm's performance is substantially attributable to foreign corporations that have, on average, larger shareholding, higher commitment, and longer-term involvement. David et al. (2010) distinguish between domestic '*relational*' owners and foreign '*transactional*' owners in Japanese corporations. They find that though transactional owners do indeed prioritize profitability when diversifying, relational owners primarily seek growth rather than profits from diversification. Furthermore, relational owners also allow managers to appropriate more of the rents arising from diversification than do transactional owners.

3.5.4 Capital structure influence

The strategic view of capital structure argues that decision-makers actively seek to direct an organization's capital structure to support its long-term strategic goals (Barton and Gordon, 1988). According to Bethel and Liebeskind (1998), two effects of diversification play a role in creating conflicts of economic interest between owners of outstanding fixed claims (i.e., debt holders) and residual claims (i.e., common equity holders)- (a) diversification changes the variance of firm revenues; and (b) diversification increases the likelihood of change in priority of claims on the firm. Jensen and Meckling (1976) posit that more leverage decreases the availability of cash, thereby forcing decision-makers to care more about the performance of the remaining resources.

Lim et al. (2009) found that firms pursuing unrelated product diversification take on less debt financing in stable environments, but more debt financing in dynamic environments. They argued that the link between diversification and capital structure is moderated by the environment in which firms operate. In India, Kakani and Reddy (1996) found firm profitability to be strongly negatively related to capital structure. Hence, leverage should be included as a control variable to isolate its influence on product diversification and performance linkage.

3.6 The Indian context

Granovetter (1994) stated that for most countries, study of business groups has received '*so little attention for so long*'. The case of India has been no different. Not much research has taken place on business groups in general, let alone the relationship between their diversification strategies and performance. The few important studies done and their conclusions are listed below.

- **Khanna and Palepu (1999)** found that Indian business groups have strengthened the ties that bind their firms together post-liberalization and that their product and geographic scope has generally increased after 1991. They argue that the existence of groups is due to their privileged access to new opportunities such as creation of internal markets and development of group brand, which connotes quality. Based on these results, the authors maintained that though the policy changes in India focused on deregulation of industries, restriction on the operation of factor markets for intermediaries continued to exist, and this facilitated increased value creation potential for groups.
- **Khanna and Palepu (2000)** aggregated the affiliate members' performance measures to construct group Tobin's Q and group ROA measures.[15] They found that accounting and stock market-based measures of firm performance initially decline with business group diversification and subsequently increase once group diversification exceeds a certain threshold level. They also observed the same quadratic

[15] Their group performance measures were weighted averages of the member firm performance measures, with firm assets used to determine the weights.

relationship between performance and group size using ROA. They constructed an industry-adjusted Tobin's Q by subtracting from group Tobin's Q a weighted average of industry Tobin's Qs. As in firm-level estimations, a regression of industry-adjusted group Tobin's Q on group size and group diversification revealed a quadratic relationship between performance and group diversification.

Nevertheless, the authors submit the non-robustness of the results. They state that their work on aggregate group performance has not been exhaustive. For example, they had taken data for just one year, 1993, for aggregate group performance analysis. Their diversification measure was also a simple count of the number of industries a business group operates in, a criterion which has been questioned in the literature (see Berry, 1975). Also, the authors had used industry-adjusted Tobin's Q and ROA; comparative figures had been taken as the unaffiliated firms' median Tobin's Q and ROA, respectively. In a country where some industry segments are altogether dominated by business groups and some other industry segments by unaffiliated single-line firms, the use of such measures might lead to spurious results.[16] A case in point is the 2-digit SIC industry code 37, consisting of all firms in transportation equipment segment is dominated in India by huge private business group firms (such as, Tata Motors, Mahindra & Mahindra, Hero Motors, and Bajaj Auto). The single segment private firms in this industry are usually the small firms manufacturing minor auto ancillaries. So, here, use of industry-adjusted measures will not give any worthy results.

Khanna and Palepu (2000) argued that the above results in Indian Economy are due to the differences in the institutional framework (including the imperfections in capital, human, and product markets in emerging economies) during the last decade in comparison to the U.S., the U.K., and Japan. They argue that these organizational contexts could diversify groups to replicate internally the functions provided by market intermediaries in advanced economies (see Khanna and Palepu, 1997, 1998a).

- **Petit et al. (2005)** examined the financial performance impact of group affiliation and diversification during two different time periods. They noticed that diversification itself seemed to exert a statistically significant negative influence on firm performance but, consistent with the traditional literature, group affiliation mitigated the negative effect.

---

[16] We have also discussed this issue while discussing the Excess Value Approach measure (Sections 3.2.1).

- **Kali and Sarkar (2005), Chacar and Vissa (2005), and Pattanayak (2009)** studied with more recent datasets and found no evidence of superior performance by business group affiliates over other firms. Pattanayak (2009) who examined the impact of block holders on firm value and performance found similar results.
- **Kedia et al. (2006)** focused on the evolution and transformation of Indian business groups over two economic eras — pre-reform era (pre-1991) and reform era (post-1991). They state that after World War I, the task of promoting new industries in India was carried out mainly by traditional merchant groups which managed to accumulate substantial wealth reaping on wartime speculation. These wealth creators participated in manufacturing activities shortly after the war. Various entrepreneurial groups that formed out of business families like Birla, Tata, Godrej, Dalmia, Juggilal Kamlapat, Jaipuria, Bangur, Goenka, and so on gradually transformed into powerful business groups (Singhal & Tagore, 2002). These conglomerates continued to grow and flourish over the years, more so after India's independence in 1947.
- **Gaur and Kumar (2009)** find in a study on Indian firms that firm performance is positively related to the degree of internationalization, while group affiliation reduces the positive effect of internationalization on firm performance.

In this chapter, we have summarized the literature on business group strategies and their performance. In the process, we also explored the role of historical and institutional linkages underlying the observations and theoretical rationales made in these studies. The study in this chapter forms the backdrop for the underlying conceptual framework and methodology that we develop in the next chapter.

4

Conceptual Framework and Research Methodology

Our first three chapters stress on the need to look differently at business groups; which are, in any way, the state of affairs in most parts of the world, except possibly in the Anglo-Saxon economies. In most economies across Europe and much of Asia and Africa, such business groups constitute a significant part of the business landscape. Business groups and their portfolio of companies have come under great criticism in recent decades, particularly from researchers using Anglo-Saxon structures of financial markets (see, for example, Claessens et al., 2000) – pitting often the interest of the financial investors (including small retail investors) with the controlling family business group. The existence of business groups have been widely ascribed to the weakness or non-development of markets, particularly of finance, in developing countries (see, for example, Khanna and Palepu, 1997). From a strategy perspective, however, it needs to be emphasized that business groups play a very important governance role; a role that a financial market possibly cannot replace (Saha et al., 2011).

Bank-based governance in Germany and Japan and public executive dominated governance in the U.S., Korea, France, China, and even (recently) Japan and Germany point out the importance of non-market executive-based governance that is not always linked to finance. In fact, the executive ambition in Japanese MITI (Ministry of International Trade and Industry) in terms of creating globally competitive domestic enterprises and acquiring technological capability[1] was very important in shaping up investment direction of several large Japanese business groups known as *Keiretsus* or *Zaibatsus*. These were large capitalist enterprises of Japan before World War II, similar to cartels or trusts usually organized around a single family. The intent of the business family and the financial investor cannot

1 As part of their notion of state power of a rising Japanese society regaining global pride.

thus be equated (Saha et al., 2011). We state that these two factions connected to an affiliate constitute different stakeholders and the primacy of the financial stakeholder (of an affiliate firm) cannot be over-riding.

Business Group, thus, is a supra-firm institution – its writ runs across several independent *often-listed* firms that constitute a closed group network (Saha et al., 2011). The institution of the business group, thus, throws up unique set of governance issues. Design of several practices in a Business Group firm, including its mode of deployment of assets, is driven on the one hand by the business family interests and on the other by the requirements to respond to the constraints imposed by '*affiliate firm specific*' financial investors. Hence, the business group's/families' perception of threat, its modes of imagination and ambition become vital. Consideration regarding bequeathal of assets, sharing of assets during the inter-generational transitions constitutes a few among its important concerns which might not bother a financial investor.

If you note, you will find that in India, most business group firms would be concentrated on narrow product/business lines and yet the group, as a whole, would be quite diversified. The practice of organizing the family business in multiple legal entities is not restricted to large groups alone – it is a ubiquitous practice in India – and fairly small businesses that would fall within the global definitions of small and medium category would have such a group structure. Several reasons, including reducing the bankruptcy risk and tax considerations play a role. Often, new businesses are started in new entities to separate the risks of the different businesses to ensure a structure which is similar to a limited liability partnership; this separation also enables outside investors (including equity investors, banks, FIs, etc.) to participate in financing separately. In many cases external financiers, including banks, prefer new business venturing in separate entities to prevent conflation of risks between the established and a new line of business controlled by the same family (Saha et al., 2011). Appendix G illustrates this aspect for the biggest Indian business group, i.e., Reliance Ambani Group.

How does a business group control its vast empire of multiple group companies? Intricate financial mechanisms, including cross-holding across companies, exercising control through friendly trusts and other such modes are quite common. Developing and deputing a group of loyal managers across group companies is also important. You can now think of Tata Groups' development of Tata Administrative Services (TAS) as an attempt to develop a group of managers, loyal to the business group and mobile across group companies. In fact, the Tata group provides an instance where considerable autonomy can be devolved on the CEOs of group companies – within a framework of trust and loyalty to the business group. Such empowering of professional managers, not necessarily at the expense of the group interest, has also been a feature of Japanese *Keiretsu*. Business groups are then a special institution in itself and we need to distinguish them from the notion of just a cluster of affiliates.

We have sequenced the flow of the sections in this chapter in the following style – In Section 4.1, we look at the reasons for which one should analyze aggregate business group performance. In Section 4.2, we look at the framework we would be using to look at financial performance of a business group. Premises and arguments behind the research study being taken are covered in Section 4.3. We look at the research methodology issues such as data source, sample size, and time span of study in Section 4.4. The section also gives an idea of the profile of the study sample. Section 4.5 discusses the control factors influencing the group diversification – performance relationship and the grounds for their being given importance as part of the work. Section 4.6 documents the variables and their measures used in the study. Section 4.7 wraps up the chapter by mentioning the econometrics used and summarizing the research questions delved in this study.

4.1 Analyzing aggregate group performance

Summarizing the discussion taken just above, we can state that 'though, each publicly listed business group affiliate is a legally separate entity that publishes its own statements and is responsible to its own shareholders, there still exists an over-riding objective of the business group which guides the associate firm's goals and strategies'. So, it would be improper to analyze only the group affiliate firms' (individual) performance and diversification strategy, and comment on overall business group performance and its characteristics. It would also be inappropriate to look at the contribution of an affiliate to the total group by a couple of select standard objective measures without taking into consideration the business affiliate's inherent importance to the group. Let us take up, as an instance, a business group affiliate firm of the Ashok Garware Group:

Garware Marine Industries Limited

Garware Marine belongs to the Ashok Garware Group. It got listed on the Bombay Stock Exchange Limited in the 1980s and has been engaged in the Manufacture and Marketing of Fishing Nets for over four decades using Nylon Yarn. The firm's website describes it as catering to the needs of fishermen and having sales of around ₹ 10 crores per annum. The Company's factory is located at Ahmednagar in Maharashtra with 24 imported Japanese machines. It has its own Twisting Division in the same factory to produce Twine for captive consumption.

Can we understand strategies of Garware Marine from an inspection of its product market only? While Garware Marine and its fishing nets remains important, one may explore several other dimensions such as the family tree of the business group; the use of this affiliate as a holding company arm of the Ashok Garware Group; to fulfill the internal capital market's objective of the business group; the use of this affiliate to ensure that the business group has control over other group companies such as Global Offshore Limited, that is the group's largest and best performing firm (with a market capitalization of ₹ 200 crores in 2012).

In other words, we can say that Garware Marine, from a broader perspective of the business group within which it remains institutionally embedded, fulfills the financing needs of the Ashok Garware Group, acts as its investment arm and ensures that the family promoters have enough control over its business empire.

Source: URL: http://www.garwaremarine.com/ and http://www.globaloffshore.in/ (accessed on 12 October 2013).

For instance, a finance subsidiary is by and large created by a business house for the sole purposes of fulfilling the group's internal financial needs rather than the usual objective of maximizing its shareholder value or financial performance (of their own self). The finance subsidiaries of Indian business groups came up primarily to bypass the regulations created by the state in a capital scarce economy as, in India; non-banking financial companies have access to specific benefits[2] such as higher leveraging which

2 In India, the advantages are due to restrictions by the Companies Act on liabilities of firms. Non-banking financial companies have access to additional financing. So, a group's finance company, a specialized firm usually collects and redistributes funds within the group and also obtains funds through: (a) national banks and financial institutions on behalf of member firms and (b) public (fixed) deposits. For example, one of the rules for the manufacturing firms says that 'manufacturing companies cannot accept deposits (from the public) of more than 25 per cent of its net worth' (see Companies Act, 1992). However, a finance company can take deposits to the maximum of 10 times its net worth. Thus, business groups could use their finance companies to bypass the restriction and access more finance for their group firms in need of capital. The business groups could also use these finance companies to make sale-and-lease-back transactions for other affiliate members of the group.

manufacturing firms do not have. Hence, we feel that it is better to look at the performance of the business group as a whole rather than look at firm-level performance for business groups (and its characteristics), which might reveal distorted results.

Several other factors also make us use aggregates of business group financial statement and capital market data, for the purpose of economic analysis. A business group with synergies would have an asymmetric influence(s) on returns of all affiliate members if the synergies do not assist all businesses in the group equally (see Brush and Bromiley, 1997). For example, in related diversification, the combination of businesses may help performance in one business (or a group of businesses) but not that of other businesses of the group. Also, a multi-affiliate diversified business group might plan to have normal or even lower returns in some affiliates to show extraordinary profits in other associate members. For instance, most finance subsidiaries in India (such as, Ashok Leyland Finance Limited of Hinduja Group) consciously have lower returns to assist other affiliates of the Business Group (in this case, other Hinduja Group entities, such as Ashok Leyland Limited).

Therefore, a firm-based study on business groups' diversification – performance relationship would not be able to capture these aspects, and might even lead to spurious results.[3] Hence, our study would focus on the aggregate performance of the business houses rather than on firms.

4.2 Performance and its components

Wealth maximization is a widely accepted objective of business organizations. Varaiya et al. (1987) demonstrated theoretically and empirically that the growth and profitability of an organization decide its shareholder value. Since the market value of a firm is a function of its financial return, given the level of its risk (Fruhan, 1979), we focus on risk as a third determinant of value. Risk affects both growth and profitability of an organization, and would indirectly determine value. Aggregate shareholder value maximization

---

[3] It is accepted that Indian business groups do not vary much in the degrees of social and economic bonds among firms and interlocks across groups (see Piramal and Herdeck, 1985; and Dutta, 1997). Hence, we can also reasonably expect that the errors (if any) would be randomly distributed among the variables (that attempt to reflect the actual economic performance of business group in the markets).

of a business group also provides a conceptual and operational framework for assessing corporate diversification strategies from a financial markets perspective (see, Alberts and McTaggart, 1979; Fruhan, 1979; also see, Section 3.2.3). This is done by identifying shareholder value as a measure and locating four determinants of value, namely profitability, growth, risk, and capital market conditions (Branch and Gale, 1983).

The Du Pont analysis (Ross et al., 1999) shows that profitability has two components: asset turnover ratio and net profit margin. The former is a production efficiency ratio, and the latter is a profit margin ratio. It may be that diversification does not have a significant effect on profitability because it is not related to profitability, but is rather related to its components (see Han et al., 1999). Hence, by using business groups' aggregated financial numbers as a starting point, it would be easy to calculate these components, margin, and asset turnover to determine if relatively focused groups are more (or less) profitable because of higher (or lower) margin or higher (or lower) sales turnover (Serrano, 1998).[4] Thus, diversification strategies can then be assessed in terms of their expected effects on risk, profitability, profitability components, growth, and ultimately on business groups' shareholder value – since capital market conditions[5] though a crucial factor driving groups' shareholder value (Branch and Gale, 1983) cannot be objectively measured.

These performance dimensions gain further importance as organizations compete not just for resources, but for political power and institutional legitimacy, for social as well as economic fitness (DiMaggio and Powell, 1983). Some of the business houses also believe in empire building in terms of asset size rather than shareholder value (see Williamson, 1985) as larger the asset

4 Similarly, growth of business groups (measured as total assets growth) can also be split into its components, fixed assets growth and current assets growth, and analyzed. This would give an idea of whether business groups were adding value through capital-intensive growth or otherwise.

5 The existence of '*diversification discount*' in developed markets (Berger and Ofek, 1995; Comment and Jarrel, 1995; Servaes, 1996; Lamont and Polk, 1999) also makes us feel that capital markets are a determining factor. A lot of work has been done by Shiller (1989) arguing that capital markets are driven by investor psychology or fashions prevailing in the markets. In Indian capital markets, there exists an analogy for the *diversification discount* that exists in the Western markets for conglomerates. It is widely seen that multinational companies and focused Indian private players have a performance similar to that of domestic companies that get a higher discounting in the markets (in terms of P/E, P/BV, and P/S ratios).

size of the group, probably larger will be its economic power and influence on society.

Another reason for going for this kind of value creation constituent analysis may be that diversification strategy does not have a significant effect on shareholder value/accounting profitability, but is related to its components that neutralize each other's influence in aggregate performance. For instance, a group pursuing a cost leadership focused strategy may improve its productivity and lower its prices (Porter, 1980). The impact of these two managerial actions may be mutually offsetting, and no change may be registered in the profitability ratio to reflect these actions (Banker et al., 1996). In these circumstances, it will be the asset turnover and margins, which will reflect this action properly.

Figure 4.1 gives a graphic view of various dimensions and their measures under which we will examine diversification.

Figure 4.1: Financial performance and its components

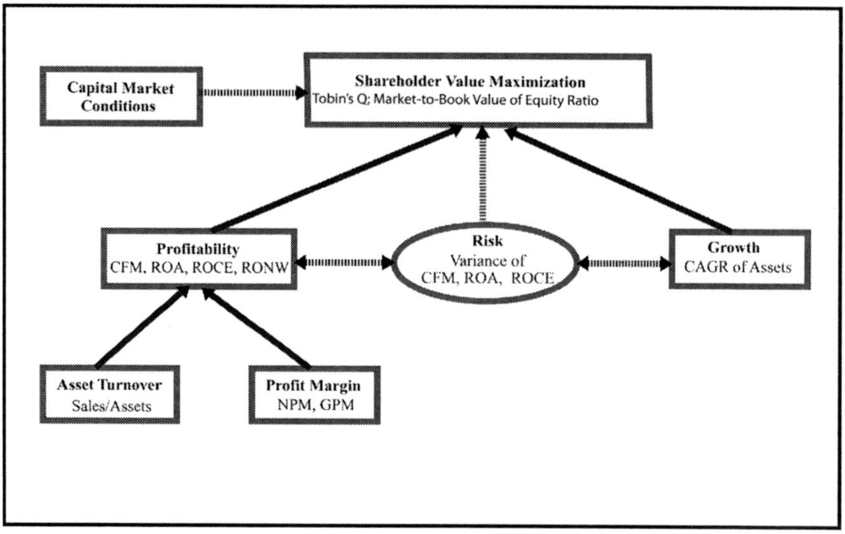

4.3 Research premise

Any diversification strategy will influence a business group's performance profile (Bettis and Hall, 1982). This will occur through potential changes in components, including

1. change in center of gravity (focus) of the group
2. change in the groups market power/position
3. change in resource dependence and scope economies
4. change in industry-specific risk
5. change in the size of the group
6. change in the number of businesses within the group
7. change in the degree of relatedness among the set of businesses[6]

For instance, Chang and Thomas (1989) held that an increase in product diversification of a business group would decrease its risk by decreasing its sector-specific risk exposure and realization of the possible benefits of relatedness.

Based on the literature reviewed, we posit that diversified groups (especially unrelated) would suffer from the extra costs of diversification (Porter, 1986) in comparison to focused groups. These extra costs would be primarily from the loss of focus and difficulty in communication by the diversified business group management while interacting with its multi-divisional arms and subsidiaries. Substantial costs in learning-by-doing and implementation of unrelated projects also exist (Claessens et al., 1998). Moreover, capital markets might get a wrong signal in the delays involved in taking decisions due to communication gaps (and delays) in the diversified groups.

Our presumption so far has been that causation flows from diversification to performance. Another key issue for examination is whether better performance influences diversification. It is likely that business groups that are not performing well in their own areas will opt for product diversification from their existing lines of business (Ansoff, 1971). A new area of operation or a new line of business would once again involve the extra costs discussed above. This could further lead to a decrease in their profitability and hurt shareholder value. This value loss could increase the diversified groups' cost of capital (Chowdhry and Nanda, 1994), driving profitability, and other performance parameters further down.

As the number of business groups in India is quite large, diversified groups having small shares in a number of markets may not be able to take advantage of the low segmental market power (Gribbin, 1976). In fact, they may suffer lower

6 See (Porter, 1985; Barton and Gordon, 1988; Hoskisson et al., 1993; Markides and Williamson, 1996; Mintzberg and Quinn, 1998).

profit margin due to lower market power, by operating in multiple segments, compared to specialized groups of similar size. We also observe that diversified business groups frequently cross-subsidize their loss, making divisions leading to misutilization of funds generated by the profitable divisions. Even scope economies may not occur as highly diversified groups face different environmental demands. Therefore, creating synergies may not be feasible especially in unrelated areas.

The Indian economy chose the path of industrial deregulation and liberalization from 1984–85 (Chopra, 1985). Major institutional changes took place, which resulted in a continuous shift toward more competitive market structures. These policy changes, to a more market-based institutional mechanism, involve stronger disclosure requirements and governance mechanisms, induced a change in the comparative costs of governance (see La Porta et al., 1998; World Bank, 2000). As the institutional foundation of a market economy is incrementally constructed, a change in these parameters resulted in a further increase in the cost of diversified business groups, and a reduction in the transaction costs for comparatively non-diversified business groups (North, 1994; Williamson, 1991).[7]

This implies that after liberalization (1990–91), the net benefits (if any) from multi-divisional diversified Indian business houses will decline over time, particularly during the latter periods of our study period.[8] Therefore, we expect that it would become gradually more difficult for highly diversified groups to create value as the Indian economy, with its policy changes, proceeds toward a more open economy and freer markets. The unrelated diversified groups would have to face more competition in multiple sectors, and this would hurt their efficacy as most of them do not have global scale of operations to achieve economies *or* synergies, whereas specialized business groups with sharper focus would be better able to cope with this competition.

Based on the above reasoning, we state that less diversified and single-segment business groups would add more value than related and unrelated diversifiers would especially after India's economic liberalization.

While the above premise largely discusses about a business groups' aggregate shareholder value creation and accounting profitability dimensions with reference to their product diversification strategy, further analysis involving all constituents of shareholder value and profitability would give a precise picture (as in Figure 4.1) of the constituents (if any) that drove the relation between a

---

7 Especially to those with large-scale operations in single segments, such as Asian Paints Choksi group, Ranbaxy group, MRF group, Dr. Reddy's group, and Gujarat Ambuja Cement group.

8 The proposition assumes, however, that deregulation of markets will lead to a reduction in transaction costs.

groups' value (or profitability) and its product diversification strategy during various phases of Indian economy (i.e., pre-liberalization, post-liberalization growth period, and post-liberalization recessionary phase).

While performing an empirical examination to test these assertions, it is important to identify and include the relevant (measurable) contextual factors (i.e., control them). Analysis related to contextual factors (discussed in Section 4.5) such as a business groups' size, its dominant industry, its ownership pattern, its international exposure, its age, its solvency position, and its capital structure would reveal the nature of linkage these characteristics have with aggregate group performance.

4.4 Research methodology

Research methods should ideally seek robustness by covering the spectrum from relatively fine grained to relatively coarse-grained methodologies within the same project to address the same set of issues. The purpose of this section is to provide a rationale for the research methodology we develop and to discuss the process for applying that methodology.

4.4.1 Data sources

The financial statement and capital market data for our research are primarily obtained from publicly available databases maintained by Centre for Monitoring the Indian Economy (CMIE) and Bombay Stock Exchange (BSE).[9] The product-wise sales data for calculating the diversification indices was also obtained from CMIE. While CMIE is a privately run, near 40 years old, Mumbai-based firm that maintains databases on private and public sector economic activity in India, BSE is India's oldest and largest stock exchange with a database of over 55 years.

These standard Indian databases are most widely used by academic researchers and business executives to analyze Indian firms/business groups (see Manuj, 1994; Ahuja and Majumdar, 1995). The databases have information drawn from annual reports, financial statements, other regulatory reports, and press releases from several thousands of companies in India, as well as daily stock prices for firms on the BSE (or National Stock Exchange).

---

9 Minor gaps in data (say, missing stock price for a year or missing financial statement for a year) were filled up using other sources such as annual reports of the group affiliates, *Capitaline* database, '*Capital Market*' Magazine, *Vans* Business Information Service, and archives of '*The Economic Times*' daily newspaper.

4.4.2 *Identifying group affiliation*

The identification of group membership in India is more reliable and easier than in several other countries (see, Khanna and Palepu, 1998b). First, unlike in a variety of countries, firms in India are members of only one group (see Strachan, 1976; Goto, 1982). Second, there is virtually little movement of affiliates across groups because of little merger activity in India.

The dataset we used in our analysis consists of all Indian business groups affiliated to private sector and listed on the stock exchanges with the required data and a listing history of at least 10 years by their affiliates.[10] For this purpose, we adopted the CMIE[11] database's classification of firms into groups. CMIE uses a variety of sources to classify firms into business groups. Prior to the repeal of the erstwhile Chapter 3 of the Monopolies and Restrictive Trade Practices (MRTP) Act in 1991, the government published a comprehensive list of affiliate firms belonging to '*large industrial houses*'.[12] This formed a starting point for the CMIE classification of a number of groups. CMIE also identifies the promoters of a firm when it was first started and traces whether the original owners retain the control of the firm.[13] CMIE also regularly monitors changes in the group structure. While shifts in a firm's business group affiliation are rare, any such changes are accounted for in the database.

There is no ambiguity between CMIEs classification of firms into groups and those attempted by other sources against which we have cross-verified. This classification was examined with *Capitaline*[14] database. As a further check

---

[10] There have been some groups (such as DLF, Nirma, Lupin, Raheja, Shobha, and Thermax) that have an existence of more than 10 years but got listed only recently (after year 1995) and, hence, are not part of the study.

[11] CMIEs database package is known as '*PROWESS*'. Please refer to the URL: http://www.cmie.com/.

[12] The commission set up in 1971 under the Monopolies and Restrictive Trade Practices (MRTP) Act, 1969 in the year defined a business house on the basis of its assets. The limit then fixed at ₹ 100 crores was later revised.

[13] Other sources of information used by CMIE involve – (a) Track announcement by individual firms of the groups of which they are a part and by the groups of lists of affiliated firms. Such announcements appear periodically in annual reports, advertisements, or at the time of public offering and news releases about the groups' and firms' future plans, and (b) identifying the interest that a group has in a particular firm through the membership of its board of directors.

[14] *Capitaline* database belongs to a reputed media-publishing house maintaining financial and capital market data of corporate India.

on the quality of group classification, we verified the CMIE database against *Business Today*[15] magazine special issue on Indian business houses classification published in the year 1997. Finally, we also verified with the names of affiliate firms that appear with that of large groups mentioned in historical accounts (Piramal, 1996, 1997; Karanjia, 1997).

In the case of family controlled groups, succession from one generation to another often results in the group being split into multiple parts. We identified several prominent groups (such as GD Birla Group, Goenka Group, Khaitan Group, and Modi Group) that had gone through such periods of succession in the past 20 years and checked to see that CMIE had indeed classified each sub-group separately. Thus, the original Birla group is classified in several sub-groups, as is the group originally run by Goenkas.

4.4.3 Sample and size

This study covers public limited companies only, quoted in any one of the Indian stock exchanges. For the purpose of our study, we take a firm as belonging to a particular business group in which the sample business group has at least 10 per cent of the control rights of the company and which is not controlled by anybody else (similar to Claessens et al., 1999).[16] Availability of data being the constraint, the study included all dominant business houses (final size of 240) in India in the sample. Appendix C lists the sample of business groups covered by the study. It also lists the sample of business groups that were eliminated from the analysis due to the following reasons:

- Business groups promoted by government or government-owned firms.
- Business groups that did not have listed affiliates for a period of more than 10 years during the time frame of the study.
- Business groups that had negative net worth during anyone of the three periods of study (as this would have generated a lot of outliers).
- Business groups whose parents were multinationals and the foreign ownership in the group was more than 50 per cent of the total share holding.
- Foreign group affiliates guided by the policies of their foreign parents (i.e., multinational interest) rather than the local interests were also deleted. In other words, a foreign business group was deleted if there

[15] A fortnightly magazine of *India Today* group.

[16] La Porta et al. (1999) had this cutoff as 20 per cent.

was an example of its strategic alignment in decisions and plans with the parent MNC during the period of study.[17]

- Groups that had an annual turnover of less than ₹ 3 crores during the time of study.

4.4.4 *Time span of the study*

Simmonds (1990) empirical work provides support to the argument that the period of study has an effect on the performance results. So, to avoid factors such as temporal stability and economic/business cycles influencing our study, we used a longer time frame of study of a 12-year period. As the business houses and firms were at liberty to choose their diversification strategy from 1985 onwards[18], the study would be carried out for the period 1987–99. This period of 12 years was divided into three sub-periods of four years each.[19] Period 1 would be from financial year 1987–88 (hereafter, FY1988) to FY1991 (period of pre-liberalization). Period 2 would be from FY1992 to FY1995 (period of post-liberalization; growth phase). Period 3 would be from FY1996 to FY1999 (period of post-liberalization; recession phase). Also, the financial performance analysis based on a longer time span of study with three equal periods of four years each would generally take care of the impact of business cycles on the various industries/sectors of the economy.

---

[17] Examples of such foreign group affiliates and their actions are – Hoechst (merger with Welcome group), Indal (was supported by Alcoa of the U.S. while having a takeover bid from Sterlite), and Glaxo (divestment of foods division based on foreign parents restructuring) and the SmithKline Beecham group (merger of local subsidiaries).

[18] Due to de-licensing of industries and starting of the policy changes.

[19] The significance of this period for the Indian firms and business houses needs hardly be emphasized as the Indian economy had to go through a stage of increased competition, deregulation, expansion, and reorientation. The rationale for these three periods was: (a) Period 1 was when de-licensing of sectors just started; (b) Period 2 was when the economy opened up rapidly, exporting industries were given more benefits, regulatory forces such as Controller of Capital Issues (CCI) gave way to SEBI, and the industrial growth rates were high; and (c) Period 3 had more liberalization and lower industrial growth rates. Appendix E provides the mean figures of the key financial. They confirm the discussion here. The industrial growth in the index of industrial production from the Central Statistical Organization (CSO) figures also confirms this (World Bank, 2000).

4.4.5 Profile of the sample

In all we had 230, 239, and 240 business groups for the periods 1987–91, 1991–95, and 1995–99, respectively. The difference in the number of business groups for the three periods is due to the fact that some groups (for example, the Khataus) had split during the period of study. A group that split during the period of study was taken as multiple groups during the next period of study.

There were also some groups that had sold or merged or divested their affiliates during the period of study[20]. A list of all the mergers and acquisitions (M&A) during the period of study was scanned for all M&A related to business group affiliates (either on the buyer side or on the seller side).[21] We then included the same accordingly in the sample of our business groups.[22]

The total sales and the total assets of the sample of business groups in our study were around ₹ 250,000 crores[23] and ₹ 370,000 crores, respectively, for the FY1999. Based on the CMIE data, we find that our sample of business groups owned more than 46 per cent of the total market capitalization of the Indian capital markets. These figures also reflect the importance of 'business group' as a unit of organizational research over 'firm'.

Table 4.1 gives the basic descriptive statistics of business groups in the sample. Section 4.6 gives detailed definitions of the measures listed below. The mean growth, profitability, and Tobin's Q figures show that average performance level of business groups in Period 3 has decreased compared to the first two periods. It also reveals that sample business groups' product and international scope increased consistently from Period 1 to Period 2, and from Period 2 to Period 3. Appendix F gives complete details of product and financial data for a sample group, i.e., Lalbhai Group.

---

[20] For example, Mehta Mahendra group took over Gujarat Sidhee Cements in 1993 from Cement Corporation of Gujarat. Similarly, Gujarat Ambuja Cement group has acquired Modi Cements Ltd. (rechristened Eastern Ambuja Cements) in 1997 from Modi Alkalies Group.

[21] The list of mergers and acquisitions for the period 1987–99 was obtained from a database generated by Professor Sushil Khanna, Economics Group, Indian Institute of Management Calcutta.

[22] The data for these merged/acquired firms was obtained from old databases of existing packages (CMIE-*PROWESS*) and the Bombay Stock Exchange Official Directory Archives.

[23] 1 crore = 10 million

Table 4.1: Descriptive statistics of select variables covering the sample business groups[24]

Name of the Variable ↓	Mean			Standard Deviation		
	Pre-liberalization Period	Post-liberalization, Growth Phase	Post-liberalization, recessionary Phase	Pre-liberalization Period	Post-liberalization, Growth Phase	Post-liberalization, recessionary Phase
Annual Growth in Total Assets (in %)	37.9	42.9	7.6	66.9	73.8	15.6
Return on Capital Employed (in %)	15.5	15.1	10.9	6.0	5.5	7.8
Modified Tobin's Q Ratio	1.2	1.6	1.1	0.3	0.7	0.5
Age of the Group (in Years)		45.7			26.5	
International Diversity of the Group (in %)	14.9	20.3	24.0	15.3	19.9	21.9
Product Diversity (Montgomery's 3-digit SIC measure)	0.45	0.52	0.54	0.28	0.26	0.24
Total Assets (in ₹crores)	271	700	1,534	667	1,695	3,722

[24] Appendix E displays the complete descriptive statistics of the sample business groups.

4.5 Other factors influencing business group performance

A potential problem with the results reported by most previous studies on the strength of the relationships between product diversification and performance is that they failed to account for the influence of moderating variables, thereby yielding potentially inappropriate conclusions. The study will use a multiple variable (regression) approach, explicitly controlling for other factors known to be important in determining business group performance. Researchers in the field (Dubofsky and Varadarajan, 1987; Varadarajan and Ramanujam, 1987) had also argued for the inclusion of potentially important moderator variables. Thus, our study includes the following variables for the reasons discussed below:

4.5.1 Size of the group

Organizational size has been proposed as an important moderator of strategy-performance relationships (Child, 1972; Morck et al., 1988). Singh and Whittington (1968) argue that as size grows, it becomes more difficult to sustain impressive performance. Presumably, this is the primary rationale behind the '*organizational size effect*' (Banz, 1981). On the other hand, Mathur and Kenyon (1998) suggested that increase in size of an organization could reduce its cost of capital by enhancing their financial clout. An increase in the financial size of a business group may conceivably improve its ability to fund itself in the following ways:

- There is a discrete jump at the point where the group affiliate can be listed on a stock exchange and raise equity in the market. Similarly, there is another discrete jump at the point where the affiliate member can raise debt by way of quoted or otherwise marketable securities, such as the bond market. There is also a discrete upward shift to access international capital markets, to get the central banks permission.[25] These three discrete jump functions will lead to wider access of sources of funds for a business group having larger size and is likely in its own right to reduce the cost of capital.
- It is possible that banks, financial institutions, and similar lenders reduce the interest rate; or rather the margin above the lender's cost of funds,

[25] In India, Reserve Bank of India (RBI) gives the permission for accessing the international financial markets such as a Euro issue, limits are set for the firm even on the amount of capital to be accessed.

to a larger borrower (Ravenscraft and Scherer, 1987) with multiple divisions. Since a larger business group will have (a) easier access to alternative sources of funds; (b) will give them a larger pie of business (reducing the running around); and (b) have larger, more valuable assets as security (such as real estate). There is also a belief among fund managers, portfolio managers, equity analysts, and retail investors that financial size itself reduces risk. The suggestion here is that the market risk premium is inversely related to its size, *ceteris paribus*.

So, a business group with a larger size could reduce its cost of capital and, hence, increase the shareholder value. Much of the negative effects of larger size and consequent difficulties on sustaining growth that Singh and Whittington (1968) talk about, does not hold in India (after liberalization), as the institutional context gives more growth opportunities and sways toward large-sized business groups.[26]

4.5.2 *Leverage of the group*

The capital structure of an organization has an effect on their financial performance. Agency theory (Jensen and Meckling, 1976) suggests that debt financing is more effective than equity financing in reducing the management's incentive to squander free cash flows, and that it induces management to improve performance. Higher leverage, on the other hand, leads organizations to have higher bankruptcy risk. Myers' (1984) '*pecking order hypothesis*' indicated that organizations prefer retained earnings to debt and they prefer debt to new equity as a form of financing new investments. Barton & Gordon (1988) suggested that organizations with high earning rate would maintain a relatively lower level of leverage because of their ability to finance themselves from self-generated funds. Empirical research in India (Kakani and Reddy, 1996) also found capital structure to be related to the performance of an organization.

4.5.3 *Short-term solvency position*

Short-term solvency position of a group measures its ability to pay its current bills with an appropriate safety margin (Cote and Latham, 1999). In other words, it gives an indication of the ability of the group to pay its bills. A stronger short-term solvency position (measured usually by either *current ratio*

---

[26] Section 5.10.5 discusses this in detail.

or *quick ratio*)[27] indicates a better ability to meet ongoing and unexpected bills, which takes the pressure off the business group's cash flows. Being in a liquid position can also enhance the ability to negotiate cash discounts with suppliers (see Johnson et al., 1980; Pinches, 1990). A weaker current ratio may indicate that the group's dominant business (or the key industries, which the group is in) is having greater difficulties meeting its short-term commitments and that additional working capital support is required.

4.5.4 Long-term solvency position

Long-term solvency position of a business group is an indication of how much liquid assets the group currently has to build its business, fund its growth, and produce wealth (Befumo, 1996). For business groups, it can be measured using the ratio of working capital[28] to total sales. This metric is also widely used by lenders to help gauge the ability for a company to weather difficult financial periods. It measures the frequency (number of times) of sales turnover annually in relation to net working capital.

The main sources of cash are receivables and long-term capital. Each component of working capital (namely inventory, receivables, and payables) has two dimensions, *time* and *money*. If a business group can get money to move faster around the cycle or reduce the amount of money tied up, the business will generate more cash. Consequently, a group can reduce the outflows of bank interest or have additional free funds available to support sales growth or investment. Similarly, if a group can negotiate improved terms with suppliers, it can effectively create finances to help fund future sales (see Johnson et al., 1982; Gup, 1983).

If a business group is growing and its current activity represents considerable increase over the corresponding activity in the previous period, the group would have increased its short-term capital requirement and/or the group may experience a reduction in its long-term solvency position. The faster a business group (*or* the industry in which it is working in) expands, the more cash it will need for working capital and investment (Martin et al., 1991). The cheapest and best sources of cash exist as working capital within a business group, bearing in mind that the cost of providing credit to customers and holding stocks can

[27] Current ratio is measured as current assets over current liabilities. Quick ratio is measured as quick assets over current liabilities (Foster, 1986; Ramachandran and Kakani, 2007).

[28] We measure working capital as *current assets* less *current liabilities*.

represent a substantial proportion of a business group's total cash and profits. Hence, good management of working capital will generate cash, could improve profits, and reduce risks (see, Lamberson, 1993).

4.5.5 *International diversification*

International diversification involves producing (or providing) the same products (or services) while developing a wider geographical reach (Buhner, 1987; Mudambi et al., 1999). Many authors (Slocum, 1997; Rees, 1998) have observed that international diversification (or geographical diversification) offers several advantages. First, it allows business groups to exploit new market possibilities (Hitt; 1998; Wan, 1998). It also helps to stabilize returns by creating economies of scale and scope (Hoskisson and Hitt, 1994). International diversification also allows groups to exploit their core competencies and distinctive capabilities across units in different international markets. International diversification also provides a broader base of markets to obtain returns from innovation. Therefore, movement into international markets may allow a business group to achieve a long-term strategic competitiveness. On the risk side, international diversification may reduce certain types of risk, but it may increase others, for example, bankruptcy risk resulting from increased debt to finance the entry into new markets (Rees, 1998).

We believe international diversification to be an important factor affecting business groups' performance. This influence would be more during the pre-liberalization period of study when import was restricted[29], and to the extent that there are large amount of imports by a business group decline in tariffs would help those business groups.

4.5.6 *Net exports of the group*

In developing countries such as India, there are several types of export incentives and credit schemes to exporters (EXIM, 1996; Puliani and Puliani, 2000):

- input stage incentives, such as duty exemption scheme and duty drawback;

[29] (For the economy as a whole) import-weighted tariff rate gradually fell from 87 per cent in FY1991 to 28 per cent in FY2001. This has further come down to near single digits (10 per cent) in FY2011.

- finished stage incentives, such as exemption/refund of terminal excise duty and exemption of sales and income tax;[30]
- other special types of incentive schemes, such as special import license, Export Credit Guarantee (ECG) scheme, 100 per cent Export Oriented Units (EOU)/Export Process Zones (EPZ) scheme and corporate tax exemption; and
- EXIM credit facility.

These sops to export-oriented business groups have increased after the liberalization phase[31] (Period 2 and 3 of our study) of the Indian economy (World Bank, 2012). This support of the state could even have a secondary effect. This may lead net exporters to have better discounting in the equity markets than others, *ceteris paribus*, and reduce their cost of equity.

Furthermore, business houses that are highly export oriented and are able to integrate across country borders by standardizing or modifying products, while coordinating critical resource functions such as research, would be able to achieve enhanced economic scale and distribute investments in critical functions over a broader base (Caves, 1982). Net exporters would also be able to learn from the global markets and adopt those techniques (or functions) in domestic markets to gain advantage over their counterparts. This implies that groups that have higher net exports may perform better than others. *Hence, net export level could also be a determinant of Indian business group performance in the post-liberalization era. We have controlled for the same in our empirical analysis.*

4.5.7 Age of the group

Researchers (Batra, 1999; Lumpkin and Dess, 1999; Kroszner, 2000) in the past had maintained that firm age has an influence on its performance. Sorenson and Stuart (1999) reasoned that the inertial forces operating on old business groups is one of the reasons why not-so-old groups, which, relatively speaking, lack capital, reputations, and brand names are able to create new market niches and compete against older and larger groups. The difficulties of keeping pace with continuous external developments often

[30] Examples: Sections 80HHC, 80HHD, 80HHE, and 80HHF of the Government of India, Income Tax Act (Puliani and Puliani, 2000).

[31] For example, (a) the setting up of EPZs to promote exports and (b) the rules and regulations have been made simpler (for example, the passbook scheme).

cause older business groups' innovative activities to diverge increasingly from modern day technology. Age can also slacken the performance of a group by making it more bureaucratic. So, we will also take age as a control variable for performance.

4.5.8 Promoters' (or business groups') stake

Agency theory proposes that owners and managers have different goals for the firm (Fama and Jensen, 1983). Nicodano (1998) pointed out that shareholders receive pecuniary benefits, such as dividends, in proportion to their ownership stake, while owner–managers also enjoy private benefits that are proportional to the amount of the controlled assets. Business groups, being owner-managed, can make decisions regarding the use of corporate resources that benefit them personally at the cost of other shareholders. As business groups' equity ownership increases in their affiliates, the owner's interests would coincide more closely with those of outside shareholders in those affiliates and, hence, the conflicts between business houses and their minority shareholders are likely to be minimized. Therefore, business groups' equity ownership helps resolve the agency problems and should probably improve the group affiliate's performance. Past studies (Khanna and Palepu, 1998a, Kakani et al., 2001) on Indian business groups and firms also suggest the possibility that performance would be associated with its ownership pattern.

4.5.9 Industry fixed effects

One variable that has been extensively used as a control variable is industry. Results by Rumelt (1991) and McGahan and Porter (1997) in developed countries indicated that industry effects exist and are important in determining performance. Porter's (1980, 1987) perspective was that the industry in which an organization competes influences its performance. On the other hand, heterogeneous organizational resources and imperfect mobility of resources lead to the existence of heterogeneous organizations within an industry. Schmalensee (1985) suggested methods for dividing business unit performance into industry, corporate, and market share effects. So, we will include the industry fixed effects in our regressions, the primary-industry in which the business group operates would be taken as the metric.

4.5.10 *Foreign ownership stake*

Agency theorists generally assume that shareholders are homogenous and that their influence on organizational performance is directly proportional to the percentage of equity they hold. However, empirical research following this approach has failed to produce definitive evidence. An interpretation provided by academicians (Kang and Sorenson, 1999) is that shareholders are not homogeneous but that certain types of shareholders use their formal authority, social influence, and expertise to *'capture'* property rights and strongly influence organizational performance.

Foreign holdings exist in business group affiliates either directly (say, through joint ventures) or by way of Foreign Institutional Investors (FII). Since 1993, when they were welcomed into Indian capital markets, FIIs have indeed come a long way. Being managers of portfolios, FIIs tend to restructure and rebalance their portfolios dynamically across countries, their primary concern being their portfolio. FIIs have been known to be ruthless and uncaring toward the companies and business groups that did not care for the interests of investors (Rajeshwar, 2000). At the same time, they have lent support to companies that have steadfastly focused on shareholders' wealth and corporate governance. Empirically, Chiibber and Majumdar (1999) show that firms with high foreign ownership display superior performance.

4.5.11 *Domestic institutional investors' stake*

Domestic Institutional Investors' (DII) ownership is the one held by financial institutions, banks, and mutual funds owing their allegiance to the Government of India. DIIs usually hold large stakes in Indian group affiliates (the mean shareholding in our study sample was around 14.5 per cent). DII ownership tempers the performance of a group by constraining their strategies and by having a lateral effect on the decision of the group. Domestic institutions do this through the board of directors and proxy voting in the group companies (see Chaganti and Damanpour, 1991). However, these DIIs typically extend more loan money to the business group than they hold as equity. Consequently, it is unclear whether their voting power is used in the interest of shareholders or fixed return holders. Empirically, DIIs involvement appears to have a negative relation with firm performance (Kakani et al., 2001).

4.5.12 Solvency position and industry influence

Short-term solvency and long-term solvency positions of an organization are primarily dictated by the industry in which the organization performs (Rees, 1990; Varazdin, 1999). So, by using them as control variables in our regression, we are also attempting to capture the industry influence on a business group's performance in terms of continuous variables. Table 5.2 displays the mean Current Ratio (CR) and Working Capital Ratio (WCM) of Period 3 for the sample of 240 business groups categorized by their dominant 2-digit SIC industry categories. Table 4.2 clearly shows that CR and WCM differ widely by industry.

Table 4.2: Average current ratio and working capital ratio of the sample business groups distributed according to their dominant industry (for post-liberalization period, i.e., Period 3)

Industry SIC Code	Industry Area	Average Current Ratio	Average Working Capital Ratio
IND20	Food and Allied Products	3.396	0.492
IND22	Textiles Mill Products	4.031	0.437
IND26	Paper and Allied Products	2.767	0.349
IND28	Chemicals and Allied Products	3.113	0.473
IND30	Rubber and Misc. Products	3.072	0.453
IND32	Stone, Clay and Glass Products	3.138	0.434
IND33	Primary Metal Industries	2.283	0.425
IND35	Industrial Machinery and Equipment	2.553	0.384
IND36	Electronics and Electrical Equipment	2.801	0.374
IND37	Transportation Equipment	2.798	0.413
INDREST	Rest of the Industries	3.262	0.611

4.6 Variables and measures used in the study

4.6.1 Measures of diversification

There are primarily two kinds of measures to differentiate between diversification categories – continuous and categorical measures. Hall et al. (1994) found that continuous and categorical measures predicted similar diversity-performance relationships. They concluded that the techniques were associated. To make our results comparable with previous studies in the area, we will use one categorical diversification measure and two continuous diversification measures. As a categorical measure, we will use Rumelt's (1974) measure due to its wide acceptance in the literature (see, Section 3.1.2). As continuous measures, we will use the entropy measures by Palepu (1985) and Montgomery (1982).

The measures have been selected due to their extensive usage in the literature on the subject. The study will use only six categories[32] of Rumelt's measures instead of the nine he proposed – *single*, *dominant constrained*, *dominant linked* (includes *dominant vertical*), *dominant unrelated*, *related* (includes both *related constrained* and *related linked*) and *unrelated* categories (includes *multi-business* and *unrelated portfolio*)[33] due to clear differences in these categories. Appendix A.1 has definitions for all nine categories. The distribution of our sample during the three periods across the six categories is given in Appendix E (Table E.2).[34]

In the study, we preferred using international Standard Industrial Classification (SIC) of United States instead of National Industrial Classification (NIC) to make the study more comparable with the other studies. Also, the NIC 1987 scheme[35] does not provide a detailed classification for the recent new economy industries such as computer hardware, computer peripherals, software programming, software designing, multi-media and so on (whereas SIC does).

We used both the 2-digit and 3-digit SIC-based Palepu's (P2 and P3) diversification variable and Montgomery's (M2 and M3) diversification variables, respectively. While the measures using the 2-digit industry

---

[32] The notations used for Single Business, Dominant Constrained, Dominant Linked, Dominant Unrelated, Related Business, and Unrelated Business categories of Rumelt's Categorization scheme in the study are RUM_SB, RUM_DC, RUM_DL, RUM_DU, RUM_RE, and RUM_UB, respectively.

[33] Most of the literature has considered only four to five categories of Rumelt's classification out of nine he proposed (see Simmonds, 1990; Barton and Gordon, 1988).

[34] Rumelt's categorization has been used only as a dummy variable (RUM_XX), which equals 1 for that particular category (XX) and 0 otherwise. The coefficient on this dummy registers a possible difference in the intercept between Rumelt's categories in regressions.

[35] Refer to the Annual Survey of Indian Industry, Government of India, 1987.

classification (P2 and M2) indicate a group's unrelated diversification, the measures using the 3-digit industry classification (P3 and M3) indicate a group's related diversification. As both these measures are based on industrial classification, we assigned the group segments as per the following procedure:

- The group affiliates' segments would be assigned as per the industries in which they operate, in accordance with the 2-digit or 3-digit SIC system. This procedure involves two steps. In the first step, we assigned the 3-digit SIC codes so that we are able to obtain one-to-one matches between SIC codes and segments. If a segment cannot be associated with a reported SIC code, we determine the segment's SIC code according to its business description. In the second step, we redefine segments at the 2-digit SIC level and aggregate segment sales to that level.
- The product-wise sales data for the group affiliates was taken for the third year of each of the four-year study periods. For example, we calculated diversification measures for pre-liberalization period (1987–91) based on the product-wise sales figures of FY1990. Wherever, the third year sales figures were not available, we took the second year (in the above example, it is FY1989) sales data. The primary reason for opting for the third year data is that it would reflect the diversification and product portfolio choice of the business group for that period to the best extent.

4.6.2 Measures of performance

As discussed in the contextual framework chapter, Section 4.2, the study will evaluate performance on the following five dimensions – shareholder value, accounting profitability, profitability components, growth, and risk. We first aggregated all the financial statement and capital market data of the individual affiliate firms to get aggregate financial statement and capital market figures of each and every individual business group in the sample. We, then, calculated all the aggregate group performance measures based on their ratios and formulas given below (see Table 4.3) for each of the four-year periods during the total study time frame from 1987–99. The discussion on the selection of these measures over others follows.

Table 4.3: Notations and measures used for the dependent variables in the study

Variable Name	Notation	Measure
1. Value Creation	TOBIN*	*{market value of equity + book value of preferred stock + book value of debt}/{book value of assets}*
	PBV*	*{market value of equity}/{book value of equity}*
2. Profitability	ROA*	*{net income + interest × (1-tax rate)}/{total assets}*
	ROCE*	*{net income + interest + tax}/{net worth + long-term liabilities}*
	RONW*	*{net income}/{net worth}*
3. Profitability Components	NPM*	*{net income}/{total sales}*
	STA*	*{total sales}/{total assets}*
4. Growth	CAGRTA	*Annual growth in total assets*
5. Risk	VROA	*Coefficient of variance in return on total assets*
	VROCE	*Coefficient of variance in return on capital employed*

Note:

- *All the notations marked with a * (asterisk) have their measures as four-year averages for the consolidated business group financial and capital market figures during the period of study.*
- *Growth variables were calculated using the aggregate business group's first and last financial year figures of the period (say, for pre-liberalization period, annualized growth between the FY1988 and FY1991).*
- *Risk category variables were calculated based on yearly aggregate profitability ratios of a business group.*

1. Measuring shareholder value creation: Tobin's Q ratio, the ratio of market value of assets to replacement cost of those assets, is the most appropriate measure of value creation. Theoretically, Tobin's Q is a much more appealing measure than accounting returns. By incorporating a capital market measure of firm rents, Q implicitly uses the precise risk-adjusted discount rate, imputes equilibrium returns, and minimizes distortions due to tax laws and accounting conventions (Wernerfelt and Montgomery, 1988). For our research purpose, we use a surrogate measure of Tobin's Q (TOBIN) defined as {market value of equity + book value of preferred stock + book value of debt}/{book value of assets}, where the market value of equity is calculated using the average[36]

[36] The average share price throughout the year is calculated as the mean of the low and high price of the share over the year (Lev, 1974).

market price of the share over the year. It has been used extensively by researchers. For example, Khanna and Palepu (1998b, 1999, 2000) used this measure extensively for studying diversification and other characteristics in emerging markets and for studying business groups.

2. Data limitations preclude us from using a better approximation to Tobin's Q as some prior studies have done.[37] We will also use another surrogate measure of Tobin's Q ratio, market-to-book value ratio (PBV) (see Varaiya et al., 1987). The usage of PBV has also been supported in literature as a measure of value creation (see Beaver and Ryan, 1993; Fama and French, 1992, 1995).

An implicit assumption behind using Tobin's Q is that stock prices reflect true firm value. Khanna and Palepu (1999) were of the opinion that this is a troubling assumption in emerging markets, where capital markets are often plagued by untimely disclosure, volatility, and other problems.[38] There are researchers, such as Shiller (1989), of the opinion that the capital markets are not efficient even in the developed countries.

Peasnell (1996) argued that stock prices suffer from the drawback of being too comprehensive, in the sense of impounding everything expected to happen in the future. Peasnell also maintained that accounting reports constitute the only systematically compiled, publicly available, alternative source of information about the financial affairs of business corporations, and are largely standardized and audited too. Also, some researchers proved accounting returns to be better measures for measuring economic returns (Brief and Lawson, 1992; Peasnell, 1996). Apart from capital market data, an analysis of the financial statement's data will also provide us more information about the relationship between the performance and product diversification strategy pursued. Hence, in our analysis, we break down value creation dimension into its analyzable constituents: growth, profitability, profitability components, and risk of the business.

1. Measuring growth: A review of empirical literature shows that the most frequently used measures for growth have been annual growth rate of sales and total assets. In the use of accounting measures, we will prefer using balance sheet-based measures rather than income statement

[37] Studies that had computed Tobin's Q in some detail include Lindenberg & Ross (1981), Montgomery & Wernerfelt (1988), Wernerfelt & Montgomery (1988), and Lang and Stulz (1994).

[38] Especially during the pre-liberalization period of our study, 1987–91, i.e., before the institution of the regulatory authority to monitor exchanges, i.e., SEBI, Securities and Exchange Board of India.

based measures as the different procedures of applying taxation rules and intra-group transactions across groups will affect their income statement figures more than the balance statement based figures. For example, growth in total assets is more preferable to growth in total sales, as the reported sales figures could be affected by varying excise tax rules, intra-group transactions, and the firm-wise accounting policies, for particular groups, across industries. Hence, we will use annual growth rate of total assets (CAGRTA) as our growth measure. Total asset growth has also been used in other studies in the literature (Dess and Robinson, 1984; Jeannet et al., 2000)[39].

2. Measuring profitability: We will use the three most used accounting measures in the literature, i.e., return on assets (ROA), return on capital employed (ROCE), and return on net worth (RONW).[40] The measures will be averaged over a period of four years to iron out any temporary swings in returns. ROCE is defined as {net income + interest + tax}/{net worth + long-term liabilities}. ROA is defined as {net income + interest × (1-tax rate)}/{total assets}, where an average tax rate is estimated and taken for each period for all the sample business groups. The tax rate was taken as 45 per cent, 40 per cent and 35 per cent for periods 1, 2, and 3, respectively (based on the marginal tax rates on corporate sector during those periods of study). A similar ROA measure is also used by Caves and Uekusa (1976) in their study of Japanese *keiretsu*, and by Khanna and Palepu (1998a) in their study of diversified Indian business groups. RONW is defined as {net income}/{net worth}.
3. Measuring risk: Risk has been widely measured in the literature as a coefficient of variance of earnings. Our study will have coefficient of variance in return on assets (VROA) and coefficient of variance in return on capital employed (VROCE) as the measures of risk. The four financial years taken for each period of study will make us calculate the variance of ROA and ROCE feasible. Though there are better measures of risk in literature (especially market-based measures such as *beta*), due to data

[39] We had also formed two components of growth, fixed assets growth, and current assets growth. Fixed assets growth rate was calculated as annual growth rate in fixed assets. Similarly, current assets growth rate was calculated as annual growth rate in current assets. Since the results did not add much value, we ignore presenting them here.

[40] Our original study also used the *cash flow ratio*. It is calculated by adding depreciation to net profits of the business group and finding its proportion to total assets of the group. Since the results did not add more value, we ignore presenting them here.

constraints, our study is not able to use them.[41] The data constraint comes from the fact that in India, business groups are not publicly listed but most of their affiliate firms are listed on the stock exchange.

4. Measuring profitability components: The two constituents of profitability are return on sales and asset turnover ratio (Ross et al., 2014). *Return on sales* or *profit margin* will be measured as net profit-to-sales ratio (NPM) averaged over the study period. Asset Turnover ratio will be calculated as sales-to-assets ratio (STA), also averaged over the four-year period.

4.6.3 Measures for control variables

We calculated all the aggregate group control variables based on their ratios and formulas given below (also see Table 4.4):

1. Age: We took the year of incorporation of the oldest affiliate of the business group. Then, we deducted this from year 1999 to get the age of the group (AGE).
2. Domestic Institutional Investors Stake: From the CMIE database, all the equity ownership held by government-owned financial institutions[42] and mutual funds were added to obtain the Domestic Institutional Investors' Stake (DIIS) in the affiliate firms. Further, these member firms stakes were added together using a weighted average based on the total assets of the group to get every individual business group's DIIS.
3. Foreign Holding: The equity stake held by all foreign entities[43] were added together to get the total foreign holding in an affiliate firm from the CMIE database. These figures were then added together using a weighted average based on the total assets of the group to get the foreign holding (FIIS) in the business house.

---

[41] A glance at the correlation matrix showed that for all the three periods of our study, most profitability measures were significantly negatively related to risk measures, i.e., VROA and VROCE. This indicates that perhaps highly profitable groups had lower risk and fluctuations in earnings and, conversely, low profit groups had higher VROA and VROCE. To an extent this justifies that VROA and VROCE are good measures of a business group's risk.

[42] Including ownership by Life Insurance Corporate of India (LIC), General Insurance Corporation of India (GIC) and Unit Trust of India (UTI) and such state-owned institutions.

[43] It can be either *foreign firms or foreign individuals or foreign institutional investors.*

4. International Diversification: {Total Exports + Total Imports}/{Total Sales} has been taken as the measure for international diversification (GEODIV). Though it is a crude measure, data constraints did not allow us to use a better measure.
5. Industry Fixed Effects: 2-digit SIC industry dummies are included in the model, a dummy variable IND_YZ is used, which equals 1 for a 2-digit SIC industry YZ wherein the group had its maximum sales and 0 otherwise. For example, if the Eicher group's maximum sales were in the Transportation Equipment Industry (2-digit SIC industry code 37) then that groups industry dummy variable will be 1 for IND37 and 0 for all other 2-digit SIC industries. The coefficient on this dummy registers a possible difference in the intercept between industries.
6. Leverage: We took long-term debt to net worth (LTD) of the business group as the measure for leverage of a group (see Kakani et al., 2001).
7. Long-term Solvency Position: One of the best measures for long-term solvency of an organization is its Working Capital Ratio (WCM) (Foster, 1986). WCM being calculated as {Current Assets – Current Liabilities}/{total sales}.
8. Net Exports: Higher the exports of a group (or lower a group's imports), the more will be the group's net exports. {Total Exports – Total Imports}/Total Sales of the consolidated financial figures of the group averaged over a four-year time period was taken as the measure for Net Exports of a group (NETEXP).
9. Promoters or Business Group's Stake: Insider ownership includes the stakes held by the group family members and by other group members. Directors' ownership and corporate holding categories in CMIE shareholding details closely capture the insider holding of business group affiliates (Khanna and Palepu, 1998b). Then, these were added together using a weighted average based on the total assets of the group to get the promoters' stake in its group (INSIDER).
10. Short-term Solvency Position: Current ratio and quick ratio are the two most used measures for short-term solvency position of an organization. Current Ratio (CR) calculated as current assets over current liabilities of the group was taken as the measure for short-term solvency position.
11. Size: The study will use multiple measures of size – natural logarithms of total assets (LNTA), total market capitalization (LNMC), and total sales of the group (LNTS). LNMC is a market-based measure and the other two, LNTA and LNTS, are accounting based measures of

size (see Kiymaz, 1999). Recently there has been an increasing use of LNMC as a measure of size (Martin, 1998; Renneboog, 2000). All the measures are the averages over the four-year period.

Table 4.4: Notations and measures used for all independent variables in the study

Variable Name	Notation	Description
1. Size	LNTA*	Natural logarithm of total assets
	LNMC*	Natural logarithm of total market capitalization
	LNTS*	Natural logarithm of total sales
2. Product Diversification	RUM_XX	Rumelt's categorical diversification index for category XX
	P2	Palepu's 2-digit SIC based continuous unrelated measure (DT)
	P3	Palepu's 3-digit SIC based continuous related measure (DU)
	M2	Montgomery's 2-digit SIC based continuous unrelated measure
	M3	Montgomery's 3-digit SIC based continuous related measure
3. Industry Effects	IND_YZ	Groups largest sales from the industry with 2-digit SIC code YZ
4. Current Ratio	CR*	{current assets}/{current liabilities}
5. Working Capital Ratio	WCM*	{current assets – current liabilities}/{total sales}
6. Age	AGE	1999 – {Year of Incorporation of the first group affiliate}
7. Net Exports	NETEXP*	{total exports – total imports}/{total sales}
8. Leverage	LTD*	{long-term debt}/{net worth}
9. International Diversification	GEODIV*	{total exports + total imports}/{total sales}
10. Promoters Stake	INSIDER	Weighted average of the business groups' stake in its affiliates. Weights being based on the total assets of the affiliate firms.
11. Foreign Holdings	FIIS	Weighted average of the foreign holders' stake in the affiliates. Weights being based on the total assets of the affiliate firms.
12. Domestic Institutions Stake	DIIS	Weighted average of the domestic institutional investors' stake in the affiliates. Weights being based on the total assets of the affiliate firms.

Note:

- *All the notations marked with * have their measures as four-year averages for the consolidated business group financial and capital market figures during the period of study.*

(Continued)

Table 4.4 (Continued)

- *The third year product-wise sales figures of the four-year period were taken for calculating the product diversification measures and industry fixed effects measures. For example, we calculated diversification measures for period 1 (1987-91) based on the product-wise sales figures of FY1990.*[44]
- *Appendix A gives the exact details of measuring all the diversification variables.*

Table E.1 (in Appendix E) presents the mean and standard deviation for the sample groups. We have also provided the Rumelt's category distribution and industry-wise distribution of the sample data in Appendix E, Table E.2, and Table E.3, respectively.

4.7 Econometrics used and summary of research questions

Econometric analysis details

We tested the hypotheses by using linear multiple regression techniques which model group performance as a function of size of the group, its diversification, leverage, and industry fixed effects among others as shown below. The regressions were computed for all the three periods for each of the dependent variable measure (namely – TOBIN, PBV, ROA, ROCE, RONW, NPM, STA, CAGRTA, VROA, and VROCE) with all the nine relevant explanatory variables. Each period consists of four years each (pre-liberalization, post-liberalization growth and post-liberalization recessionary periods). These linear multiple full model regressions were performed using both the best variables[45] and the standard variables.[46]

---

[44] In cases, where the third year sales figures were not available, we took the second year sales figures.

[45] Best variables mean variables that best fit among all the available variables for a particular category in the regression equation. For example, in size category we have three variables viz., LNMC, LNTS, LNTA which can capture the effect of size category. In regressions using best measures, we use the variable which best captures (provides highest *Adjusted R Square*) the effect of size category on the dependent variable.

[46] Standard variables are those that have been used in all the regression equations irrespective of the one which best captures the effect of a category. For example, in size category as mentioned above, we have three variables, viz., LNMC, LNTS, and LNTA which can capture the effect of size category. In regressions using the standard measures, we use the variable LNTA irrespective of the one that best captures the effect of size category on the dependent variable.

Performance = *f*(product diversification, size, leverage, long-term solvency, short-term solvency, insider ownership, foreign ownership, domestic institutional ownership, international diversification, net exports, age, industry fixed effects)

For latest period, the regressions were also performed using each of the dependent variables with the 12 explanatory variables (including the three ownership variables whose data was available for only the latest period, i.e., Period 3).

We also made use of transformations of diversification variable in the multivariate regression techniques to look into the exact fit between performance and diversification variable given all the control variables. Both the continuous and non-continuous measures of diversification were used separately for performing these multiple regressions. Also linear regressions using the 10 industry control dummy variables were performed separately to check for robustness of the results (after controlling for the industry effect).

4.8 Summary of the research questions

The objective of this empirical research is to find answers to the research questions developed in the theoretical discussion of this study. A summary list of the research questions to be answered is as follows:

1) What is the relationship of Indian business groups' shareholder value creation (market-based financial performance measure) with their product diversification strategy and such other group characteristics? Do the relationship between Indian business groups' aggregate financial performance and product diversification strategy static, irrespective of the changes in the economic policies of the state (liberalization) and the economic cycles facing the industry?
2) What is the relationship between Indian business groups' accounting profitability and their characteristics especially product diversification strategy?
3) What is the relationship between business group characteristics and their profitability components (i.e., profit margin and sales turnover) during the different study periods?
4) To what extent are growth rates of Indian business groups related to their diversification strategy and other group characteristics?
5) To what extent are Indian business groups' risk (earnings variation) related to their product diversification strategies and other group characteristics?

6) Is the relationship between product diversification strategy and aggregate performance of Indian business groups (if any) non-linear in nature (such as quadratic, cubic, etc.)?
7) Does Indian business groups' ownership pattern influence their product diversification-performance linkage?
8) Does the dominant industry category, to which these business groups belong, influence the relationship between the aggregate performance and other group-level characteristic relationships during the different study periods?
9) Does the relation (if any) between financial performance and product diversification strategy continue to hold, when Rumelt's categorical classification (non-continuous) is used as a product diversification measure instead of the continuous measures?

5

Empirical Results and Managerial Implications

Having identified a set of research questions in Chapter 4, we present in this chapter the answer to those research questions. For each research question raised, we present relevant regression results (in brief) of important variables and evaluate the performance–characteristics linkage of Indian business groups from Section 5.1 to Section 5.9. We discuss the empirical results further in Section 5.10 and deduce few take homes in the last two sections, i.e., 5.11 and 5.12.[1] Throughout this chapter, we follow the following notation for significant independent variables in the regressions based on their significance:

(a) A single asterisk (*) beside the coefficient denotes significance at the 90 per cent level of confidence.
(b) Two asterisks (**) beside the coefficient denotes significance at the 95 per cent level of confidence.
(c) Three asterisks (***) beside the coefficient denotes significance at the 99 per cent level of confidence.

5.1 Shareholder value and group characteristics

Research question # 1:

What is the relationship of Indian business groups' shareholder value creation (market-based financial performance measure) with their diversification strategy and other group characteristics? Is the relationship between the Indian business groups' aggregate

---

[1] Readers interested in having access to the correlation data and regression results can write to us.

financial performance and the product diversification strategy static, irrespective of the changes in the economic policies of the state (liberalization) and the economic cycles, facing the industry?

We had used two dependent variables for shareholder value dimension, namely *Modified Tobin's Q ratio* (TOBIN) and *Market Price over Book Value ratio* (PBV). Our regression result indicates that product diversification strategy (both related and unrelated), long-term solvency position, and size of the group were highly significant factors in determining shareholder value maximization for all the study periods.[2] While product diversification and working capital ratios were negatively related, size of the group was positively related to shareholder value maximization. Age was negatively related to value during the pre-liberalization period only. Current ratio and international diversification were positively related to value creation in the first two periods, i.e., pre-liberalization and post-liberalization growth periods. Net exports were positively related to value creation in the post-liberalization recessionary period. We also found that leverage of a business group had no impact on Tobin's Q Ratio during any of the three periods.

The highly significant negative relation between diversification strategy and value creation lends support to our hypothesis. The result exhibits that groups that were more specialized increased their shareholder value faster by reaping the benefits of being more focused while multi-divisional diversified groups probably suffered due to learning by doing costs when executing new projects and from misallocation of capital within the group among its divisions. Further analysis of the other performance dimensions (i.e., components of value creation such as profitability and growth) would yield the precise constituents that propelled the results in various periods.

---

[2] To recap, the three periods, i.e., pre-liberalization, post-liberalization growth, and post-liberalization recessionary periods correspond to 1987–91, 1991–95, and 1995–99, respectively.

Table 5.1: Relation between business groups' shareholder value creation and their characteristics: Linear multiple regression coefficients with dependent variable as Tobin's Q Ratio (TOBIN) using both 3-digit and 2-digit continuous diversification indexes as variables for diversification.

Dependent Variable →	Modified Tobin's Q Ratio (TOBIN)			Modified Tobin's Q Ratio (TOBIN)		
Independent Variable ↓	Pre-liberalization Period	Post-liberalization Growth Period	Post-liberalization Recessionary Period	Pre-liberalization Period	Post-liberalization Growth Period	Post-liberalization Recessionary Period
1. 3-digit SIC (DT) Diversification Index	-0.202***	-0.740***	-0.470***			
2. 2-digit SIC (DU) Diversification Index				-0.140**	-0.487***	-0.368***
3. Current Ratio	0.068***	0.065**	-0.015	0.068***	0.073**	-0.018
4. Working Capital Ratio	-0.276***	-0.533***	-0.302***	-0.288***	-0.581***	-0.294***
5. Net Exports	-0.001	0.0001	0.005**	-0.001	0.0001	0.005**
6. Leverage	0.007	-0.017	0.011	0.008	-0.013	0.011
7. Size	0.087***	0.238***	0.186***	0.085***	0.239***	0.192***
8. International Diversification	0.002*	0.003*	-0.001	0.003**	0.004**	-0.001
9. Age	-0.002***	-0.001	-0.001	-0.002***	-0.001	-0.002
(Constant)	0.913***	0.691***	0.631***	0.891***	0.494***	0.518***
Adjusted R Square	*0.264*	*0.337*	*0.301*	*0.253*	*0.300*	*0.286*

Note: In the above regressions, while LNMC was selected as the variable for size, Montgomery's continuous diversification index M3 and M2 were selected as the variables for diversification.

Size appears as the most significant factor influencing aggregate group value, especially during later study periods. This shows that as business houses increase in size, presumably their financial clout and market power also increases (see Mathur and Kenyon, 1998). In the liberalized scenario, larger the size of a business group, more will be the opportunities for the group (see Kilantaridis and Levanti, 2000). Also, foreign investors, institutional lenders, and fund managers target larger sized groups than smaller ones, giving them access to cheaper capital.

Apart from product diversity and size, solvency position of a business group seems to be an important factor influencing group performance. The negative significance of working capital ratio suggests that well-performing firms had tight working capital turnover ratios. The positive significance of current ratio for the first two periods suggests that poorly performing business groups had apparently tough short-term solvency positions in their balance sheets.

The positive significance of either international diversification or net exports during each sub-period of study suggests that export-oriented businesses offer several advantages and value to business groups. They allow groups to take advantage of new market possibilities (Wan, 1998) besides providing a broader base of markets to obtain returns from innovation (Hoskisson and Hitt, 1994). Therefore, movement into international markets may allow business houses to achieve a long-term strategic competitiveness and higher shareholder value.

The age-performance negative relation of business groups in pre-liberalization period suggests that older business groups were not being able to cope with the deregulation and de-licensing of industry. Perhaps, older business groups were having a hangover effect and, thus, they apparently took more time to adjust to the greater degree of competition in the changed scenario. The result that the financial leverage of business groups had no impact on their valuation was quite unexpected and interesting; further analysis into other performance parameters would probably indicate the reasons for this result.

We observe that the results were very similar using either unrelated diversification (2-digit SIC) measure or related diversification (3-digit SIC) measure. We obtained the same results while performing the regressions for all other performance variables as well. So from Sections 5.2 to 5.8, we display results using 3-digit SIC (related) continuous diversification index only.

5.2 Profitability and group characteristics

Research question # 2:

What is the relationship between Indian business groups' accounting profitability and their characteristics, especially product diversification strategy?

We used three dependent variables for the profitability dimension, namely Return on Assets (ROA), Return on Capital Employed (ROCE), and Return on Net Worth (RONW). We present summarized results here using only ROCE and ROA with 3-digit diversification index (see Table 5.2) because of their higher explanatory power, though we also performed the analysis using RONW as a dependent variable.

Our results indicate that current ratio, working capital ratio, financial leverage, and age of business group were the key factors determining the nature of the relationship between accounting profitability and product diversification in the pre-liberalization era. These were also the primary dimensions evaluated by banks and financial institutions for providing finance to business entities during this period. While diversification strategy, working capital ratio, leverage, and age were negatively related, current ratio was positively related to profitability. Unlike the pre-liberalization period, in later periods we observed that size had a significant positive influence on profitability. Age was no longer significant. Product diversification lost its significance as a determinant during the post-liberalization recessionary period, whereas international exposure had a positive influence on a business group's profitability in later periods of the study.

The finding that debt–equity ratio of a business group is significantly and negatively related to the aggregate profitability is in line with the *pecking order* theory of finance (Myers, 1984). Highly profitable business groups use internally generated funds in the form of retained earnings for funding their business plans and meeting growth needs of the group. They seek out sources of debt only as a secondary resort, whereas poorly performing business groups[3] would be having more debt in their portfolios and so would be credit constrained and would also be susceptible to financial market shocks. This is also consistent with the results of Magda Bianco and Giovanni Nicodano (Bianco and Nicodano, 2006) that where bankruptcy is costly and the cash-flow share of the promoters/entrepreneurs in the affiliate is lower than that

[3] Poorly performing business groups based on the *information asymmetry* hypothesis may be primarily opting for debt on their balance sheets as a primary resort (see Chang and Thomas, 1989).

Table 5.2: Relation between business groups accounting profitability and their characteristics: Linear multiple regression coefficients with dependent variables as Return on Capital Employed (ROCE) and Return on Assets (ROA).

Dependent Variable →	Return on Capital Employed (ROCE)			Return on Assets (ROA)		
Independent Variable ↓	Pre-liberalization Period	Post-liberalization Growth Period	Post-liberalization Recessionary Period	Pre-liberalization Period	Post-liberalization Growth Period	Post-liberalization Recessionary Period
1. 3-digit SIC (DT) Diversification Index	-1.835*	-2.497***	-1.728	-1.685**	-2.259***	-1.323
2. Current Ratio	1.609***	0.952***	0.691***	1.086***	0.809***	0.592**
3. Working Capital Ratio	-5.356***	-4.248***	-2.618**	-3.047***	-3.002***	-1.050
4. Net Exports	-0.001	-0.010	0.018	0.005	0.005	0.033*
5. Leverage	-1.072***	-0.523***	-1.737***	-0.892***	-0.371***	-1.477***
6. Size	0.357*	0.648***	1.216***	0.051	0.433***	0.843***
7. International Diversification	0.033*	0.037***	-0.004	0.022	0.015	-0.002
8. Age	-0.024**	-0.013	-0.008	-0.016*	-0.011	-0.0001
(Constant)	7.316***	4.785***	1.111	8.019***	6.062***	2.094*
Adjusted R Square	*0.379*	*0.321*	*0.421*	*0.366*	*0.260*	*0.350*

Note: In the above regressions, while LNMC was selected as the variable for size, Montgomery's continuous diversification index M3 was selected as the variable for diversification.

in the holding/parent company, the extent of external debt raised by affiliates will be high. It was pointed out in Chapter 1 that a key feature of the Indian business group structure is that the founding family/promoters/holding company/foundation owns less than a direct majority stake in most affiliates, especially the listed ones.

The observation that size has an increasingly significant and positive influence on profitability from pre-liberalization period to post-liberalization study periods is in line with the changes taking place in the economy. The dismantling of trade barriers and the rapid removal of licensing restrictions gave immense opportunities to large-sized business groups. With their financial clout, they could increase their scale and scope more easily and reap the economies therein (in sectors of their choice and focus). They also benefited from the strategic alliances (and joint ventures) with foreign firms in emerging markets, as they provide an extra-judicial mechanism for property rights' enforcement, either by investing in reputation or through their close relationships with the bureaucracy (Khanna and Palepu, 2000).

Product diversification strategy was negatively related to profitability during the pre-liberalization period and post-liberalization growth period, but during the post-liberalization recessionary period, it had not come out as a significant variable. Nevertheless, product diversification became significant in the step-wise regressions for the post-liberalization recessionary period, so the result with diversification for the post-liberalization recessionary period, though negative, was not robust. This implies that many owner-managers' (of business groups) propensity to increase their group's product diversification levels did not increase their profitability or shareholder value. Hence, we conclude that there should possibly be other reasons for business groups increasing their average product diversity levels and adopting highly unrelated diversification strategies (than increasing the group's aggregate market value). The positive *monetary* or *non-monetary* gains occurring to the owner-managers of business groups in the holding companies apart from their empire building tendencies can be a strong reason for groups increasing their diversification levels even though it does not add value (see Tricker, 1984; Williamson, 1985; Nicodano, 1998).[4]

[4] Since holding companies' structure of most business groups will make their gains from control more than their cash-flow dividends.

5.3 Profitability components and group characteristics

Research question # 3:

What is the relationship between business group characteristics and their profitability components (i.e., profit margin and sales turnover) during the different study periods?

We had used two dependent variables for profitability components, namely Net Profit Margin (NPM) and Asset Turnover Ratio (STA). These two variables indicate the two different strategies by which a business group can increase its profitability; profit margin being a price-oriented strategy and sales turnover a volume-oriented strategy.

Looking at the significant relations during all the periods from Table 5.3, we can say that while profit margin of a business group was related positively to its current ratio and size, it was related negatively to its leverage. In the first two periods, i.e., pre-liberalization and post-liberalization growth period, product diversification strategy and age of a business group had a negative relation with profit margin. Working capital ratio had a positive relation with profit margins during the post-liberalization periods.

In the case of asset utilization ratio; age, size, and working capital ratio were all significant explanatory variables during all three periods. While, size and working capital ratio had a negative relation, age had a positive relation with sales turnover. Unlike pre-liberalization period, product diversification, current ratio, and international diversification were significant factors in determining sales turnover ratio of a business house for all the post-liberalization periods. The direction of results for both product and geographic scope was negative, while it was positive for current ratio. Leverage of a business group had a negative relation with sales turnover for pre-liberalization period.

Interestingly, the increased competition from de-licensing of major sectors and the opening up of the domestic market for foreign competition seems to have influenced the profitability components and product scope relation. During a period of low competition in the economy (pre-liberalization period), we find that specialized groups were able to generate more margins in their businesses in comparison to diversified groups. However, these groups had higher asset turnovers and, thus, high utilization of assets than diversified groups during periods of relatively

Table 5.3: Relation between business groups' profitability components and their characteristics.

Dependent Variable →	Net Profit Margin (NPM)			Asset Turnover Ratio (STA)		
Group Characteristics ↓	Pre-liberalization Period	Post-liberalization Growth Period	Post-liberalization Recessionary Period	Pre-liberalization Period	Post-liberalization Growth Period	Post-liberalization Recessionary Period
1. 3-digit SIC (DT) Diversification Index	Negative	Negative	Not Significant	Not Significant	Negative	Negative
2. Current Ratio	Positive	Positive	Positive	Not Significant	Positive	Positive
3. Working Capital Ratio	Not Significant	Positive	Positive	Negative	Negative	Negative
4. Net Exports	Not Significant	Not Significant	Not Significant	Not Significant	Not Significant	Negative
5. Leverage	Negative	Negative	Negative	Negative	Not Significant	Not Significant
6. Size	Positive	Positive	Positive	Negative	Negative	Negative
7. International Diversification	Not Significant	Positive	Not Significant	Not Significant	Negative	Negative
8. Age	Negative	Negative	Not Significant	Positive	Positive	Positive

Note: In the above regressions, while LNMC and LNTA were selected as the variables for size for NPM and STA, respectively, Montgomery's continuous diversification index M3 was selected as the variable for diversification.

higher competition in the economy (post-liberalization recessionary period). In pre-liberalization period, multi-divisional diversified Indian groups had lower margins than focused counterparts probably due to low segmental market power (see Montgomery and Singh, 1984) and low-scale economies.[5] However, in post-liberalization recessionary period, multi-divisional groups probably had higher diversification overheads and lower asset utilization levels and, hence, lowers sales turnover in comparison to focused business groups.

The positive relation between size and profit margin clearly suggests that an increase in size of a business group seems to provide either increased economies or more market power, increasing its profit margins during all the periods. One possible explanation for the negative relation between sales turnover and size could be as follows – given that economies are being reaped, sales can fall if a business group with a larger size and, hence, market power, chooses to produce less, for higher unit prices.[6]

The negative relation between international diversification and asset turnover of a business group during all the post-liberalization period probably reflects the procedural delays in conducting a large number of international transactions. International diversification had a positive relation with profit margin in post-liberalization growth period, the result probably reflecting the high margins (premia) for business groups importing goods when overall import tariffs were decreasing and quantitative restrictions were being removed.[7]

The positive relation of both solvency ratios (long-term and short-term) with a business groups' profit margin throughout the study period seemingly reflects the fact that business groups adopting a higher margin strategy need more working capital funds to back the strategy.[8] The negative relation of

[5] Imagine two equal sized business groups, one diversified and another focused in one sector. Other things remaining same, focused business group would probably have more market power and scale economies than the diversified counterpart.

[6] An increase in size might also decrease asset utilization level (efficiency) of business groups, lowering their asset turnover ratio and, hence, generating a negative relation between asset turnover and size.

[7] There still existed quantitative restrictions in segments such as liquor, specific agricultural products, and fast moving consumer goods (FMCG).

[8] In fact, business groups performing in high margin businesses might have lower current liabilities in their balance sheet (given their possible power to tweak their suppliers/ vendors to get better credit).

working capital ratio with asset turnover during all periods suggests that groups with larger turnover ratios probably have lower current assets in their balance sheet.

5.4 Growth and group characteristics

Research question # 4:

To what extent are growth rates of Indian business groups related to their diversification strategy and other group characteristics?

We had used Growth in Total Assets (CAGRTA) as the dependent variable for growth dimension. The poor explanatory power (*Adjusted R Squares*) of the regression results for growth as the dependent variable suggested the need to look for better determinants (see Table 5.4). The growth variable does show a significant positive relationship with variables related to geographic scope. Thus, we deduce that business groups focused on internationalization and exports had higher growth rates than others. Perhaps these groups were also able to reap the benefits of liberalization. The majority of variation in business group growth is not associated with our explanatory variables such as size, diversification, or leverage; probably it is associated with unobservable (*idiosyncratic*) factors specific to the group or business unit such as *managerial capital* of the group (see Jensen and McGuckin, 1997). We found that product diversification was negatively related to growth in post-liberalization recessionary period.[9] The direction of the regression results is consistent with our hypothesis. The results possibly convey the fact that in the later period, with the removal of licensing and trade restrictions, focused business groups expanded and grew in their chosen sectors, reaping the benefits of scale economies, and pursued international markets for sales even during the recessionary period.

[9] In addition, we found that the 2-digit SIC continuous (unrelated) diversification variable came out as significant in the step-wise regressions in post-liberalization recessionary period.

Table 5.4: Relation between business groups' growth and risk with their characteristics: Linear multiple regression coefficients with dependent variables as Growth in Total Assets (CAGRTA) and Coefficient of Variance in ROA (VROA)

Dependent Variable →	Growth in Total Assets (CAGRTA)			Variance in ROA (VROA)		
Independent Variable ↓	Pre-liberalization Period	Post-liberalization Growth Period	Post-liberalization Recessionary Period	Pre-liberalization Period	Post-liberalization Growth Period	Post-liberalization Recessionary Period
1. 3-digit SIC (DT) Diversification Index	0.034	-0.007	-0.033*	0.441*	0.148	-0.153
2. Current Ratio	3.562	3.306	0.814	-0.069	-0.041	-0.306***
3. Working Capital Ratio	27.564	37.030*	-4.739	-0.232	-0.258*	0.371
4. Net Exports	-0.823**	-0.540	-0.106	-0.008	-0.003	-0.007
5. Leverage	1.772	-5.927	-0.871	0.408***	0.170***	0.037
6. Size	-4.043	-2.465	3.469***	-0.075	-0.101***	-0.333***
7. International Diversification	0.330	0.497**	0.083*	-0.001	0.0001	-0.004
8. Age	-0.256	-0.577***	-0.065	-0.0001	0.0001	-0.0001
(Constant)	64.018	72.624	-23.143**	0.308	0.888***	4.123***
Adjusted R Square	*0.068*	*0.130*	*0.091*	*0.284*	*0.214*	*0.071*

Note: In the above regressions, LNTA and LNTS were selected as the variable for size for CAGRTA and VROA, respectively. Montgomery's continuous diversification index M3 was selected as the variable for diversification for both the dependent variables.

5.5 Risk and group characteristics

Research question # 5:

To what extent are Indian business groups' risk (earnings variation) related to their product diversification strategies and other group characteristics?

We had used two dependent variables for the Risk dimension, namely coefficient of variance in ROA (VROA) and coefficient of variance in ROCE (VROCE). We reproduce the results for VROA in Table 5.4. For all the periods, our results indicate that size and leverage of a business group were highly significant factors influencing its risk. Size was negatively related and leverage was positively related, i.e., an increase in a business group's size reduces earnings variation, whereas an increase in leverage leads to an increase in the same. The regression results also indicate that risk had a positive and significant relation with business group's product diversification strategy for pre-liberalization period. Current ratio was a significant factor influencing the variation in earnings of a business group for post-liberalization recessionary period. The poor explanatory power (*Adjusted R Squares*) of the current explanatory variables suggests the need to look for better determinants.

Higher the debt in a business groups' capital structure, higher will be its financial risk. This evidently drives the leverage and risk relation presented above. The strong relation between a business group's size and its risk suggests that large business groups took advantage of their large financial clout and market power to lower their earnings variation (risk), especially in times of recession and import competition in many industries.

The positive relation between product scope and risk of a business group in pre-liberalization period was quite contrary to our expectations especially given the belief that groups diversify to reduce their portfolio risks (as a part of managing their portfolios). The results possibly indicate that diversified business groups having multiple divisions had probably poor overall market power due to their small positions in multiple product markets leading to large variations in their earnings (see Montgomery and Singh, 1984). Also, managerial diseconomies in overseeing multiple divisions might have led to the above result.

5.6 Performance and diversification (non-linear relation)

Research question # 6:

Is the relationship between diversification and aggregate shareholder value of Indian business groups (if any) non-linear in nature (such as quadratic, cubic and inverse)?

After evaluating the linear relations between diversification and performance, we also tested for non-linear relations in the business group data performing regressions using various transformations of product diversification variable (such as quadratic, cubic, or inverse) with all the financial performance variables. We found that '*inverse of product diversification*' was giving the best results with TOBIN (shareholder value dimension) as dependent variable. Table 5.5 lists the regression results.

Table 5.5: Relation (non-linear) between business groups' value creation and their diversification strategy: Linear multiple regression coefficients with dependent variable as Tobin's Q (TOBIN) using 'inverse of diversification' as an independent variable (INVP3)

Dependent Variable →	Tobin's Q Ratio (TOBIN)		
Independent Variable ↓	Pre-liberalization Period	Post-liberalization Growth Period	Post-liberalization Recessionary Period
1. Inverse of 3-digit SIC (DT) Diversification Index	111.31***	326.58***	216.84***
2. Current Ratio	0.068***	0.074**	--0.018
3. Working Capital Ratio	-0.280***	-0.580***	-0.314***
4. Net Exports	-0.001	0.0001	0.005**
5. Leverage	0.007	-0.017	0.009
6. Size	0.095***	0.262***	0.205***
7. International Diversification	0.002*	0.004*	-0.001
8. Age	-0.002***	-0.0001	-0.001
(Constant)	1.110***	1.117***	0.938***
Adjusted R Square	*0.272*	*0.338*	*0.316*

Note: While LNMC was selected as the variable for size, inverse of Palepu's 3-digit SIC continuous diversification index (INVP3) was selected as the measure for diversification.

Comparing Table 5.5 with Table 5.1, we conclude that '*inverse of diversification*' better explains the diversification and performance relationship than a linear relation for all study periods, the relation being positive and highly significant. The relation also does not affect the relationship of performance with other control variables (either in terms of direction or significance).

We also performed similar regressions using '*inverse of diversification*' variable and found that this transformation explains the relationship between financial performance and diversification better in a few more cases (such as Return on Assets and Net Profit Margin).

Figure 5.1: Diversification and performance relationship

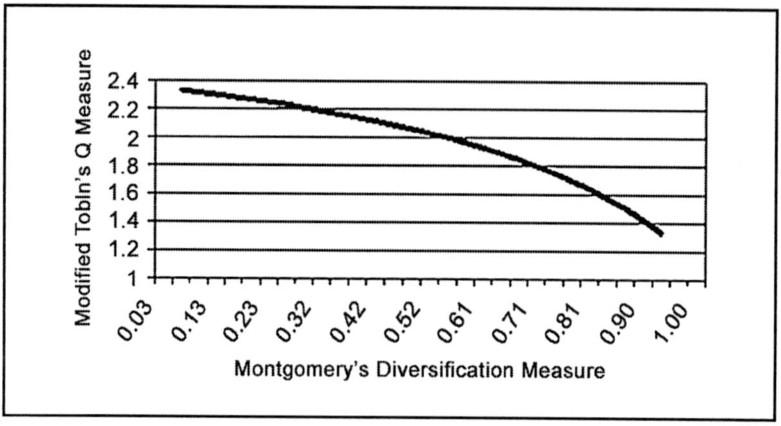

Figure 5.1 displays the non-linear relationship between diversification and shareholder value in a graphical fashion (between Montgomery's 3-digit SIC diversification index[10] and Modified Tobin's Q Ratio). The figure shows that the reduction in Modified Tobin's Q Ratio becomes increasingly higher (greater and greater) as business group's product diversity increases more and more, probably implying that a movement from related to unrelated diversification by business groups would be more value destroying in comparison to a movement from single business to dominant constrained diversification strategy by business groups.

5.7 Performance and group characteristics (including ownership)

Research question # 7:

Does Indian business groups' ownership pattern influence their diversification–performance linkage? Does ownership pattern have an influence on performance?

[10] Montgomery's diversification measure varies from 0 to 1, where 0 stands for minimum diversification and 1 for maximum diversification.

We evaluated those initial results on the diversification-performance relationship again for post-liberalization recessionary period using ownership data as control (INSIDER, FIIS, and DIIS) variables. INSIDER represents the average stake held in affiliates by business groups (owners), FIIS represents the average stake held by foreign investors in the business group affiliates, and DIIS represents the average stake held by government-owned domestic institutional investors in the business group affiliates. Non-availability of data forced us to perform this analysis only for post-liberalization period.

Using these three additional independent variables, we performed the regressions again and found that the initial regression results between dependent and independent variables did not change to a very large extent in terms of both their significance and direction of relationship for any of the variables. Table 5.6 displays these regression results for the dependent variables TOBIN, ROA, NPM, STA, CAGRTA, and VROA.

Regressions in Table 5.6 indicate that promoters stake in business groups had a negative relationship with their riskiness. The result seems to be in consonance with agency theory in the context of limited liability phenomenon. Given the positive private benefits, the smaller a business groups' stake, the larger the benefits from control (see Nicodano, 1998). In other words, the above result seems to be driven by the fact that less the ownership stakes of the promoters in their business group, the more is their propensity to take risk and make abnormal gains (by controlling a larger amount of assets or larger empire).

The positive and significant relationship of foreign ownership with profitability and growth could be due to the fact that foreign investors and funds invest only in business groups that are highly profitable and/or growth oriented. Being managers of portfolios, foreign institutional investors have portfolio performance as their primary concern and, hence, probably invest and lend support to only those organizations that are steadfastly focused on shareholders' wealth. The result also apparently suggests that foreign investors probably better use their formal authority, social influence, and expertise to strongly influence group performance through better governance (see Kang and Sorenson, 1999).

Looking at Table 5.6, we can also conclude that Domestic Institutional Investors Stake (DIIS) was not an important factor in determining any of the business houses' performance dimensions. Even though DIIS usually holds large combined debt–equity positions in business groups, the politico-economic factors probably led to an inadequate monitoring of these business groups by DIIS (see Chakravarthy, 1985), it also probably points out to an apparent lack of interest on the part of DIIS in the business group's performance.

5.8 Performance and group characteristics (including industry influence)

Research question # 8:

Does the dominant industry category, to which these business groups belong, influence the relationship between aggregate performance and other group characteristic relationships during the different study periods?

We evaluated the relationships again controlling for industry-fixed effects to look into their influence on the diversification and performance linkage as argued by some researchers (see Porter, 1985). For this, we performed the previous regressions again, using business groups' dominant 2-digit SIC industry dummy as control variables. While we found that many industries had an influence on the performance of business groups in which they were dominantly operating, industry fixed effects did not have any impact on the diversification strategy and performance relationship of aggregate business groups. Industry dummies also did not influence the relationship of performance with other business characteristics in the regressions. The results probably suggest the robustness of our previous inferences. Perhaps, they suggest the need to have better method for capturing industry- influencing performance.[11]

[11] Readers can get a copy of these results (on request)

Table 5.6: Relation between business groups; characteristics (including ownership pattern) and their financial performance[12]

Dependent Variable →	TOBIN	ROA	NPM	STA	CAGRTA	VROA
Independent Variable ↓	Post-liberalization Period	Post-liberalization Period	Post-liberalization Period	Post-liberalization Period	Post-liberalization Period	Post-liberalization Period
1. 3-digit SIC (DT) Diversification Index	-0.445***	-0.008*	-0.005	-0.232*	-0.026	0.0002
2. Current Ratio	-0.015	0.704***	1.084***	0.073***	0.813	-0.303***
3. Working Capital Ratio	-0.325***	-2.720**	2.465	-0.820***	-4.229	0.469
4. Net Exports	0.005**	0.019	0.039	-0.003*	-0.094	-0.007
5. Leverage	0.013	-1.715***	-2.522***	-0.013	-0.809	0.021
6. Size	0.190***	1.241***	1.197***	-0.099***	2.959***	-0.397***
7. International Diversification	-0.001	-0.001	0.017	-0.003**	0.068	-0.003
8. Age	-0.001	-0.003	0.011	0.003***	-0.071*	-0.003
9. Promoters Stake	0.004	0.021	0.027	-0.0001	0.128	-0.025**
10. Foreign Ownership	0.003	0.051*	0.077*	0.002	0.302***	-0.020
11. Domestic Institutions Stake	-0.001	-0.012	0.007	-0.002	0.165	0.009
(Constant)	0.434***	-4.278	-10.402**	1.707***	-28.86***	5.701***
Adjusted R Square	0.316	0.427	0.443	0.325	0.120	0.088

Note: For the same category with multiple variables (such as size), we used the same variables that were used to display the results in the previous tables.

12 Multiple regression coefficients using ownership variables (INSIDER, DIIS, and FIIS) as independent variables over select dependent variables (TOBIN, ROA, NPM, STA, CAGRTA, and VROA) for post-liberalization period.

We observe that during pre-liberalization period, industry fixed effects were rather mild, with no industry dummy variable (except for the food industry)having a highly significant relation with more than one performance measure. We found that the food industry had a significant positive relation with Tobin's Q ratio.

During post-liberalization growth period, groups dominant in rubber, plastic, and primary metal industries had a significantly negative relation with profitability, while business groups dominant in paper and primary metal industry had a significant positive relation with growth in assets. Business groups dominant in textile sector had a negative relation with shareholder value.

The poor condition of the textile sector was visible during post-liberalization recessionary period as value creation, profitability, profit margin, sales turnover, and growth had a significant negative relation with textile-sector-dominant business groups, besides, and the risk variables had a positive relation with textile category. Chemical, primary metal, stone, clay, and glass product dominant business groups had a significant negative relation with shareholder value and sales turnover ratio during the period.

We also observed that age had a significant positive relation with asset turnover during all the study periods and a significant negative relation with profit margin during pre-liberalization period and post-liberalization growth period. We conclude that older business groups due to their depreciated assets appear to be having higher sales turnover ratios in comparison to new ones. Another reason behind the result could be that newer business groups are enjoying higher profit margins in comparison to older ones, which is perhaps the result of a different strategy (price-based instead of volume-based) on their part. Since the relation holds even after accounting and controlling for industry fixed effects, the result can hardly be attributed to different industry specializations of old and new business groups.

5.9 Performance and Rumelt's diversification categories

Research question # 9:

Does the relation (if any) between financial performance and product diversification strategy continue to hold, when Rumelt's categorical classification (non-continuous) is used as a product diversification measure instead of the continuous diversification measures?

We performed the regressions again using Rumelt's diversification categories instead of the 2-digit and 3-digit SIC based continuous diversification measures. For this we used only six categories of Rumelt (1974) instead of the original nine proposed by him. Multi-business and Unrelated Portfolio categories were clubbed together into the Unrelated Business (RUM_UB) category. All related business groups were clubbed into the Related (RUM_RE) category. Dominant Vertical category business groups were also included in Dominant Linked (RUM_DL) category. The other categories used in the analysis were Single Business (RUM_SB), Dominant Constrained (RUM_DC), and Dominant Unrelated (RUM_DU) categories.

Table E.2 in Appendix E provides the distribution details of the sample based on Rumelt's categorization scheme. These results are summarized in Table 5.7. The base category in these regressions involving dummy variables was the Single Business category. In other words, all other categories were included in the regression to compare with the Single Business category. We found that business groups belonging to highly diversified categories (especially Unrelated, Related, and Dominant Unrelated) were outperformed by Single Business and Dominant Constrained category business groups in most performance dimensions (since the diversified Rumelt's categories (RUM_UB, RUM_RE, and RUM_DU) had lower levels of the performance parameters than did the less diversified Rumelt's categories (RUM_SB, RUM_DC)). However, the differences were not significant in some cases. Hence, our results using continuous diversification measures were ratified to a large extent.

Almost all the business groups in diversified categories (viz., Dominant Unrelated, Related Business, and Unrelated Business) had a negative relation with value creation. In pre-liberalization period, Dominant Unrelated was the only significant category; in post-liberalization growth period, Dominant Linked, Dominant Unrelated, Related Business, and Unrelated Business categories had a significant relation with shareholder value; and in post-liberalization recessionary period, we found that Unrelated Business and Related Business categories had a significant relation with shareholder value. The direction of the results is in confirmation with our hypothesis.

Evaluating the significant relations with profitability, in pre-liberalization period, we found that unrelated and Dominant Linked categories had a negative relation with business groups' profitability; and in post-liberalization growth period, we found that business groups in Dominant Unrelated and Related Business categories had a negative relation with profitability. On the other hand, we found that no Rumelt's category was significant in the regressions with growth and risk of business groups during any of the three periods.

Looking at the significant relations between Rumelt's categories and profitability components, profit margin and sales turnover, we find a similarity in the results with the ones we obtained in Section 5.3 with continuous product diversification variables. In pre-liberalization period and post-liberalization growth period, we found that Dominant Constrained, Dominant Linked, Dominant Unrelated, Related Business, and Unrelated Business categories had lower profit margins (had a significant and negative relation) than Single Business category business groups, while in post-liberalization recessionary period, we found that Dominant Constrained and Dominant Linked categories had higher sales turnover (had a significant and positive relation) than all other Rumelt's categories.

5.10 Analysis of results

In this section, we will review our results on the issues related to specific group characteristics and performance relation. This will include a consideration of questions that remain unanswered, along with suggestions for the kinds of research that would help to answer them.

5.10.1 Product diversification and performance: Main inference

The findings of the study are in line with our hypothesis that product diversification strategy is negatively related to consolidated performance (in terms of shareholder value creation) of Indian business groups. The results were quite robust, in the sense that the relation was negative for all three periods and for both continuous and non-continuous measures of diversification. Even when industry fixed effects were controlled for using the 2-digit SIC industry dummy variables, we found that the results did not differ greatly.

We find that the results during pre-liberalization period were propelled by the fact that specialized business groups had more profit margins than multi-divisional business houses. The poor economies of scale and low segmental market power of diversified groups (due to multi-segmental operation) probably motivated the results against the diversified business groups leading to their lower profit margins, higher earnings variation and, hence, lower value.[13]

During the post-liberalization growth period, a period of economic liberalization and growth, specialized business groups performed better than diversified business groups and added more value from their higher profit margins and higher efficiency in turnover. The higher overheads due to diversification and the lack of focus seem to the principal reasons for the poor shareholder value created by more diversified business groups.[14]

---

[13] The erstwhile industrial licensing system also played a role in the inability to benefit from economies of scale due to the low capacities licensed out to individual firms. The licensing system appears to have rested on the principle of favoring small industries that accounted for a significant, growing portion of industrial output until the mid-1980. While a number of firms took advantage of the licensing regime relaxations during the second half of the 1980s, it may well have been the case that the capacity additions were not fully operational during the first period of our study. This could in part explain the lack of economies of scale. However, in the absence of data on actual spending on new capacity and the operationalization of the same, it is difficult to verify this position.

[14] This period witnessed rapidly growing capital expenditures by large firms, partly driven by the ease of raising equity from the primary markets and debt from DFIs and banks. It is well known that the problems of excess capacity and failures to operationalize newly created capacity were important drivers of the financial problems faced by large industry during the third period. Hence, it may also be the case that the lower rates of return and turnover efficiency may be driven in part by this phenomenon.

Table 5.7: Relation between business groups' shareholder value creation and their characteristics (with non-continuous product diversification measure)[15]

Dependent Variable →	Tobin's Q Ratio (TOBIN)			Return on Assets (ROA)			Net Profit Margin (NPM)		
Independent Variable ↓	Pre-liberalization Period	Post-liberalization Growth Period	Post-liberalization Recessionary Period	Pre-liberalization Period	Post-liberalization Growth Period	Post-liberalization Recessionary Period	Pre-liberalization Period	Post-liberalization Growth Period	Post-liberalization Recessionary Period
1. Current Ratio	0.066***	0.077**	-0.020	1.543***	0.999***	0.680***	0.576**	0.609***	1.020***
2. Working Capital Ratio	-0.276***	-0.604***	-0.302***	-5.305***	-4.403***	-2.665**	1.025	4.545***	2.475
3. Net Exports	-0.002	-0.001	0.005**	-0.001	-0.013	0.015	0.014	0.015	0.040
4. Leverage	0.006	-0.013	0.013	-1.083***	-0.509***	-1.728***	-1.310***	-0.842***	-2.548***
5. Size	0.082***	0.231***	0.192***	0.358*	0.614***	1.217***	0.441**	0.830***	1.255***
6. International Diversification	0.003**	0.004**	-0.001	0.034*	0.041***	0.003	0.028	0.065***	0.021
7. Age	-0.002***	-0.002	-0.001	-0.025**	-0.015*	-0.012	-0.038***	-0.040***	0.004
8. RUM_DC	-0.034	-0.184	0.065	-0.796	-0.164	1.661	-1.521*	-2.274***	1.069
9. RUM_DL	-0.098	-0.324**	-0.052	-2.360**	-0.657	0.902	-2.227**	-1.479	-0.534
10. RUM_DU	-0.105*	-0.427***	-0.021	-0.986	-1.518**	0.454	-1.929**	-2.758***	-0.129
11. RUM_RE	-0.103	-0.348**	-0.181*	-1.559	-1.675**	-0.067	-1.885*	-2.222**	1.799
12. RUM_UB	-0.078	-0.394***	-0.273***	-1.553**	-1.077	-0.437	-1.741**	-1.482**	-0.370
(Constant)	0.921	0.663	0.490***	7.741***	4.476***	-0.157	5.656***	0.848	-6.671***
Adjusted R Square	0.236	0.297	0.271	0.374	0.306	0.401	0.339	0.540	0.437

[15] Multiple regression coefficients using Rumelt's Categorization Scheme as a measure for product diversification strategy (by having the Rumelt Single Business Category (RUM_SB) as the base category and the various other categories as Dummy Variables) over select dependent variables (TOBIN, ROA, NPM, STA, CAGRTA, and VROA)

(Continued)

Table 5.7 (Continued)

Dependent Variable → Independent Variable ↓	Asset Turnover Ratio (STA)			Growth in Total Assets (CAGRTA)			Variance in ROA (VROA)		
	Pre-liberalization Period	Post-liberalization Growth Period	Post-liberalization Recessionary Period	Pre-liberalization Period	Post-liberalization Growth Period	Post-liberalization Recessionary Period	Pre-liberalization Period	Post-liberalization Growth Period	Post-liberalization Recessionary Period
1. Current Ratio	0.032	0.047**	0.072***	3.448	4.262	0.646	-0.069	-0.048	-0.301***
2. Working Capital Ratio	-0.640***	-0.933***	-0.797***	21.645	30.331	-1.202	-0.152	-0.222	0.403
3. Net Exports	0.0001	-0.001	-0.004*	-0.826**	-0.576	-0.118	0.007	-0.003	-0.007
4. Leverage	-0.060***	-0.010	-0.016	0.929	-6.112*	-0.768	0.410***	0.169***	0.042
5. Size	-0.117***	-0.082***	-0.099***	-7.505*	-6.822	2.702***	-0.060	-0.092***	-0.340***
6. International Diversification	-0.024	-0.003**	-0.003**	0.302	0.508**	0.111**	-0.002	-0.0001	-0.005
7. Age	0.005***	0.004***	0.003***	-0.247	-0.529***	-0.076*	-0.001	0.001	-0.001
8. RUM_DC	0.122	0.080	0.219*	-14.419	-8.409	-3.426	-0.118	0.103	-0.010
9. RUM_DL	0.043	0.153	0.270**	-7.222	14.420	-0.295	0.002	-0.073	-0.269
10. RUM_DU	0.069	-0.065	0.051	14.847	7.376	-0.490	-0.079	-0.041	-0.497
11. RUM_RE	-0.131	-0.041	-0.043	10.621	0.018	-6.086	0.266	-0.054	0.092
12. RUM_UB	-0.043	-0.083	-0.042	10.943	8.093	-3.871	0.302	0.042	-0.205
(Constant)	1.708***	1.616***	1.508***	67.597***	92.307***	-5.020	0.347	0.901***	4.238***
Adjusted R Square	0.306	0.413	0.337	0.079	0.128	0.094	0.283	0.206	0.070

Note: For the same category with multiple variables (such as size), we used the same variables that were used to display the results in the previous tables. So, while LNMC was selected as the variable for size for regressions with TOBIN, ROA, and NPM; LNTA was used for the rest of the dependent variables.

Post-liberalization recessionary period was one when business groups faced recession and higher competition due to considerable relaxation of import restrictions (Balakrishnan, 2000). We find that business groups that were specialized had higher sales turnover and growth rates in comparison to their diversified counterparts. The negative relation between group product scope and their shareholder value also seems to have been driven by the fact that capital market conditions favored specialized groups. Conglomerate discount existed internationally for a long time. Globalization seems to have percolated this effect in Indian capital markets also. An analogy to this in Indian capital markets is that multinational companies and private professional Indian companies have better discounting in the stock markets even though with an exactly similar performance to business group firms.[16]

5.10.2 Product diversification and performance: Industry influence

One probable reason for the negative diversification–performance relationship could be that highly diversified groups' portfolios (in our sample) were dominated by underperforming industries.[17] This meant that most multi-segmental groups were presumably bleeding out money from the organization due to cross-subsidization of failing business segments (misallocation of capital within the divisions, Claessens et. al., 1999). International conclusions on the relationship between industry concentration and firm–industry performance generally tend to suggest that firms that participate in highly concentrated industries frequently obtain superior performance. Analyses of diversification–performance relationship of business groups, controlling for industries using their industry concentration ratios (Collin, 1980; Scherer, 1980), could generate more insights in the field.

Consider a business group in a low-yielding industry entering a high-yielding industry and improving its performance (say, due to its prudent industry selection). On the other hand, consider another business house in the same

---

[16] Readers can easily make a comparison of the historical P/E and P/BV multiples for (a) IT software firms such as Infosys Technologies vs TCS; (b) FMCG firms such as Godrej Consumer Products and Nirma vs Hindustan Unilever, ITC, and Marico. I-bankers and fund managers call it as business group discount.

[17] Take for example groups such as RPG, GP Goenka, Bangurs, Thapars, Shriram Industrial, Williamson Magor, Maharastra Jindal, Kanoria, Bajoria BP, Kothari, and Jain Shudh. These business groups were highly diversified and were in industries (such as Textiles) which were primarily value destructive during the study period.

low-yielding industry entering another low-yielding industry (say, due to its imprudent industry selection) and worsening performance further. However, both the business groups above, in an analysis such as ours, would be from the same industry and with the same diversification levels (both initially and at a later stage after entering the new industry). Here, a general analysis using large sample, as the one performed by us in this study, would not be able to capture the same. A case-based analysis within the diversifying business groups, restricting attention to specific business groups diversifying from low-yield industry to high-yield industry, and from low-yield industry to low-yield industry, would reveal more information into this area.

5.10.3 Product diversification and performance: Other inferences

A potential factor for the clearly negative relationship between diversification and performance could be that many small groups diversified too fast even though they did not attain the required economies of scale and scope in any particular industry.[18] Further research studies by – (a) separating business groups by size for an empirical analysis and (b) analyzing poorly performing and highly successful business groups in our sample could lead to a greater understanding of the current results.

5.10.4 Size and financial performance

Size comes out as the most significant business group characteristic influencing group performance (especially during post-liberalization recessionary period). This shows that, as group size increases, probably its financial clout and market power also increases. The bigger it is, the more will be the global fund managers', analysts, and foreign investors interested in (tracking) the group. A larger business group also had more opportunities for growing faster in comparison to a smaller group probably due to *existing domestic incentive sway toward larger groups* during the later period of study, e.g., permission to access overseas capital markets. Reserve Bank of India (RBI) restricted permission for the issue of Global Depository Receipts (GDRs), Euro Bonds (EBs), and American Depository Receipts (ADRs) to group affiliates and groups having a minimum size. As Kilantaridis and

[18] Some of the examples of relatively smaller business groups diversifying too fast are: SM Dyechem, Vadilal, Usha Rectifier, Andhra Sugars, and Oswals.

Levanti (2000) pointed, this incentive sway toward larger sized organizations is existent in all economies going through the policy process of liberalization, privatization, and globalization.

After considerable opening up of the economy (globalization), a lot of opportunities existed for Indian organizations to enter into alliances, joint ventures, technology transfers, and licensing agreements with foreign firms. In the changed economy by leveraging their size, large sized groups could more easily attract technological know-how from foreign partners through joint ventures and strategic alliances (see Khanna and Palepu, 1998; 2000).

5.10.5 Age and financial performance

Age of a business group was found significantly negatively related to performance parameters such as value creation, profitability, profit margins, and growth during pre-liberalization period of the study. We also found that the importance of age as a determinant of performance consistently decreased over the next two periods. The result could be due to the fact that many old business groups started to realize the change in economic scenario and were better able to re-adapt to the new environment, i.e., they overcame the hangover effect.[19]

5.10.6 International diversification, net exports, and performance

International diversification was positively related to business groups growth, profitability, profit margin, and shareholder value during pre-liberalization period and post-liberalization growth period, while in post-liberalization recessionary period, we find that net exports was positively related to business groups' profitability and shareholder value. The significance of either of these variables positively indicates benefits to the groups having higher international exposure. The results apparently convey that geographic diversification allows groups to exploit their core competencies and distinctive group capabilities across units in different international markets (Hoskisson and Hitt, 1990). International exposure might have also provided a broader base of markets for obtaining returns from innovation through economies of scale.

---

[19] For example, take the change in attitude of Mahindras, Tatas, and Aditya Birla groups (Refer: *Business Today* Magazine Anniversary Issue, January 1997).

The positive relation of performance with international diversification in the initial periods of study could be due to increased opportunities for import-intensive business groups, with the existence of protectionist policies and barriers. From a stress on import substitution till the 1980s, the national economic policies shifted their focus to export promotion in 1990s by opening up of economy, removing quota restrictions on imports, and increasing the Open General License (OGL) list for imports. The process of removal of trade barriers is still going on (World Bank, 2013). So, there existed opportunities for business groups that had a lot of global transactions to take advantage of new markets, especially those which largely depended on imported raw materials which had faced decreased import tariff rates (say, chemical intermediaries or capital goods).

The positive relation between net exports and performance in later periods probably suggests that exporters also benefited from incentives given by the state. Most importantly, higher exporting business groups gained from the learning they had in the global markets (say, in terms of better packaging, technological innovation, access to social and business networks, and so on). They were able to capitalize on the same in domestic markets as well.[20] Furthermore, capital markets seem to have also favored businesses and business groups that were net exporters during this period resulting in a reduced cost of capital for them.

5.10.7 *Solvency ratios and financial performance*

We found that the current ratio of a business group had a positive relation with profitability, and profit margins during all the periods of study. It had a positive relation with value creation for pre-liberalization period and post-liberalization growth period. A stronger short-term solvency position indicates a better ability to meet ongoing and unexpected bills and expenses, thereby taking the pressure off a group's short-term cash-flow management. Being in a liquid position also provides business groups with the ability to negotiate cash discounts with the suppliers, thus boosting the group's profitability. Conversely, a weaker current ratio apparently conveys that a business group is facing problems even in meeting its short-term commitments leading to reputational pressures (among investors) and a fall in its shareholder value.

[20] Business groups such as Dr. Reddy Labs, Hero Munjal, Lupin, and Asian Paints are quick examples regarding the same.

Working capital ratio is basically an expression of a group's ability to rotate its working capital. We find that long-term solvency position is negatively related to shareholder value, profitability, and asset utilization ratios during all the periods of study. This probably reflects that better rotation of working capital leads to savings on working capital requirements and, hence, its usage for business building and producing shareholder value.

Perhaps, the above solvency related results were also driven by the fact that better performing groups had comparatively higher sales and lower current liabilities. So, groups performing badly were not able to sell their products, could not pay their short-term commitments, and, hence, had higher current liabilities in the balance sheet (see Beaver, 1966).

5.11 Managerial implications

On some independent variables, managers and/or regulators will not have control. On some others, they will have either partial or complete control. Business group managers, group heads, financial institutions, and policymakers can use various instruments to control the latter independent variables to generate favorable dependent (here, financial performance) variables. We discuss below a few managerial implications for select dependent variables for post-liberalization period.

- Table 5.1 would help corporate houses to identify and target the independent variables to maximize the shareholder value of the group. For example, here they can do so by reducing the product diversification levels and working capital requirements of the group or by increasing the net exports and size of the group.
- Business groups that are lagging in a particular aspect of performance can shore up the same by controlling the group characteristics, which significantly affect that performance aspect and is under its control. A group which has poor asset utilization in comparison to its peers can improve the same by decreasing its product and international diversification levels (refer Table 5.3). On the other hand, a business group having poor profit margins in comparison to its peers can act according to Table 5.3 by increasing its working capital turnover and cutting its debt levels.
- Pension funds and other low-risk appetite fund managers can look for investment opportunities with large business groups having high promoters' stake and comparatively higher current ratios.

5.12 A further discussion

5.12.1 Context

Business groups are defined in the literature as collections of formally independent firms (or affiliates) under single common administrative and financial controls, owned by either families or trusts or foundations. Business groups' long-term performance would chiefly be an outcome of their corporate strategy. Such strategies comprise decisions to efficiently utilize, add, retain, or divest its resources relative to their portfolio of resources. A key objective of our study was to look into the relationship between such corporate strategy characteristics and financial performance of large Indian business groups.

Even though every publicly listed affiliates of a business group publish their own financial statements and are responsible to their own shareholders, there exists an overriding objective of the group, which guides the goals and strategies of these firms. Hence, we evaluated business groups based on their aggregated figures.

A business group's primary goal is to maximize its shareholder value, which is determined by the groups' profitability, its growth, its risk, and the capital market conditions. To look into the actual factors (or components) which drove the relationship of a group's shareholder value and its diversification, we evaluated group performance over several dimensions apart from aggregate shareholder value, namely profitability, profitability components (margin and sales turnover), growth, and risk of the group.

We performed cross-sectional regression analysis of 240 Indian business groups constituting over 45 per cent of the total market capitalization of Indian companies over a time span of 12 years. This 12-year time span was divided into three equal periods:

(a) Pre-liberalization period;
(b) Post-liberalization period of growth, and
(c) Post-liberalization period of recession.

While looking into the diversification–performance relationship, we used group size, leverage, industry fixed effects, ownership effects, age, short-term and long-term solvency position, international diversification, and net exports as control variables.

5.12.2 Main results

We found that shareholder value (or Modified Tobin's Q Ratio) was negatively related to diversification level of business houses during all the three periods. The econometric results were quite robust considering the large sample size, multiple diversification measures, long time frame, multiple aggregate group performance measures, and more control variables used.

On further analysis, we found that during pre-liberalization period and post-liberalization growth period, the result was driven by the negative relationship between a group's diversification strategy and its profitability. For pre-liberalization period, *ceteris paribus*, we found that more diversified business groups had lesser profit margins and higher levels of risk in comparison to less diversified groups driving the negative diversification–profitability relationship. For post-liberalization growth period, *ceteris paribus*, we found that highly diversified business groups had both lesser margins and asset utilization in comparison to more focused groups. *Ceteris paribus*, we found highly diversified groups growth and asset utilization to be lower than less diversified groups in post-liberalization recessionary period. Presumably, the adverse capital market outlook toward diversified business groups in India, as in other parts of the world (see Berger and Ofek, 1995; Servaes, 1996; Lamont and Polk, 1999), also drove the relation between shareholder value and product scope during the later period of study.

Figure 5.2: Indian groups' performance and performance diversification

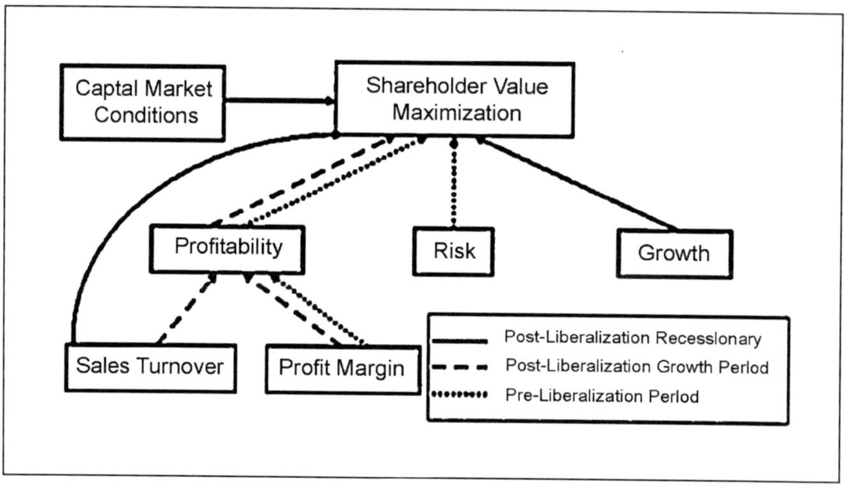

Figure 5.2 above provides a pictorial representation of only the significant relations of this study. It reveals how accounting-based performance dimensions and capital market conditions impact market value by influencing various components given diverse competitive and economic conditions. Before liberalization, the competition was relatively low; hence, focused groups had higher profit margins in comparison to their highly diversified counterparts. This may be due to their greater segmental market power and higher scale economies. However, as the level of competition increased in the next two periods, more specialized groups had higher asset utilization (captured by asset turnover ratio) than their diversified counterparts, probably due to lower diversification overheads. As the competitive conditions change, so do indicators and determinants of relative profitability.

Based on the above results, we note that product diversification benefits through economies of scope, internal capital markets, co-insurance of debt, and others either do not matter *or* are overwhelmed by the downsides. The results show that most diversified business groups yielded low segmental market power (Montgomery and Singh, 1984) and were probably bleeding out money from the business group, with cross-subsidization of failing business segments. In fact, diversified business groups would have been suffering from a value loss (*diversification discount*) due to misallocation of capital among their divisions (see Claessens et al., 1999). This value loss increases their cost of capital (Chowdhary and Nanda, 1994), which further affects their profitability and other performance parameters adversely. Apart from the above reasons, we note that diversified groups were probably paying extra costs due to distraction among the top management from their core competencies and consequent loss of focus.

5.12.2.1 Group diversification purpose

While we found that Indian business groups' diversification usually generated a relative loss for their aggregate shareholder, we also observed that most business groups had, on an average, increased their product diversification levels during the study period. One strong motive for Indian business groups with pyramidal (cross holding) structures increasing their product scope levels could be the non-efficiency based self-seeking factors rather than efficiency-oriented strategic considerations. Through holding company structures, especially while forming new divisions for entering into new sectors, business groups have more control gains than the cash-flow dividends (see Tricker, 1984; Nicodano, 1998) giving owner-managers a strong incentive to diversify. Saha et al. (2011, p.193-6) illustrates this using the example of the Tata business group.

The new opportunities existing in the deregulated Indian economy (such as in financial services) combined with their herd mentality could be an additional factor motivating greater business group diversification (see Song and Cho, 1999).

5.12.3 Other results

Contrary to most firm-level empirical conclusions that size acts as a constraint to a firm's growth and, hence, its overall performance, we find that business groups' size had a positive relation with their shareholder values. In fact, size comes out as the most important factor affecting business group performance, especially during post-liberalization recessionary period of our study. In other words, we found, *ceteris paribus*, large sized business groups had more shareholder value, profitability, and profit margins in comparison to smaller sized groups in all periods of study; and we also found large sized groups growth to be higher than small-sized groups in post-liberalization recessionary period.

Perhaps, the result indicates that (a) larger sized business groups were leveraging on their market power; and (b) liberalization has helped larger groups grow faster and perform better than smaller ones. This is possible as larger Indian business groups had superior access to international capital markets. Khanna and Palepu (2000) point this to be consistent with the larger organizations benefiting from more opportunities with foreign firms in emerging markets, as they provide an extra-judicial mechanism for property right enforcement, either by investing in reputation or through their close relationships with the bureaucracy.

Variables related to international exposure of business groups (international diversification and net exports) were found significant and positively related to performance. These results presumably appear with the opening up of Indian economy and, hence, increase in trade opportunities for importers and exporters alike. The results show that international exposure allows business groups to take advantage of new market possibilities (Wan, 1998). It also provides a broader base of markets to obtain returns from innovation (Hoskisson and Hitt, 1994). Therefore, movement into international markets may allow groups to achieve a long-term strategic competitiveness and, hence, higher shareholder value.

5.12.4 *Possible limitations of the study*

We deleted in our study all Indian business groups that had a size lower than ₹ 5 crores during the period of study; or had a negative net-worth during one of the periods of the study. Thus, the sample may contain relatively large number of better performing larger business groups.

Data constraints led us to use the coefficient of variance in earnings as the measure for risk. A better measure based on the market returns could have revealed more information. Also use of market-based performance measures such as Sharpe and Treynor measures, apart from tested strategic variables such as brand value, could have led to more insights into the factors determining excellence.

5.12.5 *Some unanswered questions: Extending the analysis*

This was a large exploratory study on business group characteristics and the kind of influence they have on business group performance in India. Further research, both quantitative and qualitative in nature, should take place to investigate these first results on aggregate business group performance. This research would add to the growing body of knowledge concerning the business group level studies.

After scrutinizing the highly diversified groups in the sample closely, we note that one of the possible reasons for the above result could be the fact the most of the diversified business groups were in industries that were not performing well (also known as, value destroying industries). These groups were not even exiting from those businesses. Interesting question is:

- Were these business groups stuck due to regulatory constraints?
- *Or* was it a case of bonding and inability to take a rational decision?
- *Or* was it something else?

Possibly a study (as above) limited to different industry sectors on business groups could reveal more information in this direction.

In many other countries (such as Argentina, Denmark, Nigeria, Sweden, and Thailand), there exist business groups with apparently many features similar to the Indian business groups. However, research work on business groups had been limited in these countries. Though the results above might also be applicable to them through international comparisons, the differences, if any, due to different structural, economic, social, and cultural characteristics and their impact on business group performance will be addressed.

Although large sample statistical research of the type in this study is a powerful device for identifying the general relationships between pairs of variables, it is a comparatively weak method to gain insight into complex interactions between business group variables. To gain this insight, detailed examination of the experiences of a sample of the individual groups is performed using four case studies in the next chapter.

Appendix A: Product diversification strategy measures

A.1 Rumelt's diversification categories

1. Single business: Any firm deriving at least 95 per cent of its revenues from one business alone.

Dominant business

Any firm which derives 70–94 per cent of its revenues from its largest business. Dominant firms were divided into four sub-classifications.

2. Dominant Vertical: Any dominant firm with a vertical ratio.
3. Dominant Constrained: Any dominant firm that diversified by building on a single strength or resource associated with the original business.
4. Dominant Linked: Any dominant firm that is diversified on the basis of one of several strengths or resources. The particular strength or resource varies across the different business in the firm.
5. Dominant Unrelated: Any dominant firm whose diversification activities are not related to the dominant business.

Related business

Any firm deriving less than 70 per cent of its sales from a single business and possessing a high-related business. Related firms were divided into two sub-classifications.

6. Related Constrained: Any related firm, which diversified by building on a single strength or resource associated with the original business.

7. Related Linked: Any related firm, which diversified on the basis of one of the several strengths or resources. The particular strength or resource varied across the different businesses in the firm.

Unrelated business

Any firm deriving less than 70 per cent of its sales from a single business and possessing lower related ratios. Unrelated firms were divided into two sub-classifications.

8. Multi-Business: Any unrelated firm containing a few large unrelated businesses.
9. Unrelated Portfolio: Any unrelated firm containing many unrelated businesses.

A.2 Continuous diversification measures

Palepu's and Montgomery's diversification measures are based on Palepu (1985) and Montgomery (1982), respectively. Unrelated and related diversification are calculated as the sum of an entropy index of 2-digit SIC and 3-digit SIC equivalent industry sales of a business group, respectively. Each index is a weighted-average of the ratio of a business group's total sale within a particular 2-digit and 3-digit SIC industry category to total group sales as illustrated in the following mathematical formulas:

Calculation of Palepu (1985) entropy measure

$$\text{Total Diversity (DT)} = \Sigma_{i=1 \text{ to } n}\{Pi \times Ln(1/P_i)\}$$

Where P_i = share of the group in the *i*th industry at the 3-digit SIC level; n = number of SIC industries at the 3-digit level

$$\text{Unrelated Diversity (DU)} = \Sigma_{j=1 \text{ to }}$$

Where P_j = share of the group in the *j*th industry at the 2-digit SIC level; n = number of SIC industries at the 2-digit level

Calculation of Montgomery product-count measures

$$\text{Diversity} = 1 - \{(\Sigma M_j^2)/(\Sigma_j M_j)^2\}$$

Where, M_j = share of the group in industry segment *j*, where *j* is measured at the 2- and 3-digit SIC code. When one uses the 2-digit SIC code, he obtains the Montgomery's unrelated diversification measure by the organization and when one uses the 3-digit SIC code, he obtains the Montgomery's related diversification measure.

Appendix B: Performance measures

B.1 Financial statement-based performance measures

Some of accounting-based measures used in the literature are:

- Annual growth rate in assets (or compounded annual growth in assets)
- Cash flow measure
- Cash flow to investment ratio
- Coefficient of variance in earnings (or returns)
- Debt to equity ratio
- Direct cost relative to competitors
- Growth in revenues
- Gross profit margin
- Multi-factor models such as Z score
- Net profit margin
- Percentage change in cash flow to investment
- Percentage change in returns *also known as* incremental returns
- Product Research and Development (R&D) and process R&D expenses
- Return on assets (ROA)
- Return on capital employed (ROCE)
- Return on equity (ROE) *also known as* return on net worth (RONW)
- Return on operating assets (ROOA)
- Sales per employee
- Sales-to-assets ratio *also known as* asset turnover ratio (other variants include receivables turnover, inventory turnover, and fixed assets turnover)

B.2 Market-based performance measures

Some of the market-based measures used in the literature are:

- Abnormal returns could be compared to the return of a controlled portfolio of similar risk profile
- Common stock returns

- Jenson's alpha = firm's capital market performance against similar market risk portfolio
- Market value of outstanding equity share (or market capitalization)
- Market-to-book value ratio
- Pretax operating cash flows normalized by the market value of assets
- Sharpe and Treynor performance measures
- Systematic risk (beta)
- Tobin's Q Ratio
- Total market return to investors

B.3 Non-financial performance measures

Some of the non-financial measures used in the literature are:

- New product activities relative to competitors
- Product quality relative to competitors
- Market share
- Market share gains
- Capacity utilization per cent

Appendix C: List of business groups

C.1 List of business groups in the sample

- A V Thomas
- Advani
- Alchemie
- Alembic
- Allana
- Alpine
- Amalgamation
- Amforge
- Amrit
- Anand D C
- Andhra Sugars
- Ansal
- Apeejay
- Apollo Hospitals
- Arihant
- Arvind Mafatlal
- Arya
- Asian Paints
- Atlas
- ATV
- Bajaj
- Bajoria B P
- Bangur B D
- Bangur L N
- Bangur P D B G
- Bangur Shree Kumar
- Bangur Shreenivas
- Batliboi
- Bharat Vijay
- Bharatiya
- Bharti Telecom
- Bhuva
- Binani
- Birla Aditya
- Birla Ashok
- Birla B K
- Birla C K
- Birla K K
- Birla M P
- Birla S K

- Borosil
- BPL
- BSES
- Chabbria
- Chemfab Alkalies
- Chidambaram M A
- Chowgule
- Cifco
- Cipla
- Continental
- Cosmo
- Dalmia Sanjay
- DCL
- DCM
- DCM Shriram Consolidated
- DCM Shriram Industries
- Dempo
- Dewan
- Dhanuka S L C K
- Dharani
- Dr. Reddy
- Eicher
- Elecon
- Elgi
- Escorts
- Essar
- Essel Packaging
- Excel
- Facor
- Finolex
- Firodia
- Flex
- G E Shipping
- G V K Reddy
- Ganesh Benzo
- Garden
- Garware
- Gaur Hari Singhania
- Ghia
- Godrej
- Goenka G P
- Goenka J P
- Goenka S P
- Goodricke
- Grauer & Weil
- GTN
- Gujarat Ambuja Cement
- Gulabchand Doshi
- Hamco
- Harishankar Singhania
- HCL
- Hero
- Himatsingka
- Hinduja
- IFB
- India Cement
- Indian Seamless
- Ispat Mittal
- ITC
- Jain Pipe
- Jain Shudh
- Jaiprakash
- Jatia
- Jayant Dalal
- Jenson & Nicholson
- Jyoti
- Kajaria
- Kalyani
- Kanoria
- KCP
- Khaitan Fan
- Khandelwal
- Khatau
- Khoday
- Kilachand
- Killick Nixon
- Kirloskar
- Kothari D C P R D P
- Kothari H C
- Krishna
- KT
- L & T
- Lakhanpal
- Lakshmi
- Lalavidya Oswal
- Lalbhai
- Lloyd Steel
- LNJ Bhilwara
- Lohia Machine
- Maharastra Jindal
- Mahendra Khatau
- Mahindra & Mahindra
- Mardia Rasik
- Mehta C K
- Mehta Mahendra
- Modern
- Modi Bhupendra Kumar
- Modi Kedarnath
- Modi Krishna Kumar
- Modi Vinay Kumar

- Modi Yogendra Kumar
- MRF
- Murugappa Chettair
- Nagarjuna
- Nath
- NCL
- Nicco
- Oberoi
- Om Prakash Jindal
- Orind
- Oswal Agro
- Oswal Spinning & Weaving
- OWM
- Paam Pharma
- Pai Manipal
- Parasrampuria
- Parijat
- Patel J V
- Patodia (Euro)
- Pearlpet
- Pennar
- Piramal Ajay
- Piramal Dilip
- Piramal Mohanlal
- Poddar Bros.
- Polar
- Prakash (Surya)
- Priyadarshini
- Punjab Tractors
- R M Gokuldas
- Raasi
- Radico Khaitan
- Raghu Mody
- Raheja Rajan
- Rajgharia
- Rajinder Steel
- Raju Shroff
- Rama
- Ramco
- Ranbaxy
- Rane
- Rasesh Mafatlal
- Rathi P C R C
- Raunaq
- Reliance Ambani
- Remi
- RPG
- Ruchi
- S M Dyechem
- Samtel
- Santogen
- Sarabhai
- Satya
- Seshasayee
- Shakthi
- Shapoor
- Shreyans
- Shri Dinesh
- Shri Ishar
- Shriram Industrial
- Shriyans Prasad Jain
- Siyaram Poddar
- Somany Enterprises
- Spartek
- Steel Strip
- Steel Tubes
- Suryalakhsmi
- Talwar Bros.
- Taparia
- Tata
- Thackersey
- Thapar
- Torrent
- Trident
- Triveni Agarwal
- TTK
- Turner Morrison
- TVS Iyengar
- UB
- Ucal Fuel
- Unipon
- Unitech
- Uniworth
- Usha Martin
- Usha Rectifier
- Vadilal
- Valecha
- Vardhman
- VBC
- Venky
- Videocon
- Vijay Singhania
- Vinod Doshi
- W S Industries
- Wadia
- Williamson Magor
- Winsome
- WIPRO
- Wockhardt
- Yogendra Mafatlal

Note: The above list of business groups is for post-liberalization recessionary period. The number of business groups for post-liberalization growth period and pre-liberalization period were 239 and 230, respectively. The number of business groups in the sample is more during later periods as some groups split – primarily an outcome of family tree issues (such as Bangurs during pre-liberalization period).

C.2 Reasons for excluding some groups

The total number of business groups we came across in the CMIE Prowess database was 450. Excluding government-owned groups such as ICICI, we ended up with nearly 430 business groups. More than 170 business groups had to be deleted due to the following reasons specified herein and, hence, we ended up with a sample size of 240 business groups.

- Business groups that did not have listed affiliates for a period of more than 10 years during the time frame of the study.
- Business groups whose data was not available completely (in all data sources including Prowess, CMIEs head office, Capitaline or BSE official directory.
- Business groups whose parents were multinationals and the foreign ownership in the group was more than 50 per cent of the total share holding. We also deleted foreign business group affiliates whose decisions were guided by the policies of their foreign parents' interest in mind rather than the local interests, e.g., SmithKline Beecham group. In other words, a foreign business group was deleted if there was an example of its strategic alignment in decisions and plans with the parent MNC during the period of study.
- All business groups promoted by government or government-owned firms.
- Groups that had a turnover of less than ₹ 3 crores during the time frame of the study.
- Business groups that were only in the service industry, such as trading and financial services, were eliminated (as their asset structure will be substantially different from that of other industries).
- Business groups that had negative net-worth during one of the three periods of study (as this would have generated a lot of outliers).

C.3 *List of excluded business groups*

- Adani
- Adhunik
- Aditya
- Ajmera
- Alsa Marine
- Ambuja (Bihar)
- Amtek
- Apar
- Apollo Earthmovers
- Apple Inds.
- Apte
- Aruna Sugars
- Ashok (Kadakia)
- Asian Consolidated
- Aspinwall
- Atul Glass
- Autoriders
- AVI
- Bajoria U.S.
- Bala Techno
- Balaji (Reddy)
- Balsara
- Bangur G.D.
- Banswara
- Berlia
- Bhai Mohan Singh
- Bhansali (CRB Capital)
- Bharat Modi
- Bhupendra
- Butterfly
- Capital Trust
- CDR
- Cepham
- Chemox Chemicals
- Chokhani
- Ciba-Geigy (F)
- Core Lab.
- Credit Capital Venture
- Dabur
- Dalal Street Journal
- Daudayal
- Delhi Flour Mills
- Dera
- Devidayal
- Dhanuka P.L.
- Dharnendra
- Dhillon
- DLF
- Dugar
- Dugar Tarachand
- Easun
- Enkay
- Esquire
- Fedders Lloyd
- Gadgil Western
- Gajra
- Ghatge Patil
- Glaxo (F)
- Goldstar
- Goodearth
- Gujarat Ambuja Proteins
- Gujarat Inject
- Gupta Carpet
- Hada
- HB
- Himadri
- Hindusthan Devl.
- Hitkari
- IMFA
- Indal (F)
- Inox
- Ipca Laboratories
- J.K. Singhania
- J.M. Financial
- Jagsonpal
- Jalan M.L.
- Jalan Sushil
- Jardine Henderson
- Jaysynth
- Jiwrajka
- JVG
- K.G.
- Kalpataru
- Kedia V
- Kings
- Kinjal
- Kongarar
- Kothari Products
- Krystal
- Lahoti
- Lamina
- Lan Eseda
- Libra
- Lupin
- Malhotra Steel
- Mardia Extrusions
- Marson
- Maxworth Orchards
- Menon (Kolhapur)
- Mesco

- Metrochem
- MGF
- Mikado Textile
- Modi Satish Kumar
- Modi Umesh Kumar
- Mohan Meakin
- Monnet
- Nachammai
- Namaste Exports
- Naterwala
- Nava Bharat
- NECO
- Nirma
- OEN
- Onida
- Orind
- Pan Asia
- Parekh
- Parekh Platinum
- Parle Products
- Partap
- Patel Roadways
- Peerless
- Pentafour
- Philips (F)
- Pioneer
- Prabhu Steel
- Pressman
- Procter & Gamble (F)
- Ram Jhunjhunwala
- Ramgopal
- Rampuria
- Reddy Obul
- Rinki
- Rohit
- S. Kumars
- Sahu Jain (Times of India)
- Samsons
- Sanghi Polyester
- Sanmar [Chemplast]
- Sayaji Hotels
- Scindia
- Shriram Transport
- Simplex (Mundhra)
- Singhal Swaroop Ispat
- SKF (F)
- SOL
- Somani B.D.
- Square D
- Star
- Sterling Holiday Resorts
- Stovec Industries
- Sujana
- Sun Pharmaceutical
- Suraj Vanaspati
- Suresh Sharma
- Surlux
- Tai
- Tainwala
- Tanna
- Tatia
- TCI-Bhoruka
- Thapar Agro (Ludhiana)
- Thermax
- Tinna
- Toshniwal
- Udyar
- Uni Lever (F)
- Uniplas India
- United
- V G P
- Walchand
- Weizmann
- Welspun
- Whirlpool (F)
- Wyeth (F)
- XLO
- Zydus

Appendix D: Variable notation and interpretation

Table D.1: Notations and interpretations of various variables used for the study on business groups.

Notation	Variable Interpretation	Measures
Dependent Variables		
CAGRCA	Annual growth in current assets	Growth
CAGRFA	Annual growth in fixed assets	
CAGRTA	Annual growth in total assets	
ROA	Return on Assets	Profitability
ROCE	Return on Capital Employed	
RONW	Return on Net Worth	
NPM	Net Profit Margin	Profitability Components
STA	Sales-To-Assets Ratio	
VROA	Coefficient of Variance in ROA	Risk (or Variance in Earnings)
VROCE	Coefficient of Variance in ROCE	
PBV	Price-to-Book Value Ratio	Shareholder Value Maximization
TOBIN	Modified Tobin's Q Measure	
Independent Variables		
AGE	Age	Age
CR	Current Ratio	Short-term Solvency
DIIS	Domestic Institutional Investors (incl. LIC, GIC, UTI, Mutual Funds, etc.) Stake	Domestic Institutional Stake

(Continued)

Table D.1 (Continued)

FIIS	Foreign Investors Stake	Foreign Stake
GEODIV	International Diversification	International Diversity
IND20	Industry Dummy Variables (with 2-digit SIC Code)	Industry Effects
INSIDER	Business Groups Ownership	Owners Stake
LNMC	Logarithm of Market Capitalization	
LNTA	Logarithm of Total Assets	Size
LNTS	Logarithm of Total Sales	
LTD	Long-term Debt over Equity Ratio	Leverage
NETEXP	Net Exports over Sales Ratio	Net Exports
M2	Montgomery's 2-digit Unrelated diversification	
M3	Montgomery's 3-digit related diversification	Product Diversification
P2	Palepu's 2-digit SIC (DU) diversification	
P3	Palepu's 3-digit SIC (DT) diversification	
WCM	Working Capital Over Sales Ratio	Long-term Solvency

Appendix E: Descriptive statistics of the sample

Table E.1: Mean and standard deviation of the independent and dependent variables[21]

Name of the Variable	Mean			Standard Deviation		
	Pre-liberalization Period	Post-liberalization Growth Period	Post-liberalization Recessionary Period	Pre-liberalization Period	Post-liberalization Growth Period	Post-liberalization Recessionary Period
Dependent Variables						
CAGRFA (Growth in FA)	63.16	80.41	12.32	113.61	117.57	24.91
CAGRTA (Growth in TA)	52.91	64.14	8.26	66.99	73.84	15.59
NPM (Net Profit Margin)	4.08	5.84	1.27	4.39	5.05	8.25
PBV (PBV Ratio)	1.81	2.69	1.26	1.29	1.87	1.39
ROA (Return on Assets)	7.37	7.71	4.75	3.44	3.03	4.97
ROCE (Return on CE)	15.54	15.13	10.86	6.04	5.46	7.77
RONW (Return on NW)	13.11	12.62	0.35	15.66	10.22	21.05
STA (Asset Turnover Ratio)	1.11	0.96	0.87	0.51	0.49	0.51
TOBIN (Tobin's Q Ratio)	1.20	1.56	1.08	0.29	0.67	0.50
VROA (Variance of ROA)	0.57	0.43	1.13	1.11	0.57	2.03
VROCE (Variance of ROCE)	0.33	0.31	0.89	0.30	0.27	1.83

21 *Note: DISS, FIIS, GEODIV, INSIDER, and NETEXP variables are given in percentage terms.*

(Continued)

Table E.1 (Continued)

Independent Variables						
AGE (Age of the Group)	45.71			26.49		
CR (Current Ratio)	2.89	3.20	3.14	1.29	1.36	1.44
DIIS (Ownership of DII)			14.01			9.82
FIIS (Foreign Ownership)			11.89			11.28
GEODIV (Marsket Diversity)	14.89	20.31	23.96	15.26	19.87	21.88
INSIDER (Owners Stake)			43.56			14.03
LNMC (Log of Market Cap.)	4.93	6.62	6.69	1.46	1.46	1.62
LNTA (Log of Total Assets)	5.61	6.55	7.33	1.34	1.23	1.29
LNTS (Log of Total Sales)	5.58	6.30	6.92	1.32	1.17	1.21
LTD (Debt-to-Equity Ratio)	1.91	1.49	1.54	1.39	1.27	1.35
M2 (Montgomery's 2-digit)	0.34	0.39	0.42	0.28	0.27	0.26
M3 (Montgomery's 3-digit)	0.45	0.52	0.54	0.28	0.26	0.24
NETEXP (Group Netexport)	-3.60	-1.48	-0.02	12.46	13.35	14.94
Total Assets (in ₹ crores)	271.14	700.59	1534.74	667.45	1695.93	3722.75
WCM (WC-to-Sales Ratio)	0.37	0.45	0.46	0.32	0.28	0.30

We had used only six categories of Rumelt's Classification in the analysis – namely Single Business, Dominant Constrained, Dominant Linked, Dominant Unrelated, Related Business, and Unrelated Business. All Related categories (viz., Related Constrained and Related Linked) were clubbed into the Related Business (RUM_RE) category. All Unrelated Categories (viz., Multi-business and Unrelated Portfolio) were clubbed into the Unrelated Business (RUM_UB) category. Dominant Linked (RUM_DL) category also includes Dominant Vertical category. The following table shows the number of sample business groups being classified based on these six Rumelt categories used in the analysis:

Table E.2: Rumelt's category distribution of the sample data[22]

RUMELT CATEGORY	Pre-liberalization Period	Post-liberalization Growth Period	Post-liberalization Recessionary Period
Single Business (RUM_SB)	52	33	20
Dominant Constrained (RUM_DC)	36	36	33
Dominant Linked (RUM_DL)	14	22	25
Dominant Unrelated (RUM_DU)	34	37	46
Related Business (RUM_RE)	21	23	23
Unrelated Business (RUM_UB)	73	88	93
Total Business Groups	230	239	240

[22] Our base Rumelt category for analyzing in the dummy variable regressions using Rumelt Category dummies was the Single Business (RUM_SB) Category.

Table E.3: Industry-wise distribution of the sample data[23]

The following table shows the number of business groups being classified based on the dominant 2-digit industry in which they were operating

2-Digit SIC Code	Name of the Industry	Notation Used	Pre-liberalization Period	Post-liberalization Growth Period	Post-liberalization Recessionary Period
20	Food and Allied Products	IND20	23	21	26
22	Textile Mill Products	IND22	38	38	33
26	Paper and Allied Products	IND26	6	5	6
28	Chemical and Allied Products	IND28	42	49	50
30	Rubber and Misc. Plastic Products	IND30	16	16	16
32	Stone, Clay and Glass Products	IND32	18	22	23
33	Primary Metal Industries	IND33	21	23	20
35	Industrial Machinery and Equipment	IND35	14	13	12
36	Electronics and Other Electrical Equipment	IND36	15	18	15
37	Transportation Equipment	IND37	14	12	14
Rest	Rest of the Industries	INDREST	23	22	25
	Total Business Groups		230	239	240

[23] Our base Industry category for analyzing the dummy variable regressions using Industry dummies was the Rest of the Industries categories (INDREST). This category constituted mostly of groups in the areas such as construction, computer software, utilities, etc.

Appendix F: Sample data of Arvind Lalbhai group

F.1 List of affiliates

Year of Institution: 1928
List of Affiliates
Amtrex Appliances Ltd.
Arvind Mills Ltd.
Arvind Polycot Ltd.
Atul Ltd.
Anagram Finance Ltd.

F.2 Group level financial data

Arvind Lalbhai group: Aggregated group financial figures (in ₹ crores)

Variable/Dimension	Pre-liberalization Period	Post-liberalization Growth Period	Post-liberalization Recessionary Period	Ownership Stake	
CURR_RATIO	2.319	6.123	5.041	FIIS	15
WCM	0.344	1.388	1.135	DIIS	20
NETEXPORT	5.414	10.921	19.283	Insider	42
LTDRATIO	1.691	1.103	1.331		
PBVRATIO	1.306	2.264	0.851		
TOTAL ASSETS	325.843	1733.240	4173.975		
SALES	329.505	758.478	1599.460		
VARROCE	0.055	0.166	0.487		
VARROA	0.165	0.102	0.530		
VARRONW	0.293	0.323	0.838		

(Continued)

Table F.2 (Continued)

ANNUAL GROWTH IN TA	71.296	118.121	7.125		
ANNUAL GROWTH IN FA	54.213	69.168	47.146		
GROWTH IN MCAP	321.733	143.747	-19.447		
TOBINSQ	1.082	1.519	0.954		
MARKET CAPITALIZATION	113.584	1609.774	1337.045		
ROCE	14.998	10.851	9.031		
ROA	7.707	7.204	5.471		
RONW	15.810	11.280	7.065		
CFM	7.232	7.073	5.769		
STARATIO	1.011	0.438	0.383		
NPM	4.173	10.574	6.937		
GEODIV	15.354	31.740	48.691		

F.3 Group level product diversity data

Arvind Lalbhai group: SIC-code-based product-wise sales data (in percentage)

SIC Codes	Pre-liberalization Period	Post-liberalization Growth Period	Post-liberalization Recessionary Period
2079	0.000	0.000	0.036
2083	0.069	0.066	0.026
2099	3.560	2.646	1.990
2241	42.745	51.118	39.115
2258	0.000	0.000	0.075
2261	0.000	0.244	0.086
2281	0.967	0.828	10.515
2329	0.000	1.518	3.832
2389	0.000	0.000	5.878

(Continued)

Table F.3 (Continued)

SIC Codes	Pre-liberalization Period	Post-liberalization Growth Period	Post-liberalization Recessionary Period
2812	1.187	1.330	0.464
2814	19.221	12.559	6.042
2819	0.000	0.342	0.156
2834	3.105	2.748	3.452
2861	5.740	3.245	8.971
2865	5.706	3.377	2.446
2869	1.399	2.151	0.575
2875	0.048	0.000	0.000
2879	0.004	0.003	0.088
2899	8.309	6.690	4.432
3088	0.000	0.018	0.089
3275	0.000	0.001	0.001
3299	0.000	0.505	0.287
3444	0.069	0.000	0.000
3462	0.308	0.025	0.000
3498	0.040	0.018	0.005
3556	0.015	0.001	0.000
3559	0.821	0.815	0.501
3585	1.420	3.114	5.546
3593	0.274	0.284	0.188
3651	3.752	0.024	0.000
3661	0.084	0.510	1.274
3669	0.000	0.000	0.055
3799	0.000	0.004	0.001
3965	1.156		
5078	0.000	0.000	0.031
5085	0.000	0.000	0.060
5113	0.000	0.000	0.249
6153	0.000	0.697	0.787
6159	0.000	0.105	0.230
6211	0.000	0.097	0.189
6289		0.396	0.000
6799	0.000	1.517	1.564
7359	0.000	3.004	0.282
7389	0.000	0.000	0.246
8711	0.000	0.000	0.237
Total	100%	100%	100%

Note: all figures above are in percentage

F.4 Affiliate level product data

Amtrex Appliances Ltd.	Pre-liberalization Period	Post-liberalization Growth Period	Post-liberalization Recessionary Period
Airconditioners & parts thereof	6.78	28.88	105.07
Chiller			1.33
Airconditioner mfd. parts			0.31
Trading in spares			1.06
Trading in Dispensers			4.74
Trading in visi coolers			0.59
Trading in packaged units			0.08
Income from service operation			0.17
Scrap			0.24
Sheet metal components	0.33	0	

Arvind Mills Ltd.	Pre-liberalization Period	Post-liberalization Growth Period	Post-liberalization Recessionary Period
Cloth	143.91	369.12	647.24
Yarn	0.83	3.95	92.89
128 port EPABX	0.4	4.73	24.2
FCBC/PBT		0.01	0.1
Garments			111.69
Wireless			1.05
Project management income			4.5
Royalty			4.68
Knit fabrics			1.43
Leasing & Bills discounting income			7.8
Misc sales			19.28
Waste	2.46	10.07	
Tablets	6.87	6.15	
Syrups	1	1.1	
Ointments	0.79	0.79	
Injectibles	0.47	0.26	
Powders	0.23	0.02	
Capsules	0.56	0	
Televisions	17.92	0.22	

Anagram Finance Ltd.	Pre-liberalization Period	Post-liberalization Growth Period	Post-liberalization Recessionary Period
Income from Hire Purchase		16.95	114.62
Lease rentals		9.33	123.82
Bills discounting		3.63	1.3
Interest income		8.42	26.75
Dividend income		0.48	1.9
Other financial income			8.16
Profit on security transactions			3.56
Income from Merchant Banking services		3.67	
Overdue compensation		0.04	
Management fees		2.35	
Share Trading Profit		3.72	
Miscellaneous income		0.06	
Profit on sale of assets		0.12	
High tensile fastener	5.52		

Arvind Polycot Ltd.	Pre-liberalization Period	Post-liberalization Growth Period	Post-liberalization Recessionary Period
Cloth	33.62	64.04	50.9
Yarn	0.84	0.56	1.53
Waste	0.7	1.37	0.71

Atul Ltd.	Pre-liberalization Period	Post-liberalization Growth Period	Post liberalization Recessionary Period
Cresol	6.5	19.58	10.82
Toluidines		0.07	0.1
Sodium sulphite	1.09	1.45	2.69
Soda ash	0.03	0.53	0
Gypsum	0	0.01	0.02
Resorcinol	0.1	0.88	0.43

(Continued)

Table F.4 (Continued)

Metanilic acid	0.18	0.3	0
Heavy duty brake fluid		0.04	0.01
Dyes & dyes intermediates	91.79	116.47	114.8
Chemicals (other than fertilizers)	20.66	37.36	45.17
Drugs & pharmaceuticals	4.06	7.34	6.03
Others - chemicals & pharmaceuticals	0.41	6.04	6.03
Caustic chlorine	4.55	10.35	6.13
Atic dyes	27.41	30.09	0
Intermediates	7.99	11.05	6.23
Para cresidine			12.48
Para anisaldehyde			38.7
Others			3.02
Dyestuff (Atic Div.)			169.54
Chemicals (Atic Div.)			0.92
Anisole			0.21
BHT			0.14
Slurry residue	0.01		
Dinitro Diphenye Sulfone	0.02		

Appendix G: Reliance group's need of creation of subsidiaries[24]

The Reliance Group, founded by Dhirubhai H. Ambani (1932–2002), is one of India's largest private sector enterprises, with businesses in the energy and materials value chain. Group's owners (currently: Mukesh D. Ambani) in the past decade have always been ranked in the Top Hundred wealthiest people of the Globe (currently valued at over ₹ 1.4 lakh crores - US$22 billion).

[24] This case is modification of an earlier summary of: Appendix 3B in Saha, Biswatosh, Parthasarthi Banerjee & Ram Kumar Kakani. *Strategic Thinking: Explorations around Conflict and Cooperation*, Sage Publications, 2011.

One of the standard strategies adopted by the group to grow has been to create manufacturing plants of massive capacities (compared to the peers at that time). Typically, the group would identify an area to get into (say, a backward integration project), create a subsidiary to execute the project, and then raise finances using a combination of innovative financial products from the investors using the public offering route. Once the group completed raising money from these new entities, the group would, then, execute the project at a fast pace without facing any resource bottlenecks. Once these new mega projects go on stream and stabilize their operations resulting in generating steady cash flows, the group would, then, merge the subsidiary company into its flagship company.

The following table gives details of the major projects undertaken, and the names of subsidiaries created and then merged with the parent entity.

G.1 Reliance group and its companies: Over the years

Name of the Firm(s) Created	Year of raising finances from retail investors through the newly created firm; Primary Products of the Project	Year of merging it with parent entity
Reliance Textile Industries Limited (flagship company)	1977; Textiles	Flagship firm renamed as 'Reliance Industries Limited'
Reliance Petrochemicals Limited (subsidiary company)	1987; Polyester Staple Fiber, Linear Alkyl Benzene & Related Intermediate Chemicals	1990
Reliance Poly Propylene Limited (RPPL) and Reliance Poly Ethylene Limited (RPEL)	1992; Polyethylene, Polypropylene and Other Petrochemical Products	1995
Reliance Petroleum Limited	1994; Petroleum Refinery & Oil Exploration	2002
Reliance Petroleum Limited (a new entity with similar name)	2006; New Petroleum Refinery (Export Oriented Unit)	2009

Source: Website of Reliance Industries Limited, URL: http://www.ril.com/ (accessed on September 2013)

The following is a list of Mukesh Ambani managed group companies in 2013:

Major group companies:

- Reliance Industries Limited, Reliance Retail Limited, and Reliance Industrial Infrastructure Limited.

Other Subsidiaries and Associates of the group include at least 100 firms including:

- Reliance Netherlands B.V., Reliance Jamnagar Infrastructure Limited, Reliance Haryana SEZ Limited, Reliance Industrial Investments and Holdings Limited, Reliance Ventures Limited, Reliance Fresh Limited, Reliance Brands Limited, and Reliance Wellness Limited.

6

Case Analyses of Business Groups' Strategies

In our empirical research (Chapter 5), we evaluated the performance of Indian business groups using their aggregated financial statement and capital market figures over a time period spanning more than a decade (1987–99). A prime objective of this chapter is to probe into the possible rationales behind our empirical results, i.e., of higher diversification of Indian groups not generating enough value and profitability in comparison to their focused counterparts. We extend the same by doing the case analysis of a few business groups. Our purpose is to gauge the strength of business groups and trail the effectiveness of their corporate diversification strategies adopted during the study period and how these impacted the group's overall performance over a period of 26 years (1987–2013). In doing so, we are also in a position to review the strategic drivers and performance during the high-growth phase in the Indian economy.

In our discussion below, we term the Indian economic conditions during 2000–13 as a period of rapid liberalization.[1] This period witnessed numerous measures such as greater easing of FDI norms, replacement of the MRTP Act with the Competition Act of 2002, privatization of a number of state owned firms, and complete abolition of quantitative restrictions on imports. Following the relaxations on current account convertibility, the erstwhile Foreign Exchange Regulation Act (FERA) was replaced by the more liberal Foreign Exchange Management Act. In addition, the relaxations on capital account convertibility allowed domestic firms to both raise and invest money in foreign countries.

[1] As we make this statement, numerous commentators have lamented about the recent 'policy paralysis' or the failure of the government to take the reforms process to the next stage. Suggestively, the constraints placed by 'coalition management' have been central in such stalling of the reform process during the second term of the UPA government.

The rapid growth of mutual funds, insurance companies, non-bank financial institutions, and the greater participation of FIIs in the Indian financial markets has played a suggestive role in driving changes in the structure of industrial activity during this period. The greater participation by these institutional investors has been both a driver and an outcome of improved corporate governance codes and practices, minority investor protection, accounting norms, bankruptcy laws and procedures, and regulations such as the takeover code that were implemented to bridge the gap with globally accepted practices.[2] This was also a period that witnessed the global financial crisis with its relatively delayed impact on the Indian economy that had achieved very high growth rates during the 2000s that slowed down during 2008–13.

The period of rapid liberalization provided numerous opportunities as well as unique challenges to Indian business groups, forcing most of them to change their approach and strategies of business conduct. One of the most important challenges was to attain improved efficiency and scale economies. During the early part of this period, the greatest hurdle to attain the same was the excess capacity built-up during the 1990s and the weakened financial position of large firms, especially those affiliated to business groups. A flurry of restructuring activities followed which included the sale of excess assets, rationalization of business segments, cost control, and change of management. While some business groups emerged stronger from these exercises, the same cannot be said for groups which lost their erstwhile dominant position in their business segments.

The growing importance of a new class of institutional investors (both domestic and foreign) that were willing to take a stance opposite to that of management to protect the value of their investments cannot be understated. The active role played by these investors meant that promoters could no longer take for granted their consent for various decisions as was the case when the erstwhile UTI, the LIC, and the DFIs were prominent passive shareholders. As pointed out in Chapter 1, most business group promoters were operating with less than a controlling stake in their larger affiliates. There was a growing recognition that promoters needed to increase their stakes in these affiliates to have better control over their decision-making or face threats of management change or takeovers.

[2] While the authors believe that much has yet to be done on these fronts to completely bridge the gap with globally accepted standards, there is no denying that significant progress has been made in that direction since 2000.

The rapid liberalization period witnessed a significant increase in promoter shareholding through measures such as creeping acquisitions, market purchases, preferential allotments, buybacks (to a much lesser extent), and rights issues (Chandrachud, 2011; Jetley and Mondal, 2012; Raju and Deepthi, 2004).[3] In fact, more than half the rights issues during 2002–08 were made by business group affiliates. Some business groups have also taken the approach of appointing non-family members and professional managers in the top management of their listed affiliates with family members being more directly involved in the parent company/trust/foundation. The increased extent of pledged promoters stake-holding as collateral for affiliate firm fund-raising has also placed an additional set of constraints for promoters. Another significant change was the much reduced dependence by large firms on external funding to finance their activities as compared to the past where such firms enjoyed much easier access to external funds from banks, the DFIs, and public sector investment institutions.[4]

In this chapter we analyze the progress and performance of seven business groups over the period 1987–2013. The background conditions and institutional features during 1987–1999 have been discussed in earlier chapters. We also make use of available data on various performance metrics during the three periods referred to in Chapter 5 and 2009–13 to supplement our analysis on the forces driving strategic decisions and performance of these business groups. The computation of the full set of metrics for all these four periods is not possible in some cases on account of lack of data availability. The case studies covered in this chapter deal with the following business groups:

---

[3] Sources:

a) 'The market for corporate control now opens up'. Economic Times, 30 June 2011; http://articles.economictimes.indiatimes.com/2011-07-30/news/29833258_1_new-takeover-regulations-acquirer-open-offer (accessed in May 2014)

b) 'SEBI tightens Corporate Governance Norms'. Times of India, 14 February 2014; http://timesofindia.indiatimes.com/business/india-business/Sebi-tightens-corporate-governance-norms/articleshow/30359220.cms (accessed in May 2014)

c) 'Private promoters' stakes in firms near all-time high'. Livemint, 11 November 2013; http://www.livemint.com/Money/rMkUT9Ml7T0qwg7NfnqrxO/Private-promoters-stakes-in-firms-near-alltime-high.html (accessed in May 2014)

d) 'Is the trend of rising promoter stake in companies beneficial for investors?' Business Standard, 25 October 2013; http://www.business-standard.com/article/markets/is-the-trend-of-rising-promoter-stake-in-companies-beneficial-for-investors-113102500144_1.html (accessed in May 2014)

[4] Source: RBI's Annual Surveys on Sources and Uses of Funds of Non-Government Non-Financial Companies. RBI Monthly Bulletin. Various Issues.

- G P Goenka Group (in **Section 6.1**)
- Dr. Reddy's Group (in **Section 6.2)**
- BPL Nambiar Group vis-a-vis Videocon Group (in **Section 6.3**)
- CK Mehta group vis-à-vis SM Dyechem Group (in **Section 6.4**)
- Thapar Group (**in Section 6.5**)

This particular selection of case studies was driven by the objective of capturing as much diversity as possible in terms of performance, strategic responses, and other unrelated factors driving decision-making. Some of these groups have performed extremely well on most fronts (e.g., Dr. Reddy's Group), especially during the rapid liberalization era, while some have become insignificant players in their erstwhile dominant industry segments (e.g., BPL Nambiar Group) or have even gone out of business (e.g., SM Dyechem Group). Some groups are still working on getting their restructuring activities right to cope with the new set of challenges raised by greater competition (e.g., Thapar Group). We discuss our findings from the case studies in Section 6.6. The analysis of this chapter combined with the empirical analysis in the previous chapter helps us present a nuanced discussion in Chapter 7 on the diversification–performance linkages for Indian business groups.

6.1 GP Goenka group

Mantle in new hands

KP Goenka divided his group in 1982 to prevent clashes among his sons. The sons, Rama Prasad Goenka, Jagdish Prasad Goenka, and Gouri Prasad Goenka, went along for a while. However, the three splinter groups that emerged from Keshav Prasad's division were not entirely free of rivalry, leading to a wasteful expending of time and resources. The adverse implications of such rivalry were so pronounced that our first case in focus, Gouri Prasad Goenka (henceforth, GP Goenka) group has not performed to its full potential even three decades after the split.

GP Goenka took over as Chairman of his splinter group on its formation. Under his stewardship, the Group received new direction and impetus. The phenomenal growth of the initial years was driven by vertical integration and diversification into unrelated, growing business activities. By the early 1990s, the GP Duncans Goenka group went on to become one of the country's fastest growing business houses with interests in segments such as electronics, tyre machinery, petrochemicals, thermosetting plastics, paper, specialty chemicals, synthetic rubber, carbon black, nylon tyre cord, synthetic fibers, leasing, healthcare, and even education. The following were the primary affiliates of the group carrying out these activities:

- *Alfred Herbert (India) Ltd.,*
- *Andhra Cements Ltd.,*
- *Bakelite Hylam Ltd.,*
- *Duncans Industries Ltd.,*
- *Herdillia Chemicals Ltd.,*
- *N R C Ltd., National-Standard Duncan Ltd.,*
- *Star Paper Mills Ltd., and Stone India Ltd.*

Thus, while the flagship firm Duncan Industries was focused on Tea & Fertilizers business, the other firms had diverse types of businesses that were capital intensive with a dominant presence of the chemical industry in the group business portfolio.

Chasing growth

The 1990s saw the Duncan Goenka Group emerge as a highly diversified group with 20 operating companies and a workforce of over 40,000 employees. Its turnover was above ₹ 2,000 crores and placed it among the top 10 industrial groups in the country.[5] The group was having an aggressive capital-intensive growth. Its fixed assets were nearly doubling every year. The product diversification index which was already high pre-liberalization increased even further as the group aggressively ventured into newer domestic avenues. Much of this growth was funded using funds borrowed from banks and the DFIs.

The poor performance of the group in terms of shareholder wealth was prominent with the wealth creation index of the group falling below 1.0 by the late 1990s. The return on equity (ROE) of the GP Goenka group which was around 9 per cent in the late 1980s reduced to 2 per cent in the mid-1990s, further going down to 0 per cent in the late 1990s and early 2000s. While both profit margins and efficiency of asset utilization were on a decline, the impact of diversification showed up in a reduction in the risk measure of the group. This indicates low earnings volatility for the group as well an inability to capture the upside from its new activities. The efforts by the group to professionalize management of its affiliates during the 1990s were also not quite successful with

[5] We provide a summary of the performance measures for the group in Table 6.1.

the group regularly facing resignations from its top management.[6] This suggests that the group was undergoing the transitional pangs from family control to professionalization of management, with continuing active involvement in day-to-day activities by controlling family members leading to clashes with professional managers.

Entering the new millennium, the Group decided to restructure itself and had identified four key areas that would drive future growth and profitability: power generation and other core sector projects, agro-based ventures, chemicals and petrochemicals, and frontier sciences like software and biotechnology. However, the weakened financial position of the group and its huge debt obligations have so far prevented the group from making any serious inroads into these arenas. On the contrary, much of the focus of the group has been on restructuring its existing companies, some of which were perpetually in the red and others struggling for survival. The group sold its chemical industry flagship Herdillia Chemicals to American multinational Schenectady. Along with the divesture, the group also gave up its right to use the Herdillia name for its firms and products. The group's flagship Duncan Industries Limited that contributed significantly to group profits went deep in the red on account of demand raised by the government in 2002 for refund of excess fertilizer subsidy and the subsequent closure and sale of the fertilizer segment in 2010.

In late 2000s, with two sell-offs in quick succession, Gouri Prasad Goenka decided to hand over the mantle to his son Srivardhan Goenka who had already been inducted into the management team of the flagship Duncans Industries. After the closure of the fertilizer plant and Andhra Cements, which subsequently got transferred to the Jaypee Group, restructuring activities are now focused on the remaining business lines, which includes listed entities like Stone India and Star Paper Mills. Stone India, which supplies high-value equipment to the railways, makes decent profits while Star Paper Mills has been in the red for a long time.

"It has been a planned strategy to get out of these industries and our focus areas would now be to invest in areas which we are left with. Tea would be one of our major focus areas while engineering would be another major one. Whichever ones are left, we will now plan to grow them." said GP Goenka.[7] As part of the move to get a slimmer look, the group also sold its share in

[6] For instance, two managing director of Duncans Industries, the groups' flagship affiliate resigned in a short time.

[7] Source: 'Son rises at Duncans, GP Goenka to retire.' Daily News and Analysis. 22 December 2011. http://www.dnaindia.com/money/report-son-rises-at-duncans-gp-goenka-to-retire-1628686 (accessed in May 2014).

healthcare outfit Duncans Gleneagles to the Apollo Group. The group flagship, Duncans has 17 tea gardens, including 2 in Darjeeling, covering 8,000 hectares producing 15 million kilograms from these gardens. Goenka senior said, referring to his son Srivardhan. "The strategy and the growth part are his baby. He wants to take Duncans Ind to the No 1 position in the tea industry, that's his ambition." In 2010s, the fortunes of the group waned further. The flagship firm of the group has also gone in for restructuring and is attempting to reorient itself away from the diversification strategy. Table 6.1 summarizes the performance of the group during the four periods of the study.

Table 6.1: Corporate characteristics and performance of 'GP Goenka' business group

Timeline ➔ == Variable 🡻	Pre-liberalization Period (end 1980s)	Post-liberalization Growth Period (early and mid-1990s)	Post-liberalization Recessionary Period (late 1990s)	Post- rapid Liberalization Period (2009-13)
1. Performance: **Shareholder Value Maximization:** Tobin's Q Ratio	1.0	1.4	0.9	Less than 0.2
2. Performance: **Shareholder Value:** *Market* Capitalization (in ₹ Crores)	126	972	519	Less than 50
3. Performance: **Profitability:** Return on Capital Employed (ROCE) (in %)	17	10	10	Negative
4. Performance: **Profitability:** Return on Net Worth (RONW)(in %)	9	2	0	Negative
5. Performance: **Profitability Component – Asset Utilization:** Asset Turnover Ratio	1.2	0.8	0.7	Not Available

(Continued)

Table 6.1 (Continued)

6. Performance: **Profitability Component – Margins:** Net Profit Margin (in %)	3.0	1.0	-0.1	Negative
7. Performance: **Risk:** Co-efficient of Variation in ROA	0.37	0.74	0.26	0.25
8. Performance: **Growth:** Annual Growth in Total Assets (in %)	20	105	13	Negative
9. Performance: **Growth:** Annual Growth in Fixed Assets (in %)	6	139	14	Negative
10. Strategy: **Product Diversification:** Rumelt's Categorical Index	Unrelated Business	Unrelated Business	Unrelated Business	Dominant Unrelated
11. Strategy: **Product Diversification:** Montgomery's Related Index	0.851	0.894	0.897	
12. Strategy: **Product Diversification:** Montgomery's Unrelated Index	0.683	0.727	0.784	
13. Strategy: **Geographical Diversification –** Internationalization (in %)	10	10	11	
14. Strategy: **Export Focus:** Net Exports (in %)	-8	-5	-4	

(Continued)

Table 6.1 (Continued)

15. Strategy: **Financial Leverage:** Long-Term Debt to Equity Ratio	0.8	1.3	1.6	
16. Strategy: **Group Size:** Total Assets (in ₹ Crores)	355	1,309	3,082	
17. Strategy: **Promoters Control:** Average Ownership in the Group (in %)			53%	53%
18. Age: Year of Incorporation	1919			
19. Strategy: **Group Structure:** Names of key affiliates Alfred Herbert (India) Ltd., Andhra Cements Ltd., Bakelite Hylam Ltd., Consolidated Fibres & Chemicals Ltd., Duncans Industries Ltd., Gujarat Carbon & Inds. Ltd., Herdillia Chemicals Ltd., Herdillia Oxides & Electronics Ltd., Herdillia Unimers Ltd., Maharashtra Polybutenes Ltd., N R C Ltd., National-Standard Duncan Ltd., Star Paper Mills Ltd., Stone India Ltd.				
20. Strategy: **Industry Landscape:** List of key revenue sources Cement, Acrylic fibre, Laminates: sheets, rods & tubes, Phenolic resins & insulating varnishes, Polyester resins, Urea, Tea, Di-Ammonium phosphate, Phenol, Phthallic anhydride, Acetone, Diacetone alcohol, EPM/EPDM rubber, Textile rayon yarn, Nylon tyre cord, Paper, Beadwire & speciality wire				

Note: (a) The Variable names indicate in bold the dimension of measure and the specific measure therein. For example, the Variable listed # 19, i.e., '**Strategy**: Geographical Diversification *– Internationalization (in percentage)' indicates within 'Strategy' Dimension, we are looking at the Business Groups' Geographical Diversification Strategy using the measure of amount of internationalization, i.e., average percentage of exports and imports done by the group. (b) Note that the above figures are for a four year period (and not just one year). (c)Note that the promoters control above is the indirect control; (d) figures for FY2013 are not audited hence – we provide the latest computed estimates.*

6.2 Dr. Reddy's group

Background

Dr. Reddy's Group has been in the pharmaceutical's business since 1981. The group produces active pharmaceutical ingredients and intermediates and finished dosage forms and biologic products, and it markets them worldwide, with a focus on India, the United States, and Europe. It conducts basic research in the areas of cancer, diabetes, metabolic disorders, cardiovascular disease, inflammation, and bacterial infection.

In 1981, Dr. Anji K. Reddy promoted a company under the name 'Cheminor Drugs Private Limited' (henceforth, *Cheminor*). It made bulk drugs, intermediates, and formulations. In 1991, it introduced import substitution drug intermediates cyclopropylamine & N Methyl-4-Piperidone. It also expanded to the U.S. and European markets through its subsidiaries Reddy Cheminor Inc and Reddy Cheminor S A, respectively. In late 1990s, it entered into a strategic alliance with Schein Pharmaceutical Inc. USA, thereby positioning itself strategically in the generic business. The firm merged with its group affiliate in the same sector to ensure benefits of larger entity.

In 1984, the group head, Dr. Anji Reddy also created Dr. Reddy's Laboratories Ltd. (henceforth, *Dr. Reddy Labs*). Dr. Reddy's Labs made its mark in transforming Indian bulk drug industry from import-dependent in mid-80s to self-reliant in mid-90s and, finally, into an export-oriented industry in late-90s. The process carried on with Dr. Reddy's and other pharmaceutical players from India becoming significant multinationals of the sector in 2000s.

In 1989, Dr. Reddy Labs introduced two new products, namely Ciprolet and Enam, by its formulation division, while its bulk drug division commenced the manufacture of Ciprofloxacin, a new drug. In 1990, it started manufacturing a new bulk drug 'Omez'. By the early 1990s, the expanded scale and profits from these unregulated developing country markets enabled the group to focus on getting approval from drug regulators for its formulations and bulk drug manufacturing plants in more-developed markets such as the U.S. and Europe. The group continued to taste success with the development of new products such as Nise, Stamlo Beta, Sparfloxacin, and Finast. Over the years, the ownership pattern has seen a dilution of the owner's stake from the initial days of above 40 per cent to near 26 per cent in 2013. The lower family stake can be explained by the spate of mergers, acquisitions, and other forms of strategic alliances pursued by the group over this period.

Group affiliates and arms

To enable pursuing growth opportunities in a *bankruptcy-risk-free* manner, Dr. Reddy's group also formed many affiliates, such as:

Company	Objective
Dr. Reddy's Diagnostics Ltd	To manufacture diagnostics kits
Reddy Biomed Ltd	Joint Venture with Russian Company for manufacturing and marketing formulation in Russia
Reddy Hong Kong Ltd	For marketing the company's products in China and Far East Countries.

The other important subsidiaries with their principal country of operation are: Aurantis Farmaceutica Ltda (Brazil; 50 per cent); Aurigene Discovery Technologies Inc. (USA.); Aurigene Discovery Technologies Limited; Dr. Reddy's Exports Limited; Dr. Reddy's Farmaceutica Do Brazil Ltda.; Dr. Reddy's Laboratories (EU) Limited (UK); Dr. Reddy's Laboratories (Proprietary) (South Africa); Dr. Reddy's Laboratories Inc. (USA.); DRL Investments Limited India; Kunshan Rotam Reddy Pharmaceutical Co. Limited (China; 51 per cent); OOO JV Reddy Biomed Limited (Russia); Pathnet India Private Limited (49 per cent); Reddy Antilles N.V. (Antilles); Reddy Cheminor S.A. (France); Reddy Netherlands B.V.; Reddy Pharma Hong Kong Limited; Reddy Pharmaceuticals Singapore; Reddy US Therapeutics Inc.; and Zenovus Biotech Limited.

Internal structure

As of 2013, the group's internal segments include Global Generics, Pharmaceutical Services and Active Ingredients, and Proprietary Products. In India, the group focuses on the therapeutic categories of cardiovascular, diabetes, gastro-intestinal, and pain management, with over 200 branded formulations by 2013. The culture of innovation inside the group has resulted in the group launching about 10 new products every year.[8] Its Global Generics

[8] For example, new products launched by the group in 2009 include Omez Insta, its brand of omeprazole powder; PECEF 200, its brand of cefpodoxime; Telsartan AM, its brand of telsartan and amlodipine; Vantej, its brand of calcium sodium phospho silicate; and Xefta, its brand of gefitinib. The company also launched Combihale, a new treatment for asthma.

Segment operates in the United States, the United Kingdom, Germany, India, Russia, Venezuela, Romania, and certain countries of the former Soviet Union (Belarus, Ukraine, and Kazakhstan). The group operates through several strategic business units, including Branded Finished Dosages; Generic Finished Dosages; Bulk Actives; Custom Chemicals; Biotechnology; Diagnostics; Critical Care; and Discovery Research.

In 2000s, the group decided to pursue the development of its own patentable molecules (also termed 'New Chemical Entity') in addition to the generics business. While the generics business can be considered as a relatively low risk, stable margin business, the successful development of a new molecule provides the opportunity to earn significantly higher margins. However, the business of developing new molecules is both a costly and highly risky activity relative to that of producing generics.

Strategic entry in Indian pharmaceutical industry

India's pharmaceutical industry has been shaped primarily by regulation with multinationals enjoying near domination of the pharmaceutical industry wherein they imported and marketed complete formulation in India, including low-cost generics along with a few highly priced specialty drugs. In 1960s, the government attempted to boost the domestic pharmaceutical sector by setting up Hindustan Antibiotics Ltd and Indian Drugs and Pharmaceuticals Ltd (IDPL) for the manufacture of bulk drugs. However, private sector firms continued to shy away from the industry on account of product patents, high cost associated with original research, and lack of scientific capabilities.

This scenario changed in 1970 with the introduction of the Indian Patent Act whereby substances used in foods and pharmaceuticals were granted process patents instead of product patents. Dr. Reddy's pioneered reverse engineering of many popular underpatent drugs broad basing its therapeutic presence. This industry quickly became one of the world's most energetic markets and by the late 1990s, there were more than 20,000 companies operating in India's pharmaceuticals industry. Indian producers were able to produce and sell drugs and their components at much cheaper prices as compared to developed country firms. This led to an enormous demand for Indian generics throughout the developing world where pharmaceutical products were prohibitively priced by developed country firms. However, the highly competitive domestic market and the low margins on generic drugs forced Indian pharmaceutical companies to develop highly costeffective manufacturing and marketing models. [9]

Dr. Anji Reddy remained with IDPL until the change of law and new opportunities in the pharmaceutical industry in the early 1970s encouraged him to set up his own business. Reddy founded a company for producing and selling bulk actives (the basic raw materials of drug compounds) to pharmaceutical manufacturers. Reddy's clientele soon featured a host of national and multinational companies, such as Burroughs Welcome and others. Following this success, Reddy decided to foray into the manufacture of complete products as a whole, leading to the formation of Dr. Reddy's Laboratories in 1984 to take advantage of the patent laws favoring generics. The venture was financed using $40,000 of his own capital backed by a bank loan for $120,000.[10] Taking advantage of the 1970 law, Dr. Reddy's Laboratories entered the market of producing generics. As Dr. Anji Reddy told Forbes: "We are products of that. But for that, we wouldn't be here. It was good for the people of India, and it was good for this company."[11]

Strategy path toward branded formulations

Though Dr. Reddy commenced business as a supplier of bulk pharmaceuticals to Indian drug manufacturers, it rapidly began exporting to other less-regulated markets. Between 1984 and 1990, Dr. Reddy's group took advantage of the opportunities presented by India's lax patent laws to reverse-engineer bulk drugs patented by MNCs at a fraction of the price charged by them. Within a year, it became the first company to export the bulk drug Methyl Idopa for cardiac patients in Europe. Dr. Reddy's started operations on branded

---

[9] The pricing of pharmaceutical products manufactured by Indian companies was subject to stringent controls under the Drug Pricing Regimes prevalent during the 1970s and 1980s with the result that profit margins for the generics business were low. Combined with the patent laws, the low profit margins reduced the incentive to invest in research for developing new drug molecules. Maintaining strict control over costs was the preferred approach to increasing profit margins which ultimately strengthened the positioning of the sector as among the lowest cost generics manufacturer in the world.

[10] Source: http://www.fundinguniverse.com/company-histories/dr-reddy-s-laboratories-ltd-history/ (accessed in May 2014)

[11] Source: Tanzer, Andrew, 'Pill Factory to the World,' *Forbes*, 10 December 2001. http://www.forbes.com/global/2001/1210/026.html (accessed in May 2014)

formulations in 1986 and achieved another crucial milestone in 1987 by obtaining FDA approval in the U.S. for its Ibuprofen formulation and the all-important FDA certification of its Hyderabad factory. This marked the commencement of international formulations exports by the group.

During the 1990s, the company introduced a slew of generic products, such as Omez, Lanzap, Peristil, Finast, and others. It launched Reclide, an anti-diabetic product, in 1997 and its first anti-cancer drug Mitotax (Paclitaxel) in 1998. The development of these products marked the entry of Dr. Reddy's into the more profitable pharmaceutical segments.

Dr. Reddy's shift toward research initially met with skepticism from the Indian pharmaceutical community. However, the company persisted and further adopted the standard practice among large multinationals of developing 'analogue' preparations of existing drugs. This took advantage of product patent laws in the US which required one to showcase sufficiently different chemical properties as compared to the existing, patented molecules. Large MNCs would take advantage of this provision by slightly altering the composition of a patented molecule or preparation and applying for a fresh patent toward the expiry of the original patent.

In 1994, the group placed a rights issue of $48 million to finance construction of a new facility dedicated to producing generic drugs capable of meeting the legislative requirements of Western markets. The group also opened a U.S. subsidiary in New Jersey that year. By 1995, Reddy's initial research and development efforts had already paid off as the group filed its first patent application for a new and promising anti-diabetes formulation. However, the lack of funds for pursuing clinical trials forced the company to license the insulin sensitizer drug to Novo Nordisk in 1997, a first for an Indian pharmaceutical company. The following year, Novo Nordisk acquired the license for Dr. Reddy's second insulin sensitizer as well.

Going global in the twenty-first century

The year 1997 marked a new era for Dr. Reddy's. In that year, the U.S. FDA adopted new rules which provided a six-month exclusivity period for the first company to gain approval to market generic versions of drugs whose patents were expiring. These rules were designed to encourage the growth of the generic drugs market in the United States and to make medications affordable. The group filed its first abbreviated new drug application (ANDA, used for registering a drug in its generic formula) for a generic version of the popular anti-ulcer medication Zantac. The head-start enjoyed by the company in terms of its research efforts had begun to pay off.

Buoyed by its early success, Dr. Reddy's moved to expand its operations by acquiring American Remedies Limited (based in Chennai) in 1999 to boost its formulations capacity. In the same year, the group set up a research and development subsidiary, Reddy US Therapeutics, in Atlanta, Georgia, placing part of its drug discovery effort closer to the U.S. market. Subsequently, it acquired Cheminor Drugs Ltd. in 2000, making it the third largest Indian pharmaceuticals player. The company followed both organic and inorganic growth strategies with the latter designed to boost its capabilities in segments where it did not have a significant presence.

In 2000, the group launched the commercial distribution of its first generics in the United States, while it filed an Investigational New Drug Application for an anti-cancer molecule developed in India. The group listed the flagship company Dr. Reddy's Laboratories Ltd. on the New York Stock Exchange in 2001. The group clearly revealed its ambitions, as Reddy told Business Week: "We want to be a truly innovative company discovering and marketing drugs the world over."[12]

The group made its first overseas acquisition in 2002 when it paid £9 million to acquire the United Kingdom's BMS Laboratories Ltd. That purchase enabled the group to expand into the U.K. and ultimately gain a foothold in the European generics market. At the end of 2002, Dr. Reddy's scored a new victory in the U.S. market, when it successfully defended lawsuits lobbied by Pfizer to prevent the Indian group's marketing of its own variant of popular pharmaceutical drugs. However, the widespread practice of pharmaceutical firms filing litigations and counter-litigations also took its toll on Dr. Reddy's when it lost the patent challenge by Pfizer for its drug Norvasc (amlodipine maleate) for the treatment of hypertension and angina. The cost involved in patent litigation and the loss of the patent challenge set back the groups' plans to start specialty business in the U.S. generic markets.

Despite these setbacks, the company followed its strategy of pursuing both organic and inorganic growth. In 2006, Dr. Reddy's acquired Betapharm Arzneimittel GmbH for about ₹3,700 crores, a transaction that was the largest

[12] Source: 'Coming at You, Merck,' Business Week, 8 April 2001; http://www.businessweek.com/stories/2001-04-08/coming-at-you-merck (accessed in May 2014).

foreign acquisition by an Indian pharmaceutical group.[13] By 2007, Dr. Reddy's group had six FDA plants producing active pharmaceutical ingredients in India and seven FDA-inspected certified plants making patient-ready medications – five of them in India and two in the U.K.

Performance analysis

Table 6.2 conveys that the business group has performed steadily on most of the performance parameters from 1990s – after achieving stability of a large sized pharmaceutical giant. We find that the market capitalization of the group rose after the group decided to focus on a combination of zero unrelated diversification and pursuing relentless internationalization efforts.

Dr. Reddy's group took advantage of India's low wage and production costs to boost its production of bulk actives. International sales were becoming an increasingly important part of the group's total revenues, a trend boosted by the group's entry into the Russian market in 1991. That country later grew into one of the group's primary export markets. The group consolidated its position in the domestic formulation market through products as well as acquisitions.

Following the opening up of the economy in 1991–92, Dr. Reddy's group adopted a strategic shift. It set up a separate unit 'Dr. Reddy Research Foundation' in 1992 to focus on drug discovery in variety of fields including metabolic disorders, such as diabetes, and cancer treatments, among others. This allowed the company to ring-fence its research activities from that of its manufacturing activities. Even now, the group spends around 6 per cent of its annual turnover on research and development efforts. Innovation combined with export-orientation allow groups to take advantage of new market possibilities (Wan, 1998) besides providing a broader base of markets to obtain returns from innovation (Hoskisson and Hitt, 1994). Therefore, movement into international markets allows businesses to achieve a long-term strategic competitiveness and higher shareholder value. The group took full advantage of opening up of the economy through greater geographical expansion that was accompanied by a rapid growth of assets in the post-liberalization era.

The growth of assets was financed primarily by borrowings during the 1990s on the strength of its generics business. However, as the group forayed

[13] Betapharm is Germany's fourth-largest generics pharmaceutical group with 150+ active pharmaceutical ingredients.

into other countries and new product development, it also substantially increased its equity to reduce its financial leverage. The new equity was partly issued as consideration for the acquisitions and for financing organic growth. On account of this new issuance, the promoters' stake-holding in the flagship company reduced to 26 per cent. Unlike other business groups that followed the practice of setting up independent affiliates for new businesses, Dr. Reddy's group adopted the conglomerate structure with most affiliates set up as subsidiaries of the flagship Dr. Reddy's Laboratories Ltd. The group was among the initial few to embrace professionalization of management.

While the net margins and asset utilization have shown continuing improvement, the return on equity was relatively low following the adoption of near zero financial leverage policy in the late 2000s. The complete focus of the group on a single industry helped it achieve high market power and maintain competitive advantage over its industry counterparts. The strategy of geographical diversification helped to diversify the business risk, resulting in low earnings variation through most of the post-liberalization period.

6.3 Videocon and BPL groups

Prior to liberalization, the consumer durables sector in India was dominated by a handful of domestic brands such as Godrej, Kelvinator, Allwyn, and Voltas that jointly controlled nearly 90 per cent of the market. They were displaced by domestic business group players BPL and Videocon in the late 1980s–90s, which invested in brand-building and in enhancing distribution and service channels. However, family rivalries and uninhibited desire to diversify further led to both the groups, i.e., BPL and Videocon becoming insignificant players in the industry by the late 2000s.

Videocon group

Videocon International Ltd., the erstwhile flagship company of the Videocon group was set up in 1985 by Nandlal Madhavlal Dhoot aided by his three sons – Venugopal, Rajkumar, and Pradeep.[14] In its initial years,

[14] Venugopal Dhoot is currently Chairman of the Videocon Group.

Table 6.2: Corporate characteristics and performance of 'Dr. Reddy's' business group

Timeline → == Variable ↓	Pre-liberalization Period (end 1980s)	Post-liberalization Growth Period (early and mid-1990s)	Post-liberalization Recessionary Period (late 1990s)	Post- rapid Liberalization Period (2009–13)
1. Performance: Shareholder Value Maximization: Tobin's Q Ratio	1.3	5.3	2.1	5.3
2. Performance: Shareholder Value: Market Capitalization (in ₹ Crores)	21	1,015	1,243	41,000
3. Performance: Profitability: Return on Capital Employed (ROCE)(in percentage)	22	26	14	19
4. Performance: Profitability: Return on Net Worth (RONW)(in percentage)	32	27	14	15
5. Performance: Profitability Component – Asset Utilization: Asset Turnover Ratio	1.1	1.0	0.6	1.0
6. Performance: Profitability Component – Margins: Net Profit Margin (in percentage)	6.1	14.9	12.7	14.9
7. Performance: Risk: Co-efficient of Variation in ROA	0.25	0.17	0.25	0.14
8. Performance: Growth: Annual Growth in Total Assets (in percentage)	122	130	23	About 15%

(Continued)

Table 6.2 (Continued)

9. Performance: Growth: Annual Growth in Fixed Assets (in percentage)	142	73	40	
10. Strategy: Product Diversification: Rumelt's Categorical Index	Single Business	Single Business	Single Business	Single Business
11. Strategy: Product Diversification: Montgomery's Related Index	0.000	0.000	0.003	
12. Strategy: Product Diversification: Montgomery's Unrelated Index	0.000	0.000	0.000	
13. Strategy: Geographical Diversification – Internationalization (in percentage)	35	55	69	76
14. Strategy: Export Focus: Net Exports (in percentage)	-6	7	18	
15. Strategy: Financial Leverage: Long-Term Debt to Equity Ratio	2.4	0.4	0.5	0.0
16. Strategy: Group Size: Total Assets (in ₹ Crores)	39	210	734	9,533
17. Strategy: Promoters Control: Average Ownership in the Group (in percentage)			47	26
18. Age: Year of Incorporation	1984			
19. Strategy: Group Structure: Names of key affiliates Dr. Reddy's Laboratories Ltd., Cheminor Drugs Ltd.				
20. Strategy: Industry Landscape: List of key revenue sources: Bulk drugs, Formulations, Diagnostic reagents & kits, Bulk drug intermediates, Chemicals, Solvents and oils				

Note: (a) The Variable names indicate in bold the dimension of measure and the specific measure therein. For example, the Variable listed # 19, i.e., '**Strategy**: Geographical Diversification – *Internationalization (in percentage)' indicates within 'Strategy' Dimension, we are looking at the Business Groups' Geographical Diversification Strategy using the measure of amount of internationalization, i.e., average percentage of exports and imports done by the group. (b) Note that the above figures are for a four year period (and not just one year). (c) Note that the promoters control above is the indirect control.*

the company was involved in the manufacturing of black and white televisions, audio systems, and assembling and packaging of integrated circuits. Following a technical tie-up with Toshiba Corporation of Japan, the company launched India's first world-class color Television under the Videocon brand. In 1988, the Videocon Appliances was set up to manufacture programmable washing machines. Videocon Appliances subsequently ventured into manufacture and marketing of air conditioners, refrigerators, vacuum cleaners, and a whole range of home appliances.

The Videocon group increased its presence in the manufacture, assembly, marketing, and distribution of consumer electronic products and home appliances in India. The company also supplied a range of components, which include glass shell panels and funnels, compressors/motors, and other components of related products to other consumer electronics manufacturers. This allowed the company to take advantage of scale economies and maintain low cost.

In 1989–90, Videocon group started Videocon Communication to engage in manufacturing of home entertainment systems, video cassette players, and recorders. In 1990, Videocon group also set up a joint venture called 'Gujarat Narmada Electronics Ltd' with Gujarat Narmada Valley Fertilizers Ltd. It was into production of glass parts (panels and funnels) for color picture tubes and black and white picture tubes. It was the first company to manufacture glass shells for color picture tubes in the country. All these entities were later merged with Videocon International. The group also commenced a search for a suitable foreign partner in the early 1990s. This was the time when foreign players such as Sony, Panasonic, and others were entering the Indian market. Samsung which was a much smaller Korean Company back then proposed a joint venture to source components from Videocon's factories at Aurangabad in Maharashtra. The belief was that the factories at Aurangabad would operate at full capacity as Samsung's business grew. It would also give the group the option to sell its stake to the Korean company at such time when foreign investment rules were to become more liberal. Videocon finally signed the joint venture with Samsung in 1995.

The group decided to further diversify in the business of lease financing, hire purchase, and investment activities by setting up Videocon Leasing & Industrial Finance Limited in 1991. In 1994, Videocon Group joined a consortium of ONGC which won the bid for oil exploration in the Ravva Oil fields. At this time, oil and gas appeared as out of place for the consumer durables group. Subsequently, it has acquired stakes in 13 more oil exploration blocks outside India. The group considers these oil and gas assets as providing significant future growth opportunities.[15] During 2004, the name of the company was changed to Videocon Industries Ltd. (VIL) to reflect the widening of its business objectives. By this time, the Videocon brand had lost significant market share in the consumer electronics segment and Videocon International Ltd. was merged with VIL in 2005.

From 2005 onwards, VIL embarked a consolidation process which comprised the amalgamation of Videocon International Ltd. (consumer electronics) and the cash-rich Petrocon India Ltd. (oil and gas) into VIL and two major acquisitions – EKL Appliances Limited (formerly: Electrolux Kelvinator Limited) and Thomson group's Color Picture Tube (CPT) business. In 2005, the acquisition of Thomson's CPT business helped Videocon in vertically integrating its existing glass-shell business and gave the company advantage in terms of economies of scale and a leadership position in the glass shell industry in addition to advanced R&D facilities in Italy. After these mergers and acquisitions, VIL has become the Flagship Company of the Videocon group. However, post-merger, Videocon has not been able to benefit from its plant in Italy and Thomson's Mexican plant largely due to the increased popularity of LCD-based screens for TVs and other display devices. In 2013, Videocon Group has over 15 production facilities in India and also has plants in Mexico, China, Italy, and Poland. All the manufacturing facilities of the group are technologically advanced. The Group's brand portfolio includes Sansui, Kelvinator, Kenstar, Akai, and Electrolux.

The Videocon group also entered into the direct-to-home (d2h) satellite TV segment in 2009 and mobile telecom services in 2010. The group attempted to revive flagging demand for its TV sets business by bundling its television sets with the d2h satellite services and charging much lower prices than its competitors.[16] This did not prove to be successful and the company quickly switched over to the traditional set-top box system adopted by other players. By August 2013, the d2h business of Videocon had the fifth largest industry

15 Source: 'Banks rework loan structure for six Videocon firms.' Livemint. 25 March 2013; http://www.livemint.com/Companies/n43w8qE9tPGssF9wO6vUxO/Banks-rework-loan-structure-for-six-Videocon-firms.html (accessed in May 2014).

16 Source: 'Videocon d2h expands in the South.' 21 February 2014; http://www.indiantelevision.com/dth/dth-operator/videocon-d2h-expands-its-business-in-the-south-140221 (accessed in May 2014)

share in terms of subscriber base.[17] More recently, the group has also entered into the grocery and lifestyle retailing business through setting up of cash and carry stores in various locations across the country, mobile handsets, and also the general insurance business through a joint venture with London based Liberty Mutual Group.

Strategy aspects

The Videocon Group started off as a manufacturer of televisions and gradually diversified into other products in the home appliances segment. The group followed a penetration pricing strategy of selling its products at very low margins to gain market share. They also pursued a cost leadership focused strategy to improve its productivity and lower its prices. The backward integration by setting up facilities for manufacture of glass for television picture tubes was an attempt to keep strict control over the cost of the primary component of TV sets. While the strategy helped it gain market share from the erstwhile industry leaders, the same did not translate into comparably high-profit growth. In fact, the penetration pricing strategy combined with the cost reduction strategy may be mutually offsetting, explaining why revenue growth has not translated into profit growth (Banker et al., 1996).

For over a decade, Videocon group held the top spot in televisions, washing machines, and similar consumer durables with a market share of 24 per cent. However, the group's fortunes in these segments waned quite fast in the 2000s, possibly driven by a lack of innovation and/or the ability to see new foreign entrants as significant threats. Similarly, the forays into unrelated segments such as lease and finance were greatly unsuccessful. As most of the growth was financed through borrowings, the huge debt service obligations possibly constrained investments in innovation. Further, the group appeared to have locked itself into large-scale manufacturing facilities and technologies that ultimately posed the threat of large write-offs and possible bankruptcy if they were closed down. As a result, the group continued to carry the baggage of unprofitable assets that have been a drain on its profitability.

---

[17] Source: 'India braced for DTH merger between Reliance and Sun.' Rapid TV News India. 13 August 2013; http://in.rapidtvnews.com/paid-tv/2452-india-braced-for-dth-merger-between-reliance-and-sun (accessed in May 2014).

Finally, facing pressures from its bankers on repayment of its roughly $4 billion plus borrowings, the group began a restructuring exercise in 2008. Under this exercise, it restructured the business into the telecom, retail, infrastructure, energy, DTH, and consumer electronics verticals with the objective of divesting a portion of its stake holding in these businesses through future public issues.[18] However, the subsequently poor primary capital market conditions did not permit such issuances. Following the recent loan restructuring agreement entered into with its lenders, the group has resorted to selling off its assets, including its oil and gas assets.[19] The proceeds from the sale of its Mozambique oil assets in 2013 have helped the group significantly reduce its outstanding debt to under $2 billion, significantly increasing its flexibility for decision-making. However, the group continues to be saddled with a number of unprofitable/low margin businesses that may hinder future profitability. The group now also faces the complex issue of succession planning with structures being worked out to ensure smooth transition in these turbulent times.[20]

Table 6.3 provides a snapshot of the performance and strategy dimensions of the firm over the years. While we observe that Montgomery's related diversification index was rising, the unrelated diversification index was stable. The group's unrelated diversification attempts that commenced in 1990s fructified in the 2000s. The result is that both value creation measure and accounting returns measures of the group have been deteriorating slowly but steadily. Poor asset utilization driven by excess capacity and loss of market share along with reduced margins have combined to reduce the accounting returns. Combined with the poor trust of investors in the group, the result was poor performance in the capital markets that led to an increase in cost

[18] 'Dhoot brothers in huddle to choose Venugopal's successor: Next Generation Being Groomed for Role, Family Trust May Be Set Up.' Economic Times; 29 August 2008; http://epaper.timesofindia.com/Repository/ml.asp?Ref-RVRELzIwMDgvMDgvMjkjQXIwMDEwMA==&Mode=HTML (accessed in May 2014).

[19] See Footnote 15 (ibid.). Also see 'Banking on Gas.' Business Today. 29 September 2013; http://businesstoday.intoday.in/story/videocon-banking-on-gas-stake-sale-business/1/198328.html (accessed in May 2014).

[20] 'Dhoots biz to witness a charge of young brigade: Pradip moves to Dubai, Venugopal's son Anirudh gets consumer goods.' Economic Times, 4 December 2012. http://articles.economictimes.indiatimes.com/2012-12-04/news/35594738_1_venugopal-dhoot-videocon-industries-vn-dhoot (accessed in May 2014). Also see footnote 18 (ibid.)

Table 6.3: Corporate characteristics and performance of 'Videocon' business group

Timeline → == Variable ↓	Pre-liberalization Period (end 1980s)	Post-liberalization Growth Period (early and mid-1990s)	Post-liberalization Recessionary Period (late 1990s)	Post-rapid liberalization Period (2009–13)
1. Performance: Shareholder Value Maximization: Tobin's Q-Ratio	1.2	1.1	0.9	0.6
2. Performance: Shareholder Value: Market Capitalization (in ₹ Crores)	411	799	407	Above 5,500
3. Performance: Profitability: Return on Capital Employed (ROCE)(in percentage)	16	14	5	8
4. Performance: Profitability: Return on Net Worth (RONW)(in percentage)	6	8	-10	7
5. Performance: Profitability Component – Asset Utilization: Asset Turnover Ratio	1.3	1.1	0.8	0.6
6. Performance: Profitability Component – Margins: Net Profit Margin (in percentage)	1.7	3.3	-4.4	4.3
7. Performance: Risk: Co-efficient of Variation in ROA	0.52	0.41	-87.41	0.34
8. Performance: Growth: Annual Growth in Total Assets (in percentage)	113	31	-7	21
9. Performance: Growth: Annual Growth in Fixed Assets (in percentage)	316	25	-3	
10. Strategy: Product Diversification: Rumelt's Categorical Index	Dominant Constrained	Dominant Constrained	Dominant Unrelated	Unrelated Business
11. Strategy: Product Diversification: Montgomery's Related Index	0.070	0.682	0.709	

Table 6.3 (Continued)

12. Strategy: Product Diversification: Montgomery's Unrelated Index	0.000	0.063	0.040	
13. Strategy: Geographical Diversification – Internationalization (in percentage)	9	8	7	
14. Strategy: Export Focus: Net Exports (in percentage)	2	1	0	
15. Strategy: Financial Leverage: Long-Term Debt to Equity Ratio	0.5	0.5	0.8	3.9
16. Strategy: Group Size: Total Assets (in ₹ Crores)	685	1,389	1,977	Above 35,100
17. Strategy: Promoters Control: Average Ownership in the Group (in percentage)			28	69
18. Age: Year of Incorporation			1924	0.6
19. Strategy: Group Structure: Names of key affiliates; Videocon Appliances Ltd., Videocon Leasing & Indl. Finance Ltd., Videocon International Ltd., Videocon Communications Ltd.				
20. Strategy: Industry Landscape: List of key revenue sources: Programmable Washing Machine, Television sets incl. sub-assemblies, Audio, assemblies/sub-assemblies of audio, Air-conditioners, Glass shell (Panels) for CTV picture tube, Glass shell (Funnels) for CTV picture tube, Profit on sale of investment, Lease rent, VCRs & VCPs, Color TVs				

Note: (a) The Variable names indicate in bold the dimension of measure and the specific measure therein. For example, the Variable listed # 19, i.e., '**Strategy:** *Geographical Diversification – Internationalization (in percentage)' indicates within 'Strategy' Dimension, we are looking at the Business Groups' Geographical Diversification Strategy using the measure of amount of internationalization, i.e., average percentage of exports and imports done by the group. (b) Note that the above figures are for a four year period (and not just one year). (c)Note that the promoters control above is the indirect control. (d) figures for FY2013 are not audited hence – we provide the latest computed estimates.*

of capital for the group. Shares of the flagship Videocon Industries Ltd. have underperformed the Sensex during 2008–13. This has resulted in the Tobin's Q Ratio deteriorating further in the late 2000s. Despite these signals, the group continued its entry into unrelated businesses with the hope of striking gold in some of these. This unrelated diversification has accounted for the growth of the group to a large extent. However, whether this round of unrelated diversification will translate into higher profits remains a question as industry profit margins in some of the key sectors that account for significant capital investments by the group will continue to drag down profits. Moreover, the value and profitability of the oil and gas assets is heavily dependent on global prices of oil and natural gas, both of which are currently at high levels.

BPL group

British Physical Laboratories Pvt. Ltd, the first company owned by the BPL group was incorporated by TPG Nambiar in 1963 in technical and financial collaboration with BPL Instruments, U.K. to manufacture precision sealed panel meters for defense applications in Palakkad, Kerala. It subsequently diversified into the manufacture of electronic testing and measuring instruments for the power sector during the 1970s. Following the minor relaxations in the industrial licensing regime in the early 1980s, the company diversified into consumer electronics such as color television receivers, black and white TV receivers, video cassette recorders, etc. in 1982. It decided to manufacture and sell these products under the brand name 'BPL'. By the late 1980s, the BPL brand had become a rising star in the consumer electronics space. The group retained its strong presence and growth in the segment during the early 1990s in the face of increased competition. The company sourced its technology through strategic alliances with international companies, helping them set benchmarks for quality standards in the industry. The most prominent among these strategic alliances were the ones with Sanyo, Siemens, US West, and Toshiba.

In 1994, the group launched its range of frost-free refrigerators and washing machines. It also commenced its mobile telephony business in 1995. The group also entered power generation by setting up BPL Power

Projects (AP) Ltd in 1994. In 1995, it also set up a unit to manufacture alkaline batteries for export. In 1996, the group led by its affiliate, BPL Display Devices Ltd. took over a sick stated owned color picture tubes manufacturer Uptron Color Picture Tubes (UCPTL), to carry out its strategy of backward integration of its core business of color televisions. In 2002, the group leveraged its expertise in speaker and transformer business and also on new products such as car speakers and car security systems. A rise in raw material prices, intense competition, and cheaper Chinese imports led to the beginning of financial problems in 2004.

Strategy path

In 1982, the BPL group made its entry into the consumer electronics business building on the manufacturing capabilities it had acquired as a precision equipment manufacturer. The technological tie-up with Sanyo, Japan provided the group access to the most modern technologies of the time. The Group promoted a new company for each business line – BPL Ltd to manufacture CTVs; BPL-Sanyo to manufacture VCRs; BPL-Sanyo Technologies for audio products; BPL-Refrigeration to make refrigerators; BPL-Sanyo Utilities & Appliances to manufacture washing machines, vacuum cleaners, and microwave ovens; and BPL Engineering for after-sales services of its products.

For over a decade, BPL group held the number two spot in CTV market with market share of 21 per cent. This in itself contributed about 50 per cent of its revenues. The group had brand ambassadors such as Amitabh Bachchan, the Indian cine superstar. It paid ₹ 8 crores for getting his endorsements – an unheard of sum in 1995. The group even started exporting its products to the Middle East and even to the U.S. The focus on quality and the strength of their marketing, distribution, and after-sales channels reflected in a positive impact on the different parameters of performance (See Table 6.4).

Table 6.4: Corporate characteristics and performance of 'BPL' business group

Timeline → == Variable ↓	Pre-liberalization Period (end 1980s)	Post-liberalization Growth Period (early and mid-1990s)	Post-liberalization Recessionary Period (late 1990s)	Post-rapid liberalization Period (2009–13)
1. Performance: Shareholder Value Maximization: Tobin's Q Ratio	1.2	1.6	1.0	0.3
2. Performance: Shareholder Value: Market Capitalization (in ₹ Crores)	66	445	573	60
3. Performance: Profitability: Return on Capital Employed (ROCE)(in percentage)	-2	8	13	11
4. Performance: Profitability: Return on Net Worth (RONW) (in percentage)	-49	-11	12	-2
5. Performance: Profitability Component – Asset Utilization: Asset Turnover Ratio	0.3	0.9	1.1	0.3
6. Performance: Profitability Component – Margins: Net Profit Margin (in percentage)	-24.9	-1.6	3.6	-4.3
7.Performance: Risk: Co-efficient of Variation in ROA	-1.19	-11.96	0.05	2.1
8. Performance: Growth: Annual Growth in Total Assets (in percentage)	35	96	7	Negative
9. Performance: Growth: Annual Growth in Fixed Assets (in percentage)	19	54	14	
10. Strategy: Product Diversification: Rumelt's Categorical Index	Dominant Constrained	Dominant Constrained	Dominant Unrelated	Single Business

(Continued)

Table 6.4 (Continued)

11. Strategy: Product Diversification: Montgomery's Related Index	0.577	0.450	0.529	
12. Strategy: Product Diversification: Montgomery's Unrelated Index	0.446	0.076	0.088	
13. Strategy: Geographical Diversification – Internationalization (in percentage)	30	24	24	
14. Strategy: Export Focus: Net Exports (in percentage)	-28	-19	-18	
15. Strategy: Financial Leverage: Long-Term Debt to Equity Ratio	4.4	5.0	1.3	0.1
16. Strategy: Group Size: Total Assets (in ₹ Crores)	174	587	1,937	400
17. Strategy: Promoters Control: Average Ownership in the Group (in percentage)			57	63
18. Age: Year of Incorporation	1963			
19. Strategy: Group Structure: Names of key affiliates: B P L Display Devices Ltd., B P L Engineering Ltd., B P L Ltd., B P L Refrigeration Ltd., B P L Sanyo Technologies Ltd., B P L Sanyo Utilities & Appliances Ltd.				
20. Strategy: Industry Landscape: List of key revenue sources; Color TV picture tubes, Speakers, Televisions, Transformers/coils, Compressor for Refrigerators, Service maintenance, Color Television & home theatre systems, Home appliances, Refrigerators, Radio cassette recorders, Washing Machines				

Note: (a) The Variable names indicate in bold the dimension of measure and the specific measure therein. For example, the Variable listed # 19, i.e., '**Strategy**: *Geographical Diversification – Internationalization (in percentage)' indicates within 'Strategy' Dimension, we are looking at the Business Groups' Geographical Diversification Strategy using the measure of amount of internationalization, i.e., average percentage of exports and imports done by the group. (b) Note that the above figures are for a four year period (and not just one year). (c)Note that the promoters control above is the indirect control.*

However, the company appeared to have timed its backward integration wrong. In addition to constraining liquidity, the additional investment of ₹ 100 crores and the efforts toward making the Uptron unit a profitable one diverted some attention of the management from the existing business. This gave some leeway to foreign players to aggressively enter the market. As with the Videocon group, the BPL group possibly underestimated the threat posed by the foreign players, especially the Koreans such as Samsung and LG.[21] Excessive debt, working capital shortage, and an inability to restructure led to the beginning of a precipitous decline of the group fortunes. The debt burden severely constrained the cash flows available to the company for carrying out its day-to-day operations and for investment. Further, the group faced numerous demands for various taxes which it could not meet due to cash flow constraints.

A double blow came to the group in the form of the acrimonious, public spat between TPG Nambiar and his son-in-law Rajeev Chandrashekhar over the issue of shareholding in BPL Communications Ltd, the mobile telephony arm.[22] When TPG Nambiar handed over the reins of the group to his son, Ajit Nambiar in the 1990s, he placed Rajeev in charge of the mobile telephony business to prevent family disputes. However, this did not seem sufficient to prevent a family feud with TPG Nambiar unsuccessfully going to court against his son-in-law to assert ownership over the BPL telecom business. The court and company law board proceedings which lasted a few years rung the death bells for the group as the promoters and the management team became more involved with the same. During this period, the company lost a large part of its market share in the consumer electronics segment which it never regained. Moreover, the allegations and

[21] Source: http://www.livemint.com/Companies/0DETNgiBEOJRHc8OfLTHYP/The-rise-and-fall-of-BPL.html (accessed in May 2014).

[22] Sources:

a) http://www.business-standard.com/article/beyond-business/newsmaker-tpg-nambiar-104100201019_1.html (accessed in May 2014).

b) http://www.business-standard.com/article/companies/bpl-family-feud-rajeev-camp-to-return-punch-104092901018_1.html (accessed in May 2014).

c) http://www.business-standard.com/article/companies/bpl-feud-rajeev-gets-a-breather-104093001003_1.html (accessed in May 2014).

d) http://timesofindia.indiatimes.com/business/india-business/BPL-family-settles-dispute/articleshow/1173944.cms (accessed in May 2014).

e) See footnote 21 (ibid).

counter-allegations of questionable allotment of shares resulted in a loss of investor faith in corporate governance practices at the group. This in turn reflected in the share prices.

In 2005, the Bombay High Court approved the Corporate Debt Restructuring (CDR) plan worked out by the group and its lenders. The plan also involved the transfer of the CTV business to a JV between BPL and Sanyo, its long-time technological partner. Under the CDR arrangement, Sanyo infused fresh equity into the business. However, the troubles of the group did not come to an end as Sanyo itself posted huge losses in 2006, partly due to a loss in global market share and partly on account of its own onerous debt burden. Sanyo itself faced a survival issue and agreed upon a merger with Panasonic that finally fructified in 2009. The BPL group also sold off a large chunk of its assets to raise the required funds for repaying lenders.

The BPL brand soon disappeared from the metros and the top cities. At present, a core team of advisors along with Ajit Nambiar is embarked on re-shaping the business portfolio and searching for potential future markets that can leverage on BPL's strengths.

Looking at both groups

We observe that both the groups, BPL and Videocon, declined from their years of glory in the 1990s. Simultaneous expansion into several unrelated areas of business and lack of financial discipline and the aggressive entry of the South Korean companies LG and Samsung are some of the common factors driving this decline. While BPL was relatively more focused and was diversifying in related areas (compared to the Videocon group), the family feud inhibited a proper response to the changing environment and competition. A business group works smoothly when its members are together and act in concert; however, in BPL's case, Rajeev Chandrasekhar and TPG Nambiar were on different paths. Thus, the impact became more severe in the face of aggressive external competitive pressures on the business.

Another common facet contributing to the problems of both groups was the heavy dependence on debt for financing their growth and poor corporate governance practices. While BPL group engaged to a much lesser degree of unrelated diversification as compared to the Videocon group, the latter having better access to capital, the outcomes were quite similar, i.e., value destruction in both cases.

6.4 CK Mehta and SM Dyechem business groups

We portray below paths of two similar sized business groups in a relatively stable sector (unlike the previous case) from the 1980s, i.e., SM Dyechem and CK Mehta Group. This is a short case with the story vividly captured in Tables 6.5 and 6.6.

CK Mehta group

CK Mehta leveraged his skills in trading and manufacturing to set up Deepak Nitrite, a specialty chemicals manufacturer in 1970. He envisaged a greater role for the company and launched Deepak Fertilizers and Petrochemicals Corporation Limited (DFPCL) and started the commercial production of ammonia, a key ingredient in chemical fertilizers, placing itself in a position of strength to take advantage of the demand created by the green revolution.[23] The group subsequently started producing a variety of premium fertilizers to cater to the needs of the agricultural sector. The group also set up its own gas pipelines from Bombay High to its plants in Tajola, thus embarking on its strategy of backward integration.

In the early 1990s, a major fire in its plants led to severe losses and disruptions in production. However, the group kept expanding and used its hard-pressed resources to undertake debottlenecking of its production facilities. The performance started improving and can be reflected in the performance parameters of late 1990s (Table 6.5). At the same time, the group infused fresh equity and significantly reduced its financial leverage, thus staving off the threat of bankruptcy.

As business got saturated from the dominant constrained strategy, i.e., a strategy restricted by the natural gas pipeline business – the group went into related diversification. During 1996–98, DFPCL added bulk fertilizers as well as specialized agro products and services to provide an enlarged basket of products to the farmers. During most of the 2000s, both group companies continued their strategy of building up on their existing strengths and expanding into related products, maintaining revenue growth in excess of 10 per cent. Further, both companies had gained a respectable position in their respective industry segments.

---

[23] Deepak Nitrite is a manufacturer of organic, inorganic, fine, and specialty chemicals and a leader in Xylidine, while DFPCL manufactures Methanol, along with various grades of Nitric Acid and Ammonia and various types of Ammonium Nitrate.

In the early 2000s, the CK Mehta group announced the group succession plans which received consent from all the family members. Under this plan, DFPCL was to be wholly under the control of Sailesh C. Mehta, while Deepak Nitrites was to be under the control of Deepak C. Mehta. While the third son Ajay C. Mehta was given a financial consideration, he continues to be associated with the management of Deepak Nitrites Ltd.[24] Thus, the group avoided needless waste of time and financial resources that many other groups spent to deal with problems involving succession planning. Subsequently, both DFPCL and Deepak Nitrites continued developing their areas of expertise with neither entering the domain of the other. Both firms have eschewed the option of unrelated diversification though the former has made a foray into the retail business by setting up a mall 'Ishanya' in Pune to monetize its excess real estate assets. The growth strategy of the group was more organic with entry into related products both providing higher revenue growth and reducing the risks of the business. Very recently, DFPCL has made a hostile takeover bid for Mangalore Chemicals & Fertilizers.[25] While the stock market performance of the group remained muted during the 2000s as reflected in the Tobin's Q ratio, the returns on both group companies have been impressive during the last one year.

SM Dyechem group

SM Dyechem Group was created in 1982 by S.M. Shetty and S.V. Shetty with the promoters setting up a large-scale organic chemicals manufacturing plant under the aegis of SM Dyechem Pvt. Ltd. The company was primarily involved in manufacturing glycol-based solvents that were in great demand due to the import restrictions in place. The company changed its name to SM Dyechem Ltd. and came out with an IPO in 1986. While the group was doing well in terms of growth and profitability, the management wanted to take advantage

---

24 Source: 'Succession plan at Deepak group,' *Times of India'* 9 January 2003; http://timesofindia.indiatimes.com/business/india-business/Succession-plan-at-Deepak-group/articleshow/33838969.cms (accessed in May 2014).

25 Source:

a) http://www.business-standard.com/article/companies/the-mehta-who-surprised-mallya-113070600024_1.html (accessed in May 2014).

b) http://www.livemint.com/Companies/Pk5zcqQxaOwW1e7FNY1zPN/Deepak-Nitrite-plans-rights-issue-to-fund-expansion-pare-de.html (accessed in May 2014).

Table 6.5: Corporate characteristics and performance of 'CK Mehta' business group

Timeline ➔ == Variable 🡓	Pre-liberalization Period (end 1980s)	Post-liberalization growth period (early and mid-1990's)	Post-liberalization recessionary period (late 1990's)	Post- rapid liberalization period (2009-13)
1. Performance: Shareholder Value Maximization: Tobin's Q Ratio	1.2	1.8	1.0	0.8
2. Performance: Shareholder Value: Market Capitalization (in ₹ Crores)	15	340	178	1,300
3. Performance: Profitability: Return on Capital Employed (ROCE)(in percentage)	10	11	-6	15
4. Performance: Profitability: Return on Net Worth (RONW)(in percentage)	159	16	-65	14
5. Performance: Profitability Component – Asset Utilization: Asset Turnover Ratio	0.8	0.7	0.3	1.3
6. Performance: Profitability Component – Margins: Net Profit Margin (in percentage)	1.3	7.0	-34.9	8.2
7. Performance: Risk: Co-efficient of Variation in ROA	2.53	0.97	-1.93	0.25
8. Performance: Growth: Annual Growth in Total Assets (in percentage)	43	148	3	10
9. Performance: Growth: Annual Growth in Fixed Assets (in percentage)	46	158	14	
10. Strategy: Product Diversification: Rumelt's Categorical Index	Dominant Constrained	Dominant Constrained	Dominant Constrained	Dominant Unrelated

(Continued)

Table 6.5 (Continued)

11. Strategy: Product Diversification: Montgomery's Related Index	0.506	0.733	0.698	
12. Strategy: Product Diversification: Montgomery's Unrelated Index	0.000	0.000	0.013	
13. Strategy: Geographical Diversification – Internationalization (in percentage)	36	21	32	
14. Strategy: Export Focus: Net Exports (in percentage)	21	12	3	
15. Strategy: Financial Leverage: Long-Term Debt to Equity Ratio	10.0	1.9	3.7	1.0
16. Strategy: Group Size: Total Assets (in ₹ Crores)	62	324	1,130	2,900
17. Strategy: Promoters Control: Average Ownership in the Group (in percentage)			71	47
18. Age: Year of Incorporation	1954			
19. Strategy: Group Structure: Names of key affiliates: Deepak Fertilisers & Petrochemicals Corpn. Ltd., Deepak Nitrite Ltd.				
20. Strategy: Industry Landscape: List of key revenue sources: Methanol, Sulphur, DAP, Ammonium Sulphate, Micro nutrients, Urea, Inorganic salt, Nitric acid, Dinitrospentamethylene tetramine (DNPT), Sodium nitrite, Dyes, Dyes intermediates, Ammonia, Nitro aromatics, Caustic soda lye, Inorganic chemicals				

Note: (a) The Variable names indicate in bold the dimension of measure and the specific measure therein. For example, the Variable listed # 19, i.e., **Strategy**: *Geographical Diversification – Internationalization (in percentage)' indicates within 'Strategy' Dimension, we are looking at the Business Groups' Geographical Diversification Strategy using the measure of amount of internationalization, i.e., average percentage of exports and imports done by the group. (b) Note that the above figures are for a four year period (and not just one year). (c)Note that the promoters control above is the indirect control. (d) In 2010, the CK Mehta group split into two groups – Shailesh C Mehta Group (managing: Deepak Fertilizers Ltd., Market Capitalization of about ₹ 1,000 crores) and Deepak C Mehta (managing: Deepak Nitrite Ltd., Market Capitalization of about ₹ 300 crores). However, we are providing combined (estimated) figures in the above table for 2013.*

of the industrial licensing reforms that were introduced in the mid-1980s. The entry into other business segments was also seen as reducing the risks from the cyclical business of organic chemicals. During the late 1980s and the early 1990s, the group chose to diversify into a wide range of business segments instead of going into further downstream chemicals or sticking to its core business.

Thus, SM Dyechem had affiliate in energy-related electronic products, namely S M Energy Teknik & Electronics Ltd.. In initial 1990s, it created a finance firm by the name S M Finance Ltd. The group also entered the foods and specialty chemicals businesses with S M Foods Ltd. and S M Z S Chemicals Ltd., respectively. Thus, by mid-1990s, the group's list of products included specialty chemicals and emulsifiers; polyesters, extruded snack foods; refined oil; soya meal; machineries; financial services; emulsifiers/de-emulsifiers; leather chemicals; and many other organic chemicals.

As with most other business groups, this expansion was financed primarily through borrowed funds. In the face of increased competition, the group found itself saddled with huge excess capacity and unsold inventories in a number of its business segments. The group flagship company SM Dyechem Ltd. finally made a filing to the Board for Industrial & Financial Reconstruction (BIFR) for revival as a sick unit in 1998. The rehabilitation scheme was finally approved by the BIFR in 2008. In the interim, the group resorted to asset sales to help it reduce the debt burden and also reduce operational losses from unviable business units.[26] The sale of business units helped the group become debt-free by 2008–09, though it also meant that the group was left with an insignificant operating asset base to carry out any further business. The memory of the losses suffered by lenders and the losses to equity investors also appear to have created hurdles for the group in raising external capital for new activities. Table 6.6 depicts its current status.

The developments at the CK Mehta group and the SM Dyechem group tell us an interesting story of the fortunes of two groups that initially started out in the same industry. While one group maintained its focus in its industry segments, the other sought to take the unrelated diversification route to achieve rapid growth in revenues and size. When faced with serious troubles in the post-liberalization era, the focused group managed to tide over the turbulent times and slowly worked toward regaining its position in the industry. On the other hand, the group that had diversified into too many unrelated businesses found

[26] Source: http://www.business-standard.com/article/specials/glycols-unit-closure-may-set-the-tone-for-sm-dyechem-agm-196091001025_1.html (accessed in May 2014).

it difficult to handle the challenges that were posed. It did not help that the growth was financed using debt, whereas the CK Mehta group had consciously worked toward reducing its dependence on borrowed funds since the early 1990s.

6.5 Thapar group

The Thapar group was started by Karam Chand Thapar (hereafter, KCT) in 1943 and was till 1980s one of the top 10 business houses of India. He built the family fortune through Karam Chand Thapar and Bros. that was into coal mining and distribution since 1929. Prior to nationalization of its coal mines in 1973, the KC Thapar group had become the second largest coal miner in Asia.[27]

The KCT group adopted the strategy of exploring new business opportunities that had immediate value potential opportunities. Considering the vast opportunities that were to come up across sectors in the wake of independence, the level of relatedness with existing business was not a major factor. The diversification was achieved by setting up or acquiring various affiliates (e.g., Greaves Cotton that was acquired from departing British owners in 1947). The group was in the forefront in the race for industrial licenses during the 1950s and 1960s. It entered textiles, molasses, and alcohol industries through JCT Limited. The group also owned Oriental Bank of Commerce (OBC) that was subsequently nationalized in 1980 and United India Insurance that was nationalized in 1972. It ventured into paper and pulp business with Ballarpur Industries Limited. The group had become a conglomerate of 25 companies spanning a large proportion of licensed industries when the founder Karam Chand Thapar died in 1962.

The group was able to raise the required finances for its activities from the LIC, SBI, OBC, and other banks on the strength of the licenses it had acquired. It was a positive feedback cycle for the group as the allotment of licenses meant that it could expand its asset base and the expanded asset base in turn made the group a relatively safe proposition for banks to lend to. In fact, the Thapar group was one of the select large business houses that was investigated for unfair licensing practices by the Hazari Committee of 1967 and the Industrial Licensing Policy Inquiry Committee of 1969.

---

27 Source: http://www.livemint.com/Companies/tTfC6YXXh54mhtAomkejKN/After-four-decades-the-Thapars-plan-a-return-to-coal-mining.html (accessed in May 2014)

Table 6.6: Corporate characteristics and performance of 'SM Dyechem' business group

Timeline → == Variable ↓	Pre-liberalization Period (end 1980s)	Post-liberalization Growth Period (early and mid-1990s)	Post-liberalization Recessionary Period (late 1990s)	Post- rapid Liberalization Period (2009–13)
1. Performance: Shareholder Value Maximization: Tobin's Q Ratio	1.4	1.2	1.0	
2. Performance: Shareholder Value: Market Capitalization (in ₹ Crores)	34	299	63	
3. Performance: Profitability: Return on Capital Employed (ROCE)(in percentage)	10	4	–4	No information about the group and its affiliates (or even its promoters) is available (in public).
4. Performance: Profitability: Return on Net Worth (RONW)(in percentage)	31	3	–58	
5. Performance: Profitability Component – Asset Utilization: Asset Turnover Ratio	0.7	0.4	0.3	
6. Performance: Profitability Component – Margins: Net Profit Margin (in percentage)	7.9	2.0	–24.7	
7. Performance: Risk: Co-efficient of Variation in ROA	0.25	0.70	–0.40	
8. Performance: Growth: Annual Growth in Total Assets (in percentage)	238	32	–5	
9. Performance: Growth: Annual Growth in Fixed Assets (in percentage)	429	23	–0	
10. Strategy: Product Diversification: Rumelt's Categorical Index	Dominant Unrelated	Unrelated Business	Unrelated Business	

(Continued)

Table 6.6 (Continued)

11. Strategy: Product Diversification: Montgomery's Related Index	0.629	0.660	0.758	
12. Strategy: Product Diversification: Montgomery's Unrelated Index	0.562	0.547	0.633	
13. Strategy: Geographical Diversification – Internationalization (in percentage)	5	13	10	
14. Strategy: Export Focus: Net Exports (in percentage)	-3	5	3	
15. Strategy: Financial Leverage: Long-Term Debt to Equity Ratio	4.1	1.7	4.0	
16. Strategy: Group Size: Total Assets (in ₹ Crores)	64	566	661	
17. Strategy: Promoters Control: Average Ownership in the Group (in percentage)			32	
18. Age: Year of Incorporation	1982			
19. Strategy: Group Structure: Names of key affiliates: S M Dyechem Ltd., S M Energy Teknik & Electronics Ltd., S M Finance Ltd., S M Foods Ltd., S M Z S Chemicals Ltd				
20. Strategy: Industry Landscape: List of key revenue sources: Specialty chemicals & emulsifiers; Extruded snack foods; Refined oil; Soya meal; Machineries; Interest earned; Income from hire purchase; Emulsifiers/De-emulsifiers; Leather chemicals; Organic chemicals; Linear alkyl benzene sulphonic acid; Alfa olefin sulfonate; Glycol ethers				

Note: (a) The Variable names indicate in bold the dimension of measure and the specific measure therein. For example, the Variable listed # 19, i.e., **Strategy**: *Geographical Diversification – Internationalization (in percentage)' indicates within 'Strategy' Dimension, we are looking at the Business Groups' Geographical Diversification Strategy using the measure of amount of internationalization, i.e., average percentage of exports and imports done by the group. (b) Note that the above figures are for a four year period (and not just one year). (c) Note that the promoters control above is the indirect control.*

After the death of Karam Chand Thapar, his third son L.M. Thapar took over the reins of the group; the other three sons, namely I.M. Thapar, B.M. Thapar, and M.M. Thapar. After the major setbacks from the nationalization of its general insurance business and extremely profitable coal business, the group decided to continue expanding in the various sectors in which it had procured licenses. By the mid-1980s, Ballarpur Industries Ltd. (paper, chemicals, and glass) accounted for 25 per cent of group's turnover, whereas three other companies Greaves Cotton (engineering products), Crompton Greaves Ltd (electricals), and Jagatjit Cotton Textiles Mills Ltd. (cotton and man-made textile) contributed another 47 per cent to group turnover. Unlike other firms and business groups that diversified into numerous activities following the industrial licensing reforms of the 1980s, the Thapar group did not diversify any further, using the opportunity to expand capacity in the existing industries. When all signs pointed to the possible opening up of the Indian economy, L.M. Thapar was not in favor of the same, adversely affecting the readiness of the group to face the challenges thrown up by liberalization.

The group adopted the same strategy in the early post-liberalization period that it had adopted post-independence. With a primary dependence on borrowed funds, the group diversified into quite unrelated areas that included leather, prawn culture, and flower exports among others. Most of these business ventures failed miserably, accounting for the poor performance of the group during the 1990s (see Table 6.7). By the late 1990s, the failure of these businesses left the group saddled with significant debt obligations and assets whose value had drastically declined (as reflected in the Tobin's Q-ratio). The group attempted to improve its cash flows by the sale of unprofitable assets such as the edible oil business and glass business. Matters were not helped by the presence of high fixed costs, over-staffing, complacence, mounting losses, and rising debt. Further, the group also introduced a number of measures to control costs that included restrictions on executive benefits like business class travel as well.

The cash crunch also forced group affiliates such as Ballarpur Industries to scrap their expansion plans. The troubles of the group increased further when the profitability of the flagship Ballarpur Industries took a beating in the face of competition from Sinar Mas (the subsidiary of Indonesia-based Asia Paper & Pulp Co.) and the crash of global paper prices. While the group finally acquired Sinar Mas in 2000, the low global paper prices continued into the 2000s, continuing to adversely impact profitability of Ballarpur and the group.

Pushed against the wall, Thapar group took a series of tough measures. It included restructuring debt, diluting equity to raise fresh capital, hiving off businesses, and selling unprofitable investments. It even sold one-third of the family holding of Ballarpur Industries to a Saudi business family to raise the cash to repay lenders. Those tough measures in late 1990s and early 2000s helped reduce the number of unrelated businesses considerably. While the market capitalization of the group in 2013 has been about ₹ 10,000 crores, the group asset size stands at ₹ 30,000 crores, indicating that the group still has a significant amount of low return assets.

Back in 1997, the family members amicably agreed to separate and divide the various businesses among themselves. I.M. Thapar was given, among other companies, KCT Coal Sales, Waterbase, India City Properties; Brij Mohan Thapar was given, among other companies, BILT Chemical, Greaves Ltd, English Indian Clays, Bharat Starch Industries and Crompton Greaves. BILT and APR Ltd, besides other companies, came under the fold of L.M. Thapar. JCT Ltd and JCT Electronics Ltd, besides other companies, came under the control of M.M. Thapar.[28] This helped in clearly demarcating the business interests with most cross-holdings and unprofitable equity investments removed from the balance sheet. However, the ultimate untangling of cross-holdings took a long time to complete with the division finally being effected in 2006–07.

After the split, the B.M. Thapar sub-group headed by Gautam Thapar renamed itself as 'Avantha Group'.[29] While the restructuring appears to have paid off for some businesses like Crompton Greaves & Ballarpur, JCT has defaulted on its foreign borrowings and is in the process of restructuring its loans from Indian bankers. The Thapar group was a product of the era of control in the Indian economy and found it unable to make the change toward a liberalized era that required it to exercise a significantly different approach to evaluate new business opportunities in an environment marked by much greater uncertainty than in the past two to three decades.

---

[28] Source: http://articles.economictimes.indiatimes.com/2006-04-14/news/27436099_1_gautam-thapar-lm-thapar-bm-thapar (accessed in May 2014).

[29] Source: http://articles.economictimes.indiatimes.com/2007-11-19/news/27676545_1_thapar-group-gautam-thapar-avantha-group (accessed in May 2014).

Table 6.7: Corporate characteristics and performance of 'Thapar' business group

Timeline → == Variable ↓	Pre-liberalization Period (end 1980s)	Post-liberalization Growth Period (early and mid-1990s)	Post-liberalization recessionary period (late 1990s)	Post-rapid liberalization period (2009–13)
1. Performance: Shareholder Value Maximization: Tobin's Q Ratio	1.1	1.4	0.9	0.5
2. Performance: Shareholder Value: Market Capitalization (in ₹ Crores)	694	2,943	2,099	10,000
3.Performance: Profitability: Return on Capital Employed (ROCE)(in percentage)	15	13	8	11
4. Performance: Profitability: Return on Net Worth (RONW)(in percentage)	13	9	2	9
5. Performance: Profitability Component – Asset Utilization: Asset Turnover Ratio	1.0	0.9	0.8	1.3
6. Performance: Profitability Component – Margins: Net Profit Margin (in percentage)	4.2	4.1	0.9	4.9
7. Performance: Risk: Co-efficient of Variation in ROA	0.11	0.09	0.50	0.34
8. Performance: Growth: Annual Growth in Total Assets (in percentage)	34	30	6	11
9. Performance: Growth: Annual Growth in Fixed Assets (in percentage)	25	31	10	
10. Strategy: Product Diversification: Rumelt's Categorical Index	Unrelated Business	Unrelated Business	Unrelated Business	Unrelated Portfolio
11. Strategy: Product Diversification: Montgomery's Related Index	0.916	0.923	0.925	

(Continued)

Table 6.7 (Continued)

12. Strategy: Product Diversification: Montgomery's Unrelated Index	0.810	0.832	0.842	
13. Strategy: Geographical Diversification – Internationalization (in percentage)	15	18	24	
14. Strategy: Export Focus: Net Exports (in percentage)	-3	-3	-4	
15. Strategy: Financial Leverage: Long-Term Debt to Equity Ratio	1.1	1.0	1.2	0.8
16. Strategy: Group Size: Total Assets (in ₹ Crores)	1,543	3,687	7,347	Above 30,000
17. Strategy: Promoters Control: Average Ownership in the Group (in percentage)			34	43
18. Age: Year of Incorporation	1922			
19. Strategy: Group Structure: Names of key affiliates: A P R Ltd., Ballarpur Industries Ltd., Bharat Starch Inds. Ltd., C G Glass Ltd., C G Igarashi Motors Ltd., C T R Manufacturing Inds. Ltd., Crompton Greaves Ltd., English Indian Clays Ltd., Foseco India Ltd., Greaves Ltd., J C T Electronics Ltd., J C T Ltd., Waterbase Ltd.				
20. Strategy: Industry Landscape: List of key revenue sources: Rayon grade pulp, Paper including wrappers, Coated paper, Caustic soda, Starch & allied products, Transformers & reactors, Motors, alternators & pumps, Switchgear control equipments & accessories, Foundry fluxes/chemicals, Diesel engines, Marine & industrial gear boxes, Spare parts for earthmoving equipment, Diesel three wheeler auto rickshaw, Cloth, Polyester staple fibres, Steel wire, Partially oriented yarn, Grey cotton – fabrics, High impact polystyrene				

*Note: (a) The Variable names indicate in bold the dimension of measure and the specific measure therein. For example, the Variable listed # 19, i.e., '**Strategy:** Geographical Diversification – Internationalization (in percentage)' indicates within 'Strategy' Dimension, we are looking at the Business Groups' Geographical Diversification Strategy using the measure of amount of internationalization, i.e., average percentage of exports and imports done by the group. (b) Note that the above figures are for a four year period (and not just one year). (c)Note that the promoters control above is the indirect control. (d) Family tree issues have forced the group to split in early 2000s. However, to ensure a single analysis, we provide above the estimated combined information for all the Thapar Group affiliates.*

However, the process of change does appear overall to be moving in the right direction. In a 2013 interview[30] to the 'Business Today' magazine, Gautam Thapar commented that "*we have done lot of work on our businesses, which are Crompton (Greaves) and Ballarpur and I think some of that work has paid off, some of that work is now restructuring for the future. ... In the case of Crompton, it has been a retooling of the business to look at driving it as a global business as opposed to driving it as an Indian business and that is going to take time.*

When we started the change in Ballarpur, it was 1998/99. It took us almost three years to revamp the way we ran the company, put the customer markets first, put the products behind and then start pushing in that direction. Similarly, for Crompton, if you look at the acquisitions, they have been for technology, because ultimately we are – despite the size of the country – still not early adopters of technology in the area of electrical engineering. We don't have a regulatory framework, where the government and the industry work together to come up with the next set of specifications to drive technology development. That's a process that happens extensively in the West."

6.6 Discussion of case observations

In the previous five sections, we have put forth the historical context and analysis of the performance of the seven groups. A common finding is that unrelated diversifiers have been poor performers on various parameters, with performance worsening after an increase in unrelated diversification. This is in line with the empirical results in Chapter 5. We summarize the key findings of these case studies in Table 6.8.

However, the story is far more nuanced with factors such as financial leverage, family succession planning, and professionalization of management also playing a significant role. What we observe from the case studies in this chapter and from articles in the news media during the period of the late 1990s on the financial troubles of large firms is that financial leverage significantly constrained restructuring moves on part of the troubled business groups.

---

30 Source:

a) http://businesstoday.intoday.in/story/gautam-thapar-avantha-group-interview/1/194755.html (accessed in May 2014).

b) http://archive.tehelka.com/story_main9.asp?filename=Ne122504thapars_fought.asp (accessed in May 2014).

Further, the presence of a huge amount of outstanding debt also prevented these business groups from entering into genuinely profitable ventures that could have increased shareholder value.

A number of success stories in the rapid liberalization era have been those of business group affiliates, and unrelated diversification for these groups has definitely been on a significant rise. One key difference between these groups and the ones that lost their dominant positions was the fact that they had emerged from the financial troubles of the late 1990s with much safer balance sheets in terms of low financial leverage. Further, the better performing groups have resorted to internal financing to a much greater extent than debt for financing their forays into new business segments.

Another key difference that also comes through, especially in the case of Dr. Reddy's group, is that the extent of professionalization of management and the willingness of the founding family to cooperate with professional managers has been crucial in determining the extent to which the groups could turn the new, uncertain external environment in their favor.

Finally, despite the increased professionalization of management, the issue of family succession planning and clarity in family ownership of group assets would continue to remain a key determinant of performance. Instability in family relationships and lack of clarity in terms of succession planning have displayed the ability to derail a well-performing group and its affiliates. The underlying cause of the same is well-summed up by Gautam Thapar of the Thapar Group "A lot of people do not understand that family businesses are social organizations and need to be treated as such. We in India still have a feudal set up, with succession planning by the family patriarch being done too late in the life span of the business when such planning should actually happen in the first generation itself. Businesses are meant to create wealth and this wealth should be shared by all in the family...."[31] It reflects the averseness of business group heads to hand over the reins to the younger generation at the right time. It also reflects that some of them pursue needless unrelated projects to ensure that the family tree needs are satisfied – than the wealth maximization goals of the shareholders.

To sum it up, while the extent of unrelated diversification is a key determinant of financial performance of business groups, the outcome depends on other factors such as access to financial resources, development

[31] Source: http://online.wsj.com/news/articles/SB125474045508264225 (accessed in May 2014).

Table 6.8: Strategy-performance path of seven Indian business groups over a quarter century period.

Business Group Name	Management Background	Group Size in Three Stages (1985 – 2000 – 2013)	Family Issues (if any)	Product Diversification Strategy (1985 – 2000 – 2013) using Rumelt Categorization	International Diversification Strategy (1985 – 2000 – 2013)	Level of Success (as on 2013)
BPL Nambiar Group	Largely Family. It also has a mix of Professionals	Small ➔ Medium ➔ Very Small	Yes, rift in family(between father and son-in-law) when the group size increased	Started with 'Dominant Constrained' category and moved toward 'Dominant Unrelated'	Medium levels throughout (due to nature of its dominant business)	Failure, left with just one small listed entity
CK Mehta Group	Largely Family members with Professional background.	Small ➔ Medium ➔ Medium	Not visible. Yet, family tree growth has led to amicable split in the groups from 2000s onwards	Largely 'Dominant Constrained'. Lately, has been attempting unrelated moves.	Medium levels throughout (due to nature of its dominant business)	Partially Successful with a decent market standing
Dr. Reddy's Group	Professionals take decisions. Vision is set by family.	Very Small ➔ Medium ➔ Large	No. Not visible.	Rumelt's 'Single Business' throughout	Started with Medium level and consciously pursued it to Very High levels	Highly Successful with a solid market standing

(Continued)

Table 6.8 (Continued)

GP Goenka Group	Family takes decisions. Professionals are asked to implement and follow.	Large → Medium → Small	Yes, rift in family when the group size was largest. Led to splits in 1980s & more	'Unrelated Business' throughout. Lately, downsizing has led to it becoming 'Dominant Unrelated'.	Low to Medium throughout. It was never been a hugely visible agenda.	Failure, left with very little
SM Dyechem Group	Completely Family Controlled	Very Small → Small → Non-existent	Not visible.	'Unrelated Business' during its short-period of existence	Very Low throughout. No conscious effort to pick it up.	Failure, has become invisible
Thapar Group	Largely Family. It also has a mix of Professionals	Very Large → Large → Medium	Yes, rift in family led to split in four groups during 1997-2002 period.	'Unrelated Business' throughout. Lately, downsizing to it becoming 'Unrelated Portfolio'.	Low to Medium throughout. It was lately become a visible agenda.	Below average with sparks of brilliance
Videocon Group	Family takes key decisions. It also has few Professionals in the family.	Medium → Medium → Medium	Not visible. Yet, family tree growth may force this in future.	'Dominant Constrained' initially and moved to 'Dominant Unrelated' and then to 'Unrelated Business'.	Very Low initially. Of late, has made effort to pick it up.	Average with a solid market standing

of capabilities to handle diversification, and the absence or otherwise of promoter-family-related problems. Business groups that have worked on developing their capabilities through means, include professionalization of management, technology upgrading, and human resource management among others. The examples of groups such as the CK Mehta group and the Thapars that have managed to survive the difficult times of the late 1990s and work toward regaining their lost position in industry are cases in point. Even the widely known examples of successful groups such as the Tatas or the Ambanis that have not been covered in this chapter corroborate these observations.

Appendix

Table 6A.1: A summary of 'family tree' and succession planning problems and actions taken by troubled business groups

Issue(s)	Troubled Business Group Stage/Actions
Large Family Tree	Huge amounts spent on unrelated diversification to enable smooth and clear division of group assets.
Lack of Clarity on Succession Plan	Time and resources of business group expended toward managing the new unrelated business
No New Investment in Traditional Successful Businesses	Competitors Succeed (in traditional businesses). Reduced market power for the group & lower economies of scale and scope (for the affiliate and the group)
Rifts in Business Group	Restructuring of the Group

7

Summary of the Work

"If human beings are not drowned,' asked the little mermaid, 'Can they live forever? Do they never die as we do here in the sea?" – *The Little Mermaid,* a fairy tale by *Hans Christian Andersen.*

<u>*What are business groups?*</u>

Business groups are a collective network of legally independent firms whose strategic and operating decisions are controlled by either members of a family or group of families. These families have control over the decision-making of these firms by virtue of holding at least a significantly influential ownership stake. Part of the ownership stakes in these business networks are usually held by the family through investment firms, trusts, or foundations set up by them with cross-holdings in affiliates making up the remaining group ownership share. The primary investment firm/trust/foundation in most cases provides direction for/controls the overall activities of the group firms. Industrial activity in a large number of countries continues to be dominated by such business groups.

They often diversify across different product lines with many divisions under them, similar to the U.S. conglomerates. In India, for instance, the Gautam Thapar Avantha group controls a host of firms predominantly in electrical and chemical industries. Another example is the Tata group controlled by the House of Tatas, operating in diverse product portfolio encompassing steel to software to salt.

Product focus based on strong core competencies combined with international diversification has been the success mantra, propounded by academicians and consultants alike. This strategy is adopted by many successful developed country transnational corporations such as Coco-Cola, Microsoft, Lafarge, and Pfizer, especially during the last three decades of increasing globalization. Contrary to some recent theories suggesting product (unrelated) diversification as a success mantra in the emerging markets vis-à-vis focused strategies as success mantra in the developed world, most developing country business groups adopting the focus strategy were also successful. Large number of business groups, which diversified more and more claiming synergies and other benefits found such benefits to be either illusory or over-rated, leading to erosion in shareholder wealth. The recent problems of big unrelated conglomerates in developing nations such as Daewoo in South Korea, Astra in Indonesia are but some of the examples that indicate all is not well with highly diversified unrelated conglomerates.

In our research, we evaluated the performance of Indian business groups using their aggregated financial statement and capital market data over a time period spanning more than one decade as empirical work and more than two decades as case study work. Our purpose was to assess the strength of business groups and the effectiveness of their corporate diversification strategies. We have found that as in the developed world, groups with large (unrelated) product scope were indeed destroying shareholder wealth in comparison to those with limited product scope. The objective of this study was also to look into the possible reasons for highly diversified Indian groups not generating enough value and profitability in comparison to their focused counterparts.

7.1 Varied institutional context

Theories proposed in the literature argue that institutional context in Argentina, Brazil, Chile, India, Korea, and many other developing nations is different from the western developed nations of Europe and the U.S. and, therefore, would give diversified conglomerates many advantages to operate (Khanna and Palepu, 1997). Organizations compete in three factor markets, i.e., labor, product, and finance.[1] The theories argue that a diversified conglomerate will have many advantages in mitigating institutional voids in comparison to their focused counterparts since these markets suffer from informational problems, misguided regulations, and inefficient judicial systems. Our research shows that this view is not borne out by empirical evidence in the Indian scenario

[1] Organizations competing in the fourth factor market, i.e., market for corporate control is, assumed to be a subset of the finance factor market.

which points to the contrary. We suggest that the following points to explain the evidence:

These institutional void arguments appear to have been highly exaggerated. To take an instance, it is often pointed out that these markets suffer from a scarcity of well-trained people. However, during the last two decades India and other emerging markets have emerged as among the largest pools of skilled and unemployed manpower. Especially in the Indian scenario, there are a sizeable number of high quality management and technical schools to train managers and engineers.

Further, the Indian capital markets are comparable to many developed markets on numerous parameters such as market turnover ratio, market capitalization as a percentage of GNP, number of listed companies, and so on. Further, the assets of the banking sector have grown at a phenomenal rate post-liberalization. Despite the large number of academic papers debating the efficiency of the Indian equity markets (e.g., Joshi, 2012; Mehla and Goyal, 2012; Poshakwale, 1996), it is widely accepted that the Indian financial system as a whole has developed by leaps and bounds in the post-liberalization era (e.g., Chakraborti, 2010; Khan, 2013; Mohan 2007a, 2007b). Against this background, the internal capital markets arguments appear to lack a strong foundation in the Indian scenario.

Unlike the claims made in the institutional voids literature, such voids create different sets of difficulties for both diversified and focused groups which may be more or less equal in terms of their impact. As the case studies show, the penchant of diversified groups to seek favors from political parties in power to fill these institutional voids makes them particularly vulnerable to onslaught from regulatory agencies and the opposition political parties especially when they come in power. That is, in addition to economic cycles, such diversified groups may also have to contend with 'election cycles' where their fortunes also depend on outcomes of national and state government elections. For instance, when the politically powerful Autoriders group made a high-profile acquisition bid for Saurashtra Cements, the securities regulator (SEBI) took more than a year to clear the matter, forcing the group to subsequently withdraw the offer. Large unrelated diversified groups using such political linkages and liasoning also risk falling out of favor following changes in political and regulatory agency structures. The Tata Group faced widespread difficulties in West Bengal state due to its perceived closeness to the erstwhile ruling party (currently the opposition party).

The institutional delays coupled with complicated linkages within the group operations are so severe that it may often become very difficult for diversified groups to exit a business operation without consequences for the rest of the group. Despite repeated attempts, Hindustan Motors of CK Birla group has not been able to close their Uttarpara operations for the last one-decade and the group has to continue subsidizing the loss-making divisions. It took the reputed Tata group around three years to divest itself off an affiliate company operating in soaps and detergents sector (TOMCO). The complex favors given and taken during iron ore mining allocations by the Naveen Jindal group in the Karnataka state appears to have come back to haunt them after nearly a decade.

7.2 Unrelated conglomerates as sources of institutional deficiencies

Many economists, bankers, traders, lawmakers, and academicians equate diversified groups with corruption and unhealthy business practices and believe that these conglomerates play a major part in contributing to the underlying sources of institutional deficiencies, i.e., informational problems, misguided regulations and inefficient judicial systems. In the absence of reliable information for decision-making, participants in both factor and product markets would tend to be reluctant to enter into economic transactions. Unrelated diversified groups in developing countries have typically been wary of revealing detailed information to their transacting counterparties in product and factor markets. In fact, they are alleged to be the most opaque business organizations unlike developed country conglomerates (such as Moller-Maersk of Denmark) which are usually a single overarching company and publish clear consolidated financial statements indicating the status of each asset. For example, diversified groups seldom reveal their cross-holdings or their ownership stake in the affiliates beyond the minimum legal requirement.[2]

It is widely known that organizations are reluctant to transact without ways of ensuring that their partners will hold up their end of the bargain. As most developing countries do not yet have efficient regulatory and judicial systems, contract enforcement mechanisms followed by the group and its reputation for fair play become significant drivers of credibility of the group. Affiliate companies from groups having well-developed, transparent contract enforcement mechanisms, and a high reputation for fair play are typically preferred by product and factor market counterparts. Our study suggests that unrelated diversified

---

[2] Lately, public outcry and intellectual media has forced some of the unrelated conglomerates to come clean.

groups[3] have typically been found to engage in poor treatment of minority shareholders, weak disclosure norms, and questionable intra-group transactions and end up losing their credibility in product/labor/financial markets.[4]. Some diversified groups such as NEPC have a negative record even in the payment of dividends and poor contract enforcement practices; adversely affecting the extent of support they received from their investors, partners, and clientele. There are others that have a 'moral economy' within the group such as Tatas which have built a reputation for a very good contract enforcement mechanism leading to their enjoying continued support from their stakeholders. However, the analysis in this book suggests that not every diversified group destroys value or faces credibility problems unlike the focused groups. Rather, the underlying causes can be traced to the historical development of the group activities and the drivers of unrelated diversification in the first instance.

7.3 Contrasting industry structures

The study also suggests that institutional features, particularly, as the financial system, government policies, regulatory enforcement have played an important role in determining the nature and extent of activities of Indian business groups. In other words, the development of business group structures and activities are path dependent with changes in institutional context opening up opportunities and, in some cases, the necessity to follow a different development path. We observed that diversified business groups in many cases grew not out of any conscious strategic decisions, but rather due to historical circumstances and succession planning problems within the controlling families. The case studies in Chapter 6 do point to the fact that unrelated diversification was often driven by the desire to avoid any family rifts (or to resolve one at a later point in time).

Integrating affiliates engaged in varied businesses and managing them from the headquarters is a very tough task as each business operates within its own distinctive market structure. For instance, affiliates operating in product markets such as electricity or steel tend to be highly capital intensive, whereas affiliates such

[3] Except for a select few (such as Aditya Birla Group, Mahindra and Mahindra Group, and Tata Group) most diversified conglomerates fall in this category (please look at the list of business groups at the end of this book for a list of unrelated diversifiers).

[4] For instance, during the placement session in the top business schools of India, candidates have typically been found to prefer focused Indian organizations such as Infosys, Asian Paints, and Ranbaxy over diversified groups despite similar pay packages being offered.

as those in software sector would have lesser requirements for long-term capital, but would require high intellectual (human) capital to consistently perform and stay with them for long. Capital allocation for investment decisions, performance evaluation of business lines, and intra-group transfer pricing decisions rank among the most complex decisions that come to the fore during the annual planning process. As the dynamics of world markets and the technology of serving them are rapidly changing, top management, therefore, needs to be highly adaptable in its approach to corporate strategy and selection of portfolio of businesses and their composition within a group. Business groups managed by families are less likely to have a professional team at the top with such wide range of skill sets and, hence, it is imperative for them to concentrate on select lines of businesses rather than managing a wide array of businesses with no synergies between them. The case becomes stronger especially when the twin forces of globalization and domestic deregulation subject even the sleepiest industry to fierce competition. The impact of the changing dynamics post-liberalization has been witnessed in the Indian scenario with business groups increasingly appointing professional managers for a number of their affiliate companies. The post-2000 developments in the market for corporate control, the market for managerial talent, and increased activism of institutional investors have all played a significant role in driving this change.

7.4 Value loss of diversified groups

Diversified groups have been found to destroy value in three important ways. Firstly, they have complex structures hindering innovation. For instance, in the Indian cement sector, conglomerates such as MP Birla, LN Bangur, and BK Birla have been manufacturing cement in the segment for decades without much innovation to talk about.[5] In contrast, Gujarat Ambuja Cements, a young focused group, has become one of the most cost-efficient producers of cement in the world

[5] The term 'innovation' is used in a broader sense to include process and organizational innovation in addition to product innovation. It is frequently bemoaned that developing country firms do not spend as much on R&D (or rather, product innovation) as they should be doing. However, it is the view of the authors that those holding this point of view fail to take into consideration 'process innovation' which is not easily captured in the traditional metrics for evaluating innovativeness efforts. In the absence of such process innovation, it is difficult to imagine how a number of developed country firms have continued to remain low cost producers despite the increasing trend in labor costs which has typically been considered their source of competitive advantage.

due to their constant innovation.[6] Secondly, diversified groups misallocate capital and shield loss-making affiliates. In fact diversified entities have been found to engage in 'socialist' reallocation of funds across divisions with stronger divisions/entities cross-subsidizing weaker ones (Scharfstein & Stein, 2000). When one affiliate in a group faces declining prospects, its assets and cash flows (in some cases, even liabilities) are transferred to other group affiliates that are doing well despite their operating in otherwise unrelated areas. The numerous transfers of the loss making Birla Tyres' division shifting hands within the other BK Birla group affiliates during the late 1990s is a case in point. More recently, the losses of Kingfisher Airlines being funded by other UB Mallya group affiliates is another case in point. Thirdly, they have poor governance due to which most investors, both foreign and domestic, are wary of investing their funds in diversified group affiliates. The result is many diversified group affiliates trade at discounts in the stock markets to their peers in the same industry.

Studies on developed country diversified conglomerates examining the diversification discount (e.g., Berger and Ofek, 1995; Lins and Servaes, 1999; Scharfstein and Stein, 2000; Rajan et al., 2000) have emphasized the misallocation of capital investments by corporate headquarters and the drivers for the same. However, as we have pointed out in Chapter 1, Indian business group affiliates are largely characterized by 'significant influence' rather than 'control' by the 'parent company/promoters'. Unlike the parent/holding company in the case of developed conglomerates, the 'parent company/promoters' are generally not listed on a stock exchange in India (Tata Sons is a case in point). Moreover, the case studies show that whereas the business group as a whole may be diversified, each individual affiliate tends to focus in one or related lines of business. This was in part due to the nature of the licensing system adopted post-independence and the resort to long-term capital provision through the 'project finance' route by banks and DFIs which encouraged business groups to form separate legal entities to apply for licenses across different business lines. In the post-liberalization era, the continued choice of 'project finance' by providers of capital meant that new activities/business lines continued to be carried out by setting up a separate legal entity. In most cases, the controlling stake, if any, was made of the combined stake-holding of the 'parent company/promoters' and other affiliates.

Since neither the parent company nor the other affiliates had a sole controlling stake, there was no requirement to present consolidated financial statements as is

[6] In 2000s, Gujarat Ambuja Cements group owned by Sanghvi's sold itself to the multinational Holcim group.

the requirement for developed country conglomerates with controlling stake in their subsidiaries/business divisions. Hence, the diversification discount in the Indian scenario may not show up or even exist at the level of the listed individual affiliates who for the most part would display a focused strategy. This suggests that in addition to the negative influence of diversification on performance (especially profitability) that is borne out of this study, the presence of an equity market diversification discount for Indian business group affiliates can also be partly explained by a combination of poor treatment of non-promoter shareholders and the ability of the parent company/family dominated management to divert resources to other affiliates through means such as inter-company loans and even dividends (which the parent company could use to finance other affiliates). The IT giant, TCS (part of Tata Group) provides a fine example of how a business group affiliate even though performing extremely well has historically traded at a discount to its more focused compatriots such as Infosys and Wipro. Some other examples include CEAT (RP Goenka Group) and JK TYRE (Singhania Group) in the automotive tyre segment as compared to focused TYRE players such as MRF and Apollo Tyres.

7.5 Advantages of international exposure

International exposure allows business groups to exploit core competencies and distinctive capabilities across units in different international markets. It also helps in stabilizing returns by creating economies of scale and scope and by providing a broader base of markets for obtaining returns from innovation. Exporters can also take advantage of the numerous sops, cheaper finance sources, and taxation benefits given by the states. All these advantages make investors prefer groups with high international exposure earning them higher discounts in the markets. Asian Paints and Dr. Reddy's were two industrial houses that adopted a strategy of being highly export-intensive early on during the post-liberalization era and were able to integrate across country borders by standardizing or modifying products while coordinating critical research functions to achieve enhanced scale economies and, hence, achieve a long-term strategic competitiveness.

Lately, most business groups have realized this and have been pursuing aggressive acquisition and expansion strategies in other countries as well. The recent overseas ventures and acquisitions of the AV Birla group, Jindal group, Sanjay Kirloskar group, and Baba Kalyani group are some prominent examples. Most of them have been successful. Kirloskar Brothers, a pumps manufacturer owned by Sanjay Kirloskar group, in the early 2000s was struggling to survive.

However, after a spate of overseas acquisitions and expansions, Kirloskar Brothers today enjoys a leadership position in its pumps business.

7.6 Primary findings of statistical analysis

We performed empirical analysis on 240 large Indian business groups (constituting over 45 per cent of total market capitalization of India) over a time-span of 12 years, using multiple measures of performance and diversification. Our work also controlled for a large set of variables such as size and industry fixed effects. The time-span was selected to reflect the different phases of Indian economy, viz. pre-liberalization period, post-liberalization growth period, and post-liberalization recessionary period. The following box with two figures gives an essence of the research findings.

We found a positive relation between international exposure and performance, and a negative relation between product diversification and performance. Figure 1 gives a pictorial view of the results. The bubbles represent the business groups in the sample and the size of the bubble represents their financial performance. A larger sized bubble indicates a better aggregate group performance than a smaller sized bubble business house.

FIGURE 1: Product Diversification, International Exposure and Financial Performance of Indian Business Groups

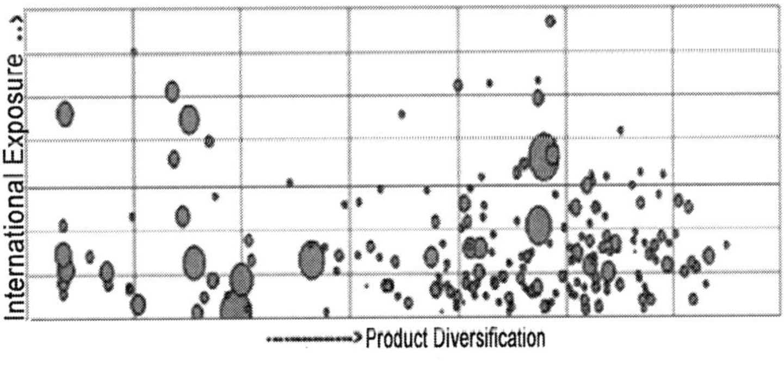

Figure 2 gives a graphic view of this non-linear relationship. The figure conveys that the reduction in shareholders' wealth becomes greater and greater as business group's product diversity increases more and more. This probably implies that a movement from Related to Unrelated diversification by business groups would be more value destroying in comparison to a movement from Single Business to Dominant Constrained product diversification strategy.

Figure 2: Diversification and Performance Relationship

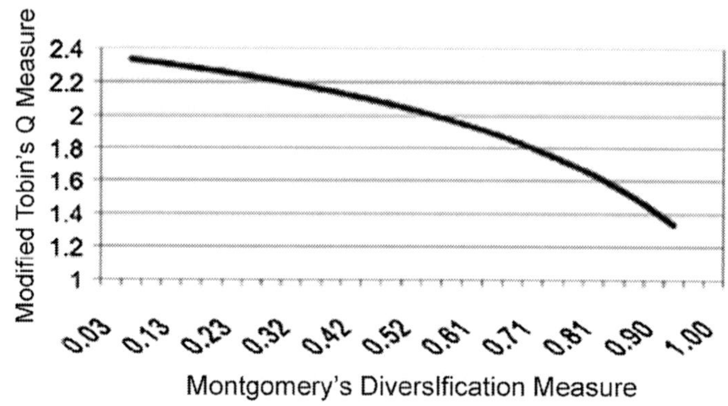

7.7 Primary findings from analysis of case studies

In Chapter 6, we used a case-study approach to dig deeper into some of the key findings from the statistical analysis. The analysis suggests that there is a wide dispersion of performance of diversified groups with some diversified groups standing out as better performers in contrast to the negative statistical relation for the entire sample. We identified some common themes that could account for such divergence in performance which are summarized below:

7.7.1 *What went wrong with diversified groups?*

- **Stretching brands**: Brand stretching is a phenomenon when an established brand name is applied to an increasing variety of products/ product categories that are not similar to each other. Failures in one or more of these products have the ability to diminish the value of the brand. While some brands may be strong enough to recover from these failures, the same may not be the case with other brands as the case studies of SM Dyechem and BPL groups suggest. For instance, the Tatas have made unsuccessful forays into unrelated areas in the rapid liberalization period. However, the strength of the brand and the improving performance of the other products/affiliates of the group significantly negated the impact of these failures.

- **Changing direction frequently**: The key to successful diversification is to diversify into areas that are congruent with the core competencies of the group. Business interests by a group could be stretched in many directions, however, if they are not going in a direction that is congruent with the core competencies of the group, then groups are at a risk of being wiped off. To succeed, Alpine group ventured into three new lines of businesses, viz. metals, chemicals, and financial services during the last one decade and has failed in all of them. The cases of SM Dyechem and Vadilal groups are no different.
- **Lacking success formula**: To understand why successful groups such as Videocon, GE Shipping, and Uniworth failed, it is necessary to examine their origins of success. All these once successful groups owed their success to their distinctive combination of focused strategies, processes, and relationships. Then, almost in a business cycle, everything for these groups changed. They ventured into new lines of business, where they had no prior knowledge or a competitive formula, and all of them failed.

7.7.2 *How some diversified groups did well/recovered?*

- **Cutting unrelated exposure**: After venturing into unrelated areas, ITC group realized its folly and cut down on its exposures in select areas such as agriculture and agricultural commodities, exited financial services sector completely, and limited its exposure in the paper industry. Obviously, issues such as diversifying have to be dealt with lot of caution.
- **Concentrating on core**: The approach we recommend diversified groups is to look for cutting down on businesses that are outside the group's core business. Punjab Tractors, MRF, and Ranbaxy

are examples of groups moving out of their other businesses to concentrate on its core business of manufacturing Tractors, Tyres, and Pharmaceuticals, respectively, and reaping dividends.

- **Seeking external markets**: Another alternative is to seek international markets and leverage the strengths in the existing businesses. Wipro, Dr. Reddy, Ramco, and Hero are some of the groups to have entered international markets and made dramatic transformations in their business fortunes.

7.8 Managerial implications

Top management of business groups in developing nations while formulating their group's corporate strategy should take into account the costs and the negative impact of product diversity and the problems arising from this in the organization. A plan with a higher degree of product diversity for the group will need to be justified in terms of the capital costs spent and management time. These business groups competing against multinationals should consider it vital that to stay in world market; they would need to have competitiveness. Presence in large number of product portfolios with no distinct economies or strategic advantage in any of them would leave these groups by the wayside in the face of global competition, whereas those with superior performance in a limited number of select lines of business would be better placed to face global competition. There is a strong case for quitting businesses that are not part of their core competencies and consolidating in a range of product lines with distinct advantage with emphasis on increasing international exposure.

However, it cannot be denied that on account of their long experience in doing business in the home markets, business groups have a unique understanding of the ground realties faced in the conduct of business in the domestic market. This does place them in a position to take advantage of opportunities thrown up in new areas, even if they are unrelated to existing businesses. In event that a business group does decide to implement a strategy of unrelated diversification, it must ensure that it has in place certain mechanisms that would enable it to benefit from the same. The success stories of diversified business groups in the 2000s and those of groups that recovered from the setbacks in the late 1990s point to the importance of having in place clear succession plans and plans for division of assets among the family. A number of groups had diversified into unrelated areas during the 1980s and 1990s to ensure that there is a clear demarcation of assets to be divided. As our study shows, this is similar to putting the cart before the horse with clarity on succession planning being an important driver of success in diversification efforts. Further, the strategy of unrelated diversification using borrowed funds has turned out to be a recipe for disaster for business groups during the 1990s. The recent financial troubles in the Indian corporate sector suggest that this strategy is as dangerous in these more developed[7] times as it was back then.

Delegation of decision-making powers to professional management is important for two reasons. First, it allows the examination of the decisions from an alternate point of view. Second and more important, as a group diversifies into areas which require a different set of competencies, the development of the same would divert a significant amount of time and resources of the promoter family to develop the same. This in turn could has an adverse impact on existing businesses that would receive less managerial attention from the family. As the case studies show, having affiliates that manage to maintain their leadership position in the industry has a positive impact on performance of the group. Hence, it becomes all the more imperative for the group to keep a close watch on the performance of its flagship businesses as the group diversifies into unrelated areas. In most of the cases where such diversification ended in significant failures for the group, management attention was diverted toward making the new businesses profitable. The lack of attention to the flagship businesses during these times made management less alert to environmental changes in these industries. This was illustrated by the case studies of BPL and the Thapar group examined in Chapter 6.

[7] We refer to 'developed' in the context of the financial system, corporate governance practices and norms, regulations, and so on.

References

Ahuja, Gautam and Sumit Majumdar. 1995. 'An Assessment of the Performance of the Indian State-owned Enterprises'. University of Michigan, School of Business Administration. Working Paper 9550-610.

Alberts, William and James McTaggart. 1979. 'The Divestiture Decision: An Introduction; Mergers and Acquisitions; Fall' 18-30.

Alberts, William and James McTaggart. 1984. 'Value Based Strategic Investment Planning; Interfaces'. 138-151.

Almeida, H. and Wolfenzon, D. 2006. 'Should Business Groups Be Dismantled? The Equilibrium Costs of Efficient Internal Capital Markets'. *Journal of Financial Economics* 79: 99–144.

Amihud, Y. and B. Lev. 1981. 'Risk Reduction as a Managerial Motive for Conglomerate Mergers; Bell'. *Journal of Economics 12(2): 605*-617.

Amsden, Alice and Takashi Hikino. 1991. 'Project Execution Capability, Organizational Know-How and Conglomerate Corporate Growth in Late Industrialization; Industrial and Corporate Change'. 111-148.

Ansoff, H. Igor. 1971. *Strategies for diversification in 'Long Range Planning for Marketing and Diversification'* by (editors) Bernard Taylor and Gordon Wills. London: Bradford University Press: 172-195.

Aoki, M. 1988. *Information, Incentives, and Bargaining in the Japanese Economy.* Cambridge, UK: Cambridge University Press.

Aoki, M. 1984. 'The Economic Analyses of The Japanese Firm', North-Holland.

Aoki, M. 1990. 'The Participatory Generation of Information Rents and the Theory of Firm; in The Firm as a Nexus of Treaties' by (editors) Aoki, M. et al. Sage: London 26-52.

Arnould, R. J. 1969. *Conglomerate Growth and Public Policy.* In L. Gordon (ed.), Economics of Conglomerate Growth; Department of Agricultural Economics. Corvallis, OR: Oregon State University.

Ashiq Ali, Ashiq, Tai-Yuan Chen and Suresh Radhakrishnan. 2007. 'Corporate Disclosures by Family Firms'. *Journal of Accounting and Economics* 44 (1–2): 238–286.

Bae, K. H. and Jeong, S. W. 2007. 'The Value-Relevance of Earnings And Book Value, Ownership Structure, and Business Group Affiliation: Evidence from Korean Business Groups'. *Journal of Business Finance and Accounting* 34 (5): 740–66.

Bagchi, Amiya Kumar, ed. 2000. *Indian Institution under the Neo-Liberal Regime.* New Delhi: Sage Publishers.

Bagozzi, R. P. and L. W. Phillips. 1982. 'Representing and Testing Organizational Theories: A Holistic Construal; Administrative Science Quarterly' 17: 59.

Balakrishnan, Pulapre. 2000. 'Agriculture and Economic Reforms: Growth and Welfare; Economic and Political Weekly' 999-1004.

Banker, Rajiv D., Hsi-Hui Chang and Sumit K. Majumdar. 1996. 'A Framework for Analyzing Changes in Strategic Performance' *Strategic Management Journal* 17: 693-712.

Banz, R. 1981. 'The Relationship between Return and the Market Value for Common Stocks.' *Journal of Financial Economics* 9(1): 1-19.

Barney, J. B. 1991. 'Firm Resources and Sustained Competitive Advantage.' *Journal of Management* 17(1): 99-120.

Barton, Sidney L. and P. J. Gordon. 1988. 'Corporate Strategy and Capital Structure.' *Strategic Management Journal* 9(6): 623-632.

Batra, Geeta. 1999. 'Job Reallocation, the Export Market, and Firm Performance: Microeconomic Evidence; World Bank Policy and Research; Business Environment Unit' 10(1): 683-626.

Beaver, William H. and S. G. Ryan. 1993. 'Accounting Fundamentals of the Book-To-Market Ratio.' *Financial Analysts Journal* 49(6): 50-56.

Beaver, William H. 1966. 'Financial Ratios as Predictors of Failure.' *Empirical Research in Accounting; Supplement in Journal of Accounting Research* 71-111.

Befumo, Randy and Liquid. 1996. How to Read a Balance Sheet.' *The Motley Fool www.fool.com.*

Berger, P. and E. Ofek. 1995. 'Diversification's Effect on Firm Value.' *Journal of Financial Economics* 37: 39-65.

Berger, Phillip and Eli Ofek. 1996. 'Bustup Takeovers of Value-Destroying Diversified Firms' *Journal of Finance* 51: 1175–1200.

Berry, Charles H. 1975. *Corporate Growth and Diversification.* Corporate Growth and Diversification. Princeton, New Jersey: Princeton University Press.

Bethel, Jennifer E. and Julia Porter Liebeskind. 1998. *Diversification and the Legal Organization of the Firm* Organization Science 9(1): 49-67.

Bettis, IL A. and W. K Hall. 1982. 'Diversification Strategy, Accounting Determined Risk, and Accounting Determined Return.' *Academy of Management Journal* 25: 254-64.

Bettis, IL A. 1981. 'Performance Differences in Related and Unrelated Diversified Firms.' *Strategic Management Journal* 2: 379-83.

Bettis, Richard A. and Vijay Mahajan. 1985. 'Risk/return Performance of Diversified Firms.' *Management Science* 31(7): 785–99.

Bianco, Magda and Nicodano, Giovanna. 2006. 'Pyramidal Groups and Debt.' *European Economic Review* 50(4): 937–61

Biggadike, R. E. 1979. *Corporate Diversification: Entry, Strategy, and Performance.* Cambridge, MA: Harvard University Press.

Bower, J. L. 1970. *Managing The Resource Allocation Process: A study of Corporate Planning and Investment.* Boston, MA: Harvard Business School Press.

Branch, Ben, and Bradley Gale. 1983. Linking Corporate Stock Price Performance to Strategy Formulation.' *Journal of Business Strategy* Boston. 4(1).

Brealey, R. and S. Myers. 1988. *Principles of Corporate Finance* New York: McGraw-Hill.

Brief, Richard P. and R. A. Lawson. 1992. 'The Role of the Accounting Rate of Return in Financial Statement Analysis.' *Accounting Review* 67(2):: 411–26.

Brush, Thomas H. and Philip Bromiley. 1997. 'What Does a Small Corporate Effect Mean? A Variance Components Simulation of Corporate and Business Effects.' *Strategic Management Journal* 18: 825–35.

Buhner, Rolf. 1987. 'Accessing International Diversification of West German corporations.' *Strategic Management Journal* 8: 25–37.

Burgelman, R. A. 1983. ;A process model of internal corporate venturing in the diversified major firm.' *Administrative Science Quarterly* 28: 223–44.

Carney, Michael, Daniel Shapiro and Yao Tang. 'Business Group Performance in China: Ownership and temporal Considerations.' *Management and Organization Review* 5(2): 167–93.

Caves, R. E., Porter, M. E., Spence, M. A. and Scott, J. T. 1980. *Competition in the open economy: A model applied to Canada.* Cambridge, MA: Harvard University Press.

Caves, R. E. 1982. *Multinational Enterprise and Economic Analysis.* Cambridge: England: Cambridge University Press.

Caves, Richard and Uekusa, M. 1976. *Industrial Organization* Japan: Brookings.

Chacar, A. and Vissa, G. 2005. 'Are Emerging Economics Less Efficient? Performance Persistence and Business Group Affiliation.' *Strategic Management Journal* 26: 933–46.

Chaganti R. and F. Damanpour. 1991. 'Institutional Ownership, Capital Structure, and Firm Performance. *Strategic Management Journal* 12: 479–91.

Chakraborty, Indrani. 2010. 'Financial Development and Economic Growth in India – An Analysis of the Post-reform Period.' *South Asia Economic Journal* 11(2): 287–308.

Chakravarthy, Balaji S. 1986. 'Measuring Strategic Performance.' *Strategic Management Journal* 7(5): 437–58.

Chakravarty, Sukhamoy. 1985. *Report of the committee to review the working of the money market;* Committee chaired by Sukhamoy Chkravarthy, Reserve Bank of India, Mumbai.

Chandler, A.D. 1962. *Strategy and Structure: Chapters in the History of the Industrial Enterprise* Cambridge, MA: MIT Press.

Chandrachud, Abhinav. 2011. 'The Emerging Market for Corporate Control in India: Assessing (and Devising) Shark Repellents for India's Regulatory Environment.' *Washington University Global Studies Law Review* 10(2).

Chang, S.-J. 2006. 'Business Groups in East Asia: Post-Crisis Restructuring and New Growth; Asia Pacific.' *Journal of Management* 23(4): 407–18.

Chang, S. J. and Hong, J. 2000. 'Economic Performance of Group-Affiliated Companies in Korea: Intragroup Resource Sharing and Internal Business Transactions.' *Academy of Management Journal* 43(3): 429–48.

Chang, Sea Jin and Unghwan Choi. 1988. 'Strategy, Structure and Performance of Korean Business Groups: A Transactions Cost Approach.' *The Journal of Industrial Economics* 37(2): 141–58.

Chang, Y. and H. Thomas. 'The Impact of Diversification Strategy on Risk-return Performance *Strategic Management Journal* 10: 271–84.

Chatterjee, S. and Blocher, J. 1992. 'The continuous measurement of firm diversification: Is it robust?' *Academy of Management Journal* 35: 874–88.

Chen, Chun-Chung, C. Nehrt and S. Guisinger. 1998. *Product, international market, and international operation diversification: relationship with firm performance in the U.S. computer peripheral industry* University of Texas; Working paper proceedings II.

Chibber, Pradeep K. and Sumit K. Majumdar. 1999. 'Foreign ownership and profitability: Property rights, control, and the performance of firms in Indian industry.' *The Journal of Law and Economics* 42(1).

Child, J. 1972. 'Organization structure, environment and performance: the role of strategic *choice.' Sociology* 6: 2–22.

Chopra, BS KS. 1985. Business Policy for Indian Industries. Pune: The Times Research Foundation 68–76.

Christensen, H. K. and C.A. 1981. 'Montgomery; Corporate economic performance: diversification strategy versus market structure.' *Strategic Management Journal* 2(4): 327–43.

Chowdhary, Bhagwan and Vikram Nanda. 1994. 'Repurchase premia as a reason for dividends: a dynamic model of corporate payout policies.' *Review of Financial Studies* 7: 321–50.

CIFAR (Center for International Financial Analysis and Research Inc.). 1995. *International Accounting and Auditing Trends* New Jersey, USA: CIFAR 1: 4(e).

Claessens, Stijn, Simeon Djankov, Joseph P.H. Fan, and Larry H.P. Lang. 1998. *Diversification and efficiency of investment by East Asian corporations.* The World Bank. Economic Policy Research Working Paper. 2033.

Claessens, Stijn, Simeon Djankov, Joseph P.H. Fan, and Larry H.P. Lang. 1999. *Corporate diversification in East Asia: The role of ultimate ownership and group affiliation* The World Bank. Policy Research Working Paper. 2089.

Coase, R. H. 1937. 'The nature of the firm.' *Economica* 4 (New Series): 386–405.

Collin, Sven-Olof. 1998. *Why is there no relationship between ownership concentration and performance?* Lund University: Department of Business Administration. Presented at International Conference on Accounting and Governance; Napoli. 23-24.

Comment, Robert, and Gregg A. 1995. 'Jarrell; Corporate focus and stock returns.' *Journal of Financial Economics* 37: 67–87.

Cote, Jane M., and C. K. Latham. 'The merchandising ratio: A comprehensive ratio of working capital management.' *Issues in Accounting Education; American Accounting Association* 14(2): 1999.

Datta, Deepak K., Nandini Rajagopalan, and Abdul M.A. Rasheed. 1991. 'Diversification and performance: critical review and future directions.' *Journal of Management Studies* 28: 529–58.

David, Parthiban, Jonathan P. O'Brien, Toru Yoshikawa, and Andrew Delios. 2010. 'Do Shareholders or Stakeholders Appropriate the Rents from Corporate Diversification? The Influence of Ownership Structure.' *Academy of Management Journal* 53(3): 636–54.

Davis, Peter S., R. B. Robinson, Jr., J. A. Pearce II, and S. H. Park. 1992. 'Business unit relatedness and performance: a look at the pulp and paper industry.' *Strategic Management Journal* 13: 349–61.

Denis, David J., Diane K. Denis, and Atulya Sarin. 1999. 'Agency problems, equity ownership, and corporate diversification.' *Journal of Finance.*

Dess, Gregory G., and Robinson, Richard B., Jr. 1984. 'Measuring organizational performance in the absence of objective measures: the case of the privately-held firm and conglomerate business unit.' *Strategic Management Journal* 5(3): 265–73.

Diamond, Douglas. 'Financial intermediation and delegated monitoring.' *Review of Economic Studies* 51: 393–414.

DiMaggio, Paul J., and Walter W. Powell. 1983. 'The iron cage revisited: Institutional isomorphism and collective rationality in organization fields.' *American Sociological Review* 48: 147-60.

Dubofsky, P. and P. R. Varadrajan. 1987. 'Diversification and measures of performance: additional empirical evidence.' *Academy of Management Journal* 30: 597–608.

Dutta, Sudit. 1997. *Family Business in India* New Delhi: Response Books Sage Publications.

Easterly, William, and Levine Ross. 1997. 'Africa's growth tragedies: Policies and ethnic divisions.' *Quarterly Journal of Economics* 107: 1203–50.

Encaqua, David and Alexis Jacquemin. 1982. 'Organizational efficiency and monopoly power.' *European Economic Review* 19: 25–51.

Encarnation, D. 1989. *Dislodging Multinationals: India's Comparative Perspective*. Ithaca, New York: Cornell University Press.

EXIM (Export Import Bank of India). 1996. Exim banks in Asia: A comparative analysis. Occasional paper no. 47. Mumbai: Export import bank of India.

Faccio, M., & Lang, L. H. P. 2002. 'The ultimate ownership of Western European corporations.' *Journal of Financial Economics* 65: 365–95.

Fama, Eugene F., and K. R. French. 1995. 'Size and book-to-market factors in earnings and returns.' *Journal of Finance* 50(1): 131–55.

Fama, Eugene F., and K. R. French. 1992. 'The cross-section of expected stock returns.' *Journal of Finance* 47: 427–65.

Fama, Eugene F., and M. Jensen. 1983. 'Separation of ownership and control.' *Journal of Law and Economics* 26: 74–98.

Farjoun, Moshe. 1998. 'The Independent and Joint Effects of the Skill and Physical Bases of Relatedness in Diversification.' *Strategic Management Journal* 19: 611–30.

Fauver, L., J. Houston, and A. Naranjo. 1998. *Capital market development, legal systems and the value of corporate diversification: a cross-country analysis.* Mimeo: University of Florida.

Fields, Karl J. 1995. Enterprise and the State in Korea and Taiwan Ithaca, New York: Cornell University Press.

Fisman, Raymond, and Tarun Khanna. 1998. *Facilitating development: The role of business groups* Harvard Business School. Working Paper.

Fisman, Raymond. 2001. 'Estimating the Value of Political Connections.' *American Economic Review* 91: 1095–102.

Foster, George. 1986. *Financial Statement Analysis* Second edition. New Jersey: Englewood Cliffs. Prentice Hall, Inc.

Fruhan, William E. Jr. 1979. *Financial Strategy: Studies in the Creation, Transfer and Destruction of Shareholder Value.* Homewood, IL: R. D. Irwin.

Gadgil, D. R. 1951. *Notes on the rise of Business Communities in India Poona:* Gokhale Institute of Politics and Economics.

Galbraith, Jay R. 1998. *Strategy and organization planning – in 'Readings in the Strategy Process* by H. Mintzberg and J. B. Quinn. 3(e) Prentice Hall International Inc. 134–42.

Galbraith, Jay and D. A. Nathanson. 1978. *Strategy Implementation: The Role of Structure and Process* New York: West Publishing Company.

Gaur, Ajai S. and Kumar, Vikas. 2008. 'International Diversification, Business Group Affiliation and Firm Performance: Empirical Evidence from India.' *British Journal of Management* 20: 172–86.

Gerlach, M. L. 1992. *Alliance capitalism: The social organization of Japanese business* Berkeley: University of California Press.

Gertner, Robert H., David S. Scharfstein, and Jeremy C. Stein. 1994. Internal versus external capital markets. *The Quarterly Journal of Economics* 1211–30.

Ghemawat, P. and Khanna, T. 1998. 'The nature of diversified business groups: A research design and two case studies.' *Journal of Industrial Economics* 46: 35–61.

Ghosal, Sumantra. 1987. 'Global strategy: An organizing framework.' *Strategic Management Journal* 8: 425–40.

Gleuck, W. F. 1980. *Business Policy and Strategic Management.* McGraw-Hill.

Gort, M. 1962. *Diversification and Integration in American Industry* Princeton, NJ: Princeton University Press.

Goto, Akira. 1982. 'Business groups in a market economy.' *European Economic Review* 19: 53–70.

Granovetter, Mark. 1994. '*Business groups*' – in Handbook of Economic Sociology; by Neil J. Smelser and Richard Swedberg, eds. Princeton, NJ: Princeton University Press.

Granovetter, Mark. 1995. 'Coase revisited: Business groups in the modern economy.' *Industrial and Corporate Change* 4: 93–130.

Granovetter, Mark. 1985. 'Economic Action and Social Structure: The Problem of Embeddedness.' *American Journal of Sociology* 91: 481–510.

Grant, Robert M., Azar P. Jammine, and Howard Thomas, 1972–84. 'Diversity, Diversification, and Profitability among British Manufacturing Companies.' *Academy of Management Journal* 31(4): 771–801.

Gribbin, J.D. 1992. 'The conglomerate merger.' *Applied Economics* 8: 19–34.

Griliches, Zvi. 1992. 'The search for R&D spillovers.' *National Bureau of Economic Research.* NBER Working Paper Series no. 3768.

Guille´n, M.F. 1987–95. 'Experience, imitation, and the sequence of foreign entry: Wholly owned and joint-venture manufacturing by South Korean firms and business groups in China.' *Journal of International Business Studies* 34(2000b) 185–98.

Guille´n, M.F. 2000. 'Business Groups in Emerging Economies: A Resource-Based View.' *Academy of Management Journal* 43(3): 362–80.

Guillen Mauro. 1997. 'Business Groups and Economic Development.' *Academy of Management Proceedings.*

Gup, Benton. 1983. *Principles of Financial Management.* New York: John Wiley & Sons.

Hall, Ernest H. Jr., St. John and H. Caron. 'A methodological note on diversity measurement.' *Strategic Management Journal* 15(2): 153–68.

Hall, Ernest H., Jr. 1995. 'Corporate Diversification and Performance: An Investigation into Causality.' Australian Journal of Management 20(1).

Hamilton, G. (ed). 1996. *Asian Business Networks.* De Gruyter Studies in Organization. New York: Walter de Gruyter.

Han, Ki C., Suk Hun Lee, and David Y. Suk. 1999. 'Ownership structure and firm performance: International evidence'. *Multinational Business* Review. Spring 92–97.

Harun R. Khan. 2013. *Indian Financial Markets: Fuelling the Growth of the Indian Economy* Address delivered by Shri. Harun R Khan, Deputy Governor, Reserve Bank of India, at the inaugural session of the conference on Indian Financial Markets:

Fuelling the Growth of the Indian Economy organized by the Confederation of Indian Industry at the ADB Annual Conference at Greater NOIDA, Delhi NCR.

Herdeck, Margaret, and Gita Piramal. 1985. Indias' Industrialists, 1. Washington DC: Three Continents Press.

Hill, C. W. L. and R. E. Hoskisson. 1987. 'Strategy and structure in the multiproduct firm.' *Academy of Management Review* 2: 331–41.

Hill, Charles W. L. 1985. 'Diversified growth and competition: The experience of twelve large UK firms.' *Applied Economics* 17: 827–47.

Hirschman, A. O. 1945. *National Power and the Structure of Foreign Trade.* Berkeley: University of California Press.

Hirschman, A. O. 1964. 'The paternity of an index.' *American Economic Review* 54: 761.

Hitt, Michael A., and R. Duane Ireland. 1986. 'Relationships among corporate level distinctive competencies, diversification strategy, corporate structure and performance.' *Journal of Management Studies* 23(4): 401–16.

Holderness, Clifford G., and Dennis P. Sheehan. 1991. 'Monitoring an owner.' *Journal of Financial Economics* 30: 325–46.

Holmstrom, B.; Moral hazard and observability; Bell Journal of Economics; Volume 10; 1979; p. 74-91.

Holzmann, Oscar J., Ronald M. Copeland, and Jack Hayya. 1975. 'Income measures of conglomerate performance.' *Quarterly Review of Economics and Business* 15(3): 67–78.

Hoshi,Takeo, Anil Kashyap, and David Scharfstein. 1991. 'Corporate Structure, Liquidity and Investment: Evidence from Japanese Industrial Groups.' *The Quarterly Journal of Economics* 106(1): 33–60.

Hoskisson, Robert E. and Michael A. Hitt. 1990. 'Antecedents and performance outcomes of diversification: A review and critique of theoretical perspectives.' *Journal of Management* 16: 461–509.

Hoskisson, Robert E., and Michael A. Hitt. 1994. *Downscoping: How to tame the diversified firm.* New York: Oxford University Press.

Hoskisson, Robert E., C. W. L. Hill, and H. Kim. 1993. 'The multidivisional structure: organizational fossil or source of value?' *Journal of Management* 19: 269–98.

Ito, Takatoshi. 1992. *The Japanese Economy.* Cambridge: The MIT Press.

Jacquemin, A. P., and C. H. Berry.1979. 'Entropy measure of diversification and corporate growth.' *Journal of Industrial Economics* 27: 359–69.

Jahera, John S. Jr., William P. Lloyd, and Daniel E. 1987. 'Page; The relationship between financial performance and stock market based measures of corporate diversification.' *The Financial Review* 22(4): 379–89.

Jeannet, Jean-Pierre, Sean Meehan, Bill Currie, and Frank Kolhatkar. 2000. 'Growth strategies for globalizing financial services companies.' *A study by Deloitte Touche Tohmatsu and IMD – International Institute for Management Development.*

Jensen M. and W. Meckling. 1976. 'Theory of the firm: managerial behavior, agency costs, and ownership structure.' *Journal of Financial Economics* 3(4): 305–60.

Jensen, B. and R. H. McGuckin. 1997. 'Firm performance and evolution: Empirical regularities in the US micro-data.' *Industrial and Corporate Change* 6: 25–47.

Jetley, Gaurav, and Mondal, Shamim S. 2013. 'Rights Issues and Creeping Acquisitions in India (on July 6, 2012).' *Midwest Finance Association* Annual Meeting Paper, available at SSRN: http://ssrn.com/abstract=2142841.

Johnson, James M., David R. Campbell, and James L. Wittenbach. 1982. 'Identifying and resolving problems in corporate liquidity.' *Financial Executive* 41–46.

Johnson, James M., David R. Campbell, and James L. Wittenbach. 1980. 'Problems in corporate liquidity.' *Financial Executive* 44–53.

Jones, Leroy P., and I. Sakong. 1980. *Government Business and Entrepreneurship in Economic Development: The Korean Case.* Cambridge: Council of East Asian Studies.

Joshi, Divyang J. 2012. 'Testing Market Efficiency of Indian Stock Market.' *International Journal of Scientific and Research Publications* 2(6).

Joshi, Vijay, and Little I.M.D. 1997. *Indias' Economic Reforms: 1991-2001.* New Delhi: Oxford University Press.

Journal of Finance 51: 1175–200.

Kahloul, Ines, and Slaheddine Hallara. 2010. 'The Impact of Diversification on Firm Performance and Risk: An Empirical Evidence.' *International Research Journal of Finance and Economics*(35): 150–62.

Kakani, Ram Kumar, and V. N. Reddy. 1996. 'Econometric analysis of the capital structure determinants.' 23: 73–98.

Kakani, Ram Kumar, B. Saha, and V. N. Reddy. 2001. 'Corporate performance of Indian firms.' NSE Research Initiative Paper 18. Mumbai: National Stock Exchange.

Kakani, Ram Kumar. 2000. 'Financial performance and diversification strategy of Indian business groups.' Working Paper 411. Calcutta: Indian Institute of Management.

Kali, R. and Sarkar, J. 2005–06. 'Diversification, propping and monitoring: Business groups, firm performance and the Indian economic transition.' Working Papers. Mumbai, India: Indira Gandhi Institute of Development Research.

Kang, David L., and Aage B. Sørensen. 1999. 'Ownership organization and Firm Performance.' *Annual Review of Sociology* 25: 121–44.

Karanjia, B. K. 1997. *Godrej: A Hundred Years, 1897-1997.* New Delhi: Penguin Books.

Katz, Jeffrey P., and Brian P. Niehoff. 1998. 'How Owners Influence Strategy – A Comparison of Owner-Controlled And Manager-Controlled Firms.' *Long Range Planning* 31(5): 755–61.

Keats, Barbara W. 1990. 'Diversification and Business Economic Performance Revisited: Issues of Measurement and Causality.' *Journal of Management* 16(1): 61–72.

Kedia, Ben L, Debmalya Mukherjee, and Somnath Lahiri. 2006. 'Indian business groups: Evolution and transformation.' *Asia Pacific Journal of Manage* 23: 559–77

Keister, Lisa A. 1998. 'Engineering Growth: Business Group Structure and Firm Performance in China's Transition Economy.' *American Journal of Sociology* 104(2): 404-40.

Kelkar, Vijay, and V.V.N. Bhanoji Rao. 1996. *India: Development Policy Imperatives* New Delhi: Tata McGraw Hill Publishing Company.

Kester, W. C. 1991. *Japanese takeovers: The global contest for corporate control.* Boston: Harvard Business School Press.

Khanna, T. and Palepu, K 2004. 'Globalization and Convergence in Corporate Governance: Evidence from Infosys and the Indian Software Industry.' *Journal of International Business Studies* 35(6): 484–507.

Khanna, T. and Palepu, K. 2005. *The evolution of concentrated ownership in India: Broad patterns and a history of the Indian software Industry* National Bureau of Economic Research working paper series. 2004a; July 16, 2005. retrieved from http://www.nber.org/papers/w10613.

Khanna, Tarun and Krishna Palepu. 1998. *The future of business groups in emerging markets: Long run evidence from Chile* Harvard Business School. Working Paper 99-077 [forthcoming, Academy of Management Journal, 2000].

Khanna, Tarun, and Krishna Palepu. 1998. *Emerging market, business groups, foreign investors, and corporate governance; forthcoming NBER Volume on Concentrated Ownership.* University of Chicago Press [formerly Harvard Business School. Working Paper 99-017].

Khanna, Tarun, and Krishna Palepu. 2000. 'Is group affiliation profitable in emerging markets? An analysis of diversified Indian business groups.' *Journal of Finance* 867-91 [formerly, Harvard Business School Working Paper 96-051].

Khanna, Tarun, and Krishna Palepu. 1999. 'Policy shocks, market intermediaries, and corporate strategy: Evidence from Chile and India.' *Journal of Economics and Management Strategy* 8(2).

Khanna, Tarun, and Krishna Palepu. 1997. 'Why focused strategies may be wrong for emerging markets.' *Harvard Business Review*41-51.

Khanna, Tarun, and Jan W. Rivkin. 1999. 'Estimating the performance effects of networks in emerging markets.' *Academy of Management Best Paper Proceedings* [formerly, Harvard Business School Working Paper # 99-108].

Kilantaridis, Christos, and Areti Levanti. 2000. *Internationalization and the size of the firm.* UK: University of Lutton. www.sbaer.uca.edu/DOCS/2000asbe/00asbe076.htm.

Kim, H., Hoskisson, R. E., and Wan, W. P. 2004. 'Power dependence, diversification strategy, and performance in keiretsu member firms.' *Strategic Management Journal*613–636.

Kiymaz, Halil. 1999. *Long run performance of IPOs: Case of Istanbul stock exchange.* University of Houston-Clear Lake and Bilkent University. Working paper proceedings 3.

Kroszner, Randall S.; 2000. 'Stock ownership by officers and directors of publicly traded firms.' *Capital Ideas* 2(3).

La Porta, Rafael, F. Lopez-de-Silanes, A. Shleifer, and R. Vishny. 1997. 'Legal determinants of external finance.' *Journal of Finance* 52: 1131–150.

La Porta, Rafael, F. Lopez-de-Silanes, A. Shleifer, and R. Vishny. 1998. 'Law and finance.' *Journal of Political Economy* 106(6): 1113–155.

La Porta, Rafael, F. Lopez-de-Silanes, A. Shleifer, and R. Vishny. 1999. 'Corporate ownership around the world.' *Journal of Finance* 54(2): 471–517.

Lamberson, Morris. 1993. *The Response of the Working Capital Position of Smaller Firms to Changes in the Business Cycle.* University Of Central Arkansas. Working paper proceedings.

Lamont, Owen and Christopher Polk. 1999. 'The Diversification Discount: Cash Flows Vs Returns.' *National Bureau of Economic Research.* NBER Working Paper: W7396.

Lang, Larry and Rene Stulz. 1994. 'Tobin's Q, corporate diversification and firm performance.' *Journal of Political Economy* 1248–280.

Langlois, Richard N. 2009. *Economic Institutions and the Boundaries of the Firm: The Case of Business Groups* Department of Economics Working Paper Series. Working Paper 2009-23. University of Connecticut.

Lecraw, Donald J. and Allen H. Morrison. *Transnational Corporations and Business Strategy.* London: Routledge.

Lecraw, Donald J. 1984. 'Diversification Strategy and Performance.' *Journal of Industrial Economics* 33: 179–198.

Lee, K. and Xuehua Jin. 2009. 'The origins of business groups in China: An empirical testing of the three paths and the three theories.' *Business History* 51(1): 77–99.

Lee, K., Peng, M. W., and Lee, K. 2008. 'From Diversification Premium to Diversification Discount during Institutional Transitions.' *Journal of World Business* 43: 47–65.

Leff, Nathaniel H. 1978. 'Industrial organization and entrepreneurship in the developing countries: the economic groups.' 661–75.

Leff, Nathaniel. 1976. 'Capital Markets in the Less Developed Countries – In "Money and Finance in Economic Growth and Development"' by Mckinnon, Ronald (ed.). New York: Marcel Dekker.

Lemelin, Andre. 1982. 'Relatedness in the patterns of inter-industry diversification.' *Review of Economics and Statistics* 64: 646–57.

Lev, Baruch. 1974. *Financial Statement Analysis: A New Approach.* New Jersey: Prentice-Hall; 1974.

Levy, David T., and L. J. Haber. 1986. 'An Advantage of the Multiproduct Firm: The Transferability of Firm-Specific Capital.' *Journal of Economic Behavior & Organization* 7(3): 291–302.

Levy, David T. 1989. 'Predation, firm-specific assets and diversification.' *Journal of Industrial Economics* 38: 227–233.

Lewellen, Wilbur G., and S. G. Badrinath. 1997. 'On the measurement of Tobin's Q.' *Journal of Financial Economics* 44: 77–122.

Lewellen, Wilbur G. 1971 'A Pure Financial Rationale for the Conglomerate Merger.' *Journal of Finance* 26: 527–37.

Li, David D., and Shan Li. 1996 'A Theory of Corporate Scope and Financial Structure.' *Journal of Finance* 51(2): 691–706.

Lincoln, J., Gerlach, M., and Ahmadjian, C. 1996 'Keiretsu Networks and Corporate Performance in Japan.' *American Sociological Review* 61: 67–88.

Lindenberg, E. B. and S. A. Ross. 1981. 'Tobin's Q Ratio and Industrial Organization.' *Journal of Business* 54: 1–32.

Lins, Karl and H. Servaes. 1999. 'International Evidence on the Value of Corporate Diversification.' Journal of Finance 54: 2215–240.

Lins, Karl and H. Servaes. 1998. *Is Corporate Diversification Beneficial in Emerging Markets?* Working Paper. University of North Carolina.

Lins, Karl and Henri Servaes. 1999. 'International Evidence on the Value of Corporate Diversification.' *Journal of Finance* 54: 2215–39.

Lins, Karl and Henri Servaes. 1999. 'International Evidence on the Value of Corporate Diversification.' *Journal of Finance 54: 2215–39.*

Liu, G. and Pei, S. 2005. 'The Class of Shareholdings and its Impacts on Corporate Performance: A Case of State Shareholding Composition in Chinese Public Corporations.' *Corporate Governance* 13(1): 46–59.

Lloyd, William P., and John S. Jr. Jahera. 1994. 'Firm-diversification effects on performance as measured by Tobin's Q.' *Managerial & Decision Economics* 15(3): 259–66.

Lumpkin, G. T. and Gregory G. Dess. 1999. 'Linking Two Dimensions of Entrepreneurial Orientation to Firm Performance: The Moderating Role of Environment, Firm Age, and Industry Life Cycle.' *Journal of Business Venturing (forthcoming).*

Ma, X., & Lu, J. 2005. 'The Critical Role of Business Groups in China.' *Ivey Business Journal* 69(5): 1–12.

Mahajan, Vijay, and Y. Wind. 1988. 'Business synergy does not always pay off.' *Long Range Planning* 21(1): 59–65.

Majluf, Nicolas, Nureya Abarca, Dario Rodriguez, and Luis A. Fuentes. 1998. 'Governance and Ownership Structure in Chilean Economic Groups.' *Revista ABANTE* 1 111–39.

Manuj, Hemant Kumar. 1994. *An Analysis of Statistical Properties of Financial Ratios.* Unpublished Doctoral Dissertation. Calcutta: Indian Institute of Management.

Markides, Constantinos C., and P. J. Williamson. 1996. 'Corporate diversification and organizational structure: a resource-based view.' *Academy of Management Journal* 39(2): 340–67.

Martin, John D., William J. Petty, and David F. Scott Jr. 1991. *Basic Financial Management.* New Jersey: Prentice Hall Inc. 873–907.

Martin, R. Douglas. 1998. 'Trellis Displays for Deep Understanding of Financial Data.' *Financial Engineering* 2(1).

Mathur, Shiv S., and Alfred Kenyon. 1998. *Creating Value: Shaping Tomorrow's Business.* Oxford: Butterworth Heinemann.

McGahan, Anita M., and M. E. Porter. 1997. 'How Much Does Industry Matter, Really?' *Strategic Management Journal* 18 (summer special issue): 15–30.

Mehla, Sunita, and S. K. Goyal. 2012. 'Empirical Evidence on Weak Form of Efficiency in Indian Stock Market.' *Asia-Pacific Journal of Management Research and Innovation* 8(1): 59–68.

Mendes-Da-Silva, Wesley, and Black, Ervin L. 'Is There an Association Between Corporate Governance and Firm Diversification?' An Empirical Study with Brazilian Companies. Available at SSRN: http://ssrn.com/abstract=623182.

Michael, A. and I. Shaked. 1984. 'Does business diversification affect performance?' *Financial Management* 13 (winter): 18–25.

Milgrom, Paul, and John Roberts. 1992. *Economics, Organization and Management.* New Jersey: Prentice-Hall Inc.

Mintzberg, H. and J. B. Quinn (eds.). 1998. *Readings in the Strategy Process* 3(e) Prentice Hall International Inc.

Mintzberg, Henry. *The diversified organization and the generic corporate strategies – in 'Readings in the Strategy Process'* by (eds.) H. Mintzberg and J. B. Quinn. 3(e). Prentice Hall Intl. Inc. 335–51.

Mohan, Rakesh . 2007. *Development of Financial Markets in India –Reserve Bank of India Monthly Bulletin.*

Mohan, Rakesh. Recent Financial Market Developments and Implications for Monetary Policy.

Montgomery, C. A. 1985. 'Product market diversification and market power.' *Academy of Management Journal* 28(4): 789–98.

Montgomery, Cynthia A., and B. Wernerfelt. 1988. 'Diversification, Ricardian rents, and Tobin's Q.' *Rand Journal of Economics* 19: 623–32.

Montgomery, Cynthia A., and H. Singh. 1984. 'Diversification strategy and systematic risk.' *Strategic Management Journal* 5(2): 181–91.

Montgomery, Cynthia A. 1982. 'The measurement of firm diversification: some new empirical evidence.' *Academy of Management Journal* 25(2): 299–307.

Mookherjee, D. (ed.). 1995. *Indian Industry Policies and Performance.* Delhi: Oxford University Press. Myers, Stewart; Financial theory and financial strategy. Interfaces. 126–37.

Morck, R, A. Shleifer, and W. Vishny. 1988. 'Management ownership and market valuation: an empirical analysis.' *Journal of Financial Economics* 20: 293-315.

Morck, R.,Wolfenzon, D., and Yeung, B. 2005. 'Corporate Governance, Economic, Entrenchment, and Growth.' *Journal of Economic Literature* 43: 655–720.

Mudambi, Ram, A. Khurshed; and M. Goergen. 1999. *The effect of multi-nationality on the performance of initial public offerings.* Manchester School of Management. EIBA Paper.

Nathanson, D. A. and J. S. Cassano. 1982. *'Organization, Diversity and Performance.' The Wharton Magazine* 6(4): 19-26.

Nayyar, P. R. 1992. 'On the measurement of corporate diversification strategy: evidence from large U.S. service firms.' *Strategic Management Journal* 13: 219-35.

Nicodano, Giovanna. 1998. 'Corporate groups, dual-class shares and the value of voting rights.' *Journal of Banking & Finance 22: 1117*-137.

Noble, G. W. 1998. *Collective Action In East Asia: How Ruling Parties Shape Industrial Policy*. Ithaca: Cornell University Press.

North, D. C. 1994. *Institutions, Institutional Change and Economic Performance* Cambridge: Cambridge University Press.

Orru, Marco, Garry G. Hamilton, and Mariko Suzuki. 1989. 'Patterns of inter-firm control in Japanese business.' *Organization Studies* 10(4): 549-74.

Palepu, K. 1985. 'Diversification strategy, profit performance and the entropy measure.' *Strategic Management Journal* 6(3): 239-55.

Pant, P Narayan and Vasant G. Rajadhyaksha. 1996. 'Partnership with an Asian family business – what every multinational corporation should know.' *Long Range Planning* 29(6): 812-20. Pattanayak, Manoranjan. 2009. *Business Groups, Strategic Ownership and Firm Value* (October 15, 2009); available at SSRN: http://ssrn.com/abstract=1523751.

Peasnell, Kenneth V. 1996. 'Using Accounting Data to Measure the Economic Performance of Firms.' *Journal of Accounting and Public Policy* 15: 291-303.

Peng, M. W. 2002. 'Towards an institution-based view of business strategy.' *Asia Pacific Journal of Management* 19(2-3): 251-67

Peng, M. 2003. 'Institutional Transitions and Strategic Choices.' *Academy of Management Review* 28(2): 275–85. Perotti, E. and Gelfer, S. 'Red barons or robber barons? Governance and investment in Russian financial-industrial groups.' *European Economic Review* 45: 1601-617.

Perry, Susan Ross.. 1998. *A meta-analytical review of the diversification-performance relationship findings in strategic management.* Doctoral Dissertation. Florida Atlantic University.

Peters, Thomas J. and Robert H. Waterman. 1982. *In Search of Excellence. New York:* Harper and Row.

Petitt, P. B., Ramaswamy, K., and Li, M.. 2005. 'A temporal study of diversification, group affiliation and performance among Indian manufacturers.' *Academy of Management Proceedings* E1–E6.

Pinches, George. . 1990. *Essentials of Financial Management*. New .York: Harper & Row Publishers.

Piramal, Gita and Margaret Herdeck. 1985. *India's Industrialists*. Washington, DC: Three Continent Press Inc.

Piramal, Gita. 1997. *Business Legends*. Mumbai: Viking Press.

Piramal, Gita. . 1996. *Business Maharajas*. Mumbai: Viking Press.

Pitts, R A. and H. D. Hopkins. 1982. 'Firm diversity: conceptualization and measurement.' *Academy of Management Review* 7: 620–29.

Pitts, R. A. 1974. 'Incentive compensation and organizational design.' *Personnel Journal* 53: 338–44.

Porter, M. A. 1980. *Competitive Strategy: Techniques for Analyzing Industries and Competitors*. New York: Free Press.

Porter, M. E. 1986. *Competition in global industries: A conceptual framework*. in M. E. Porter (ed.), Competition in global industries. *15*–60. Boston: Harvard Business School Press.

Porter, M. E. 1985. *Competitive Advantage: Creating and Sustaining Superior Performance*. New York: Free Press.

Porter, Michael E. 1987. 'From competitive advantage to corporate strategy.' *Harvard Business Review*. 43-59.

Poshakwale, Sunil. 1996. 'Finance India.' *Evidence on Weak Form Efficiency and Day of the Week Effect in the Indian Stock Market* 10 (3): 605–16.

Prahalad, C. K. and Richard A. Bettis. 1986. 'The dominant logic: a new linkage between diversity and performance.' *Strategic Management Journal* 7(6): 485–501.

Prasad, Dev, G.D. Bruton, and A. Merikas. 1997. 'Long-run strategic capital structure.' *Journal of Financial and Strategic Decisions* 10(1).

Puliani, Ravi and Mahesh Puliani. 2000. *Bharat's Income Tax Act*. New Delhi: Bharat Law House.

Quinn, James Brian and John Voyer. 1994. *The Strategy Process*. Prentice Hall.

Raja Kali and Jayati Sarkar. 2011. 'Diversification and tunneling: Evidence from Indian business groups.' *Journal of Comparative Economics* 39 (3): 349–367.

Rajan, Raghuram G. and Luigi Zingales. 1998. *'Financial dependence and growth.'* The American Economic Review 88(3): 559–86.

Rajan, Raghuram, Henri Servaes, and Luigi Zingales. 2000. 'The Cost of Diversity: The Diversification Discount and Inefficient Investment.' *Journal of Finance* 55: 35–80.

Rajeshwer, Ch. 2000. *Foreign institutional investors: A new force of support and discipline; Analyst*. Hyderabad: ICFAI.

Raju, M. T. and L. S. Deepthi. 2004. *Market for Corporate Control and Takeover Regulations: Trends and Analysis*. SEBI Working Paper no. 10.

Ramanujam, Vasudevan and P. Vardarajan. 1989. 'Research on Corporate Diversification: A Synthesis.' *Strategic Management Journal* 10: 523–51.

Ramu, Shiva S. 1998. *Corporate Growth through Mergers and Acquisitions.* New Delhi: Response Books.

Rappaport, Alfred. 1986. *Creating Shareholder Value.* New York: Free Press.

Ravenscraft, D. and F. Scherer. 1987. *Mergers, sell-offs, and economic efficiency.* Working Paper; The Brookings Institution.

Reed, Richard, and George A. Luffman. 1986. 'Diversification: The Growing Confusion.' *Strategic Management Journal* 7: 29–35.

Rees, B. 1990. *Financial Analysis.* Prentice Hall.

Rees, William. 1998. 'International Diversification and Firm Value.' *European Financial Management Association.*

Renneboog, L. 2000. *Prediction of Control Concentration in German and UK Initial Public Offerings.* Document 2010. Working Paper Series 2000. Manchester School of Management.

Rhoades, Stephen A. '1974. A Further Evaluation of the Effect of Diversification on Industry Profit Performance.' *Review of Economics and Statistics* 56: 557–90.

Riahi-Belkaoui, Ahmed. *Diversification Strategy as a Determinant of the Earnings Persistence of U.S. Multinational Firms* available at SSRN: http://ssrn.com/abstract=451323 or doi:10.2139/ssrn.451323.

Richter, Frank Jurgen. 1999. *Business Networks in Asia: Promises, Doubts and Perspectives.* Greenwich, CT: Quorum Books.

Risseeuw, Peter. 1997. *Estimating Determinants of Financial Performance of Small Service Firms.* Economic & Social Institute. Amsterdam: Vrije Universiteit.

Ronald C. Andersona, Augustine Durua, and David M. Reeb. 2009. 'Founders, Heirs, and Corporate Opacity in the United States.' *Journal of Financial Economics* 92 (2): 205–22.

Ronald W. Masulis, Peter Kien Pham, and Jason Zein. 2009. *Family Business Groups Around the World: Costs and Benefits of Pyramids.* ECGI Working Paper Series in Finance.

Rose, N. L. and Shepard, A. 1997. 'Firm diversification and CEO compensation: Managerial ability or executive entrenchment?' *Rand Journal of Economics* 28:489–514.

Ross, Stephen A., R. W. Westerfield, and B. D. Jordan. 1999. *Essentials of Corporate Finance.* 2(e). Irwin/McGraw-Hill.

Roth, K. 1992. 'Implementing international strategy at the business unit level: The role of managerial decision-making characteristics.' *Journal of Management* 18(4): 769–89.

Rumelt, R. P. 1982. 'Diversification strategy and profitability.' *Strategic Management Journal* 3(4): 359–69.

Rumelt, Richard P.; How Much Does Industry Matter? Strategic Management Journal; Volume 12; 1991; 167–85.

Rumelt, Richard P. 1974. *Strategy, Structure and Economic Performance Cambridge* MA: Harvard University Press.

Saha, Biswatosh, Parthasarathi Banerjee, and Ram Kumar Kakani. 2011. *Strategic Thinking: Explorations Around Conflict and Cooperation*. New Delhi: Sage Publications. 193-96.

Salter, M. and W. Weinhold. 1979. *Diversification through Acquisition: Strategies for Creating Economic Value*. New York: Free Press.

Saple, Vardhana. 2000. *Diversification, Merger and Their Effect on Firm Performance: A Study of the Indian Corporate Sector*. Unpublished Doctoral Dissertation. Mumbai: Indira Gandhi Institute of Development Research.

Scharfstein, D. S. 1998. *The Dark Side of Internal Capital Markets II: Evidence from Diversified Conglomerates*. Working Paper. MIT Sloan School of Management.

Scharfstein, David S., and Jeremy C. Stein; The Dark Side Of Internal Capital Markets: Divisional Rent-Seeking and Inefficient Investment, Journal of Finance, 2000, Volume 55, (6,Dec), 2537-64.

Scharfstein, David S., and Jeremy C. Stein; The Dark Side of Internal Capital Markets: Divisional Rent-Seeking and Inefficient Investment, Journal of Finance, 2000, Volume 55 (6, Dec), 2537-64.

Scherer, F.M. 1980. *Market Structure and Economic Performance*. Chicago III: Rand McNally and Co.

Schmalensee, Richard. 1985. 'Do Markets Differ Much?' *The American Economic Review*. 75(3): 341-51.

Schwartz, Adam. 1992. *A Nation in Waiting: Indonesia in the 1990s. Allen and Unwin:* Sydney; 1992.

Serrano, C. 1998. 'From Financial Information to Strategic Groups – A Self-Organizing Neural Network Approach.' *Journal of Forecasting* 17: 415-28.

Servaes, Henri. 1996. 'The Value of Diversification During the Conglomerate Merger Wave.' *Journal of Finance* 51: 1201-225.

Seth, A. and Thomas, H. 1994. 'Theories of the Firm: Implications for Strategy Research.' *Journal of Management Studies* 31: 165-91.

Shiller, Robert J. 1989. *Market Volatility*. Cambridge: The MIT Press.

Shin, H. and Park, Y. S. 1999. 'Financing Constraints and Internal Capital Markets: Evidence from Korean Chaebols.' *Journal of Corporate Finance* 5(2): 169–191.

Simmonds, P. G. 1990. 'The Combined Diversification Breadth and Mode Dimensions and the Performance of Large Diversified Firms.' *Strategic Management Journal* 11: 399-410.

Singh, A. and Whittington, G. 1968. *Growth, Profitability and Valuation: A Study of United Kingdom Quoted Companies*. Cambridge University Press.

Slocum, Dr. John W., Jr. 1997. 'Address, An Analysis of Structured Cumulative Argument in Research Concerning Diversification and Firm Performance.' *Strategic Management Society* Barcelona: Spain.

Smallbone, D. and P. Wyer. 1995. Export activity in SMEs. CEEDR. Working Paper Series 9.

Song, Jaeyong and Dong-Sung Cho. 1999. *Diversification Strategies and the Formation of Korean Big Business Groups (Chaebols): Resource Based and Institutional Perspectives on the Causes of Diversification* Discussion Paper no. 9. APEC Study Center. Columbia University.

Sørensen, Jesper B. and Toby E. Stuart. 1999. *Aging, Obsolescence, and Organizational Innovation* GSB Chicago: University of Chicago.

Sridev R. 1998. *Corporate governance in the 21st century: The Role of Institutional Investors* Chapter 10, in New Dimensions in Global Business. ed. Bhattacharyya B. and Gupta A. Excel Books.

Strachan, Harry. 1976. *Family and Other Business Groups in Economic Development: The Case of Nicaragua.* New York: Praeger.

Teece, David, J. 1980. 'Economics of Scope and the Scope of Enterprise.' *Journal of Economic Behavior and Organization* 1: 223–47

Teece, David, J. 1982. 'Towards an Economic Theory of the Multi-Product Firm.' *Journal of Economic Behavior and Organization.* 3: 39–63;

Tobin, James and William Brainard. 1968. 'Pitfalls in Financial Model Building.' *American Economic Review* 99-122.

Tobin, James. 1969. 'A General Equilibrium Approach to Monetary Theory.' *Journal of Money, Credit and Banking* 1: 15–29.

Tricker, R. I. 1984. *Corporate Governance: Practices, Procedures, and Powers in British Companies and Their Board of Directors.* Harts: Gower.

Utton, M. A. 1977. 'Large Firm Diversification in British Manufacturing Industry.' Economic Journal 87: 96–113. Valedictory address at IIFs inaugural Asia Regional Economic Forum on 20 September 2007.

Varadarajan, P. and V. Ramanujam. 1987. 'Diversification and performance: a reexamination using a new two-dimensional conceptualization of diversity in firms.' *Academy of Management Journal* 30(2): 380–93.

Varaiya, Nikhil, Roger A. Kerin, and David Weeks. 1987. 'The Relationship between Growth, Profitability, and Firm Value.' *Strategic Management Journal* 8: 487–97.

Varazdin, Marizana Z. S. 1999. *Neural Networks in Investment Profitability Predictions.* Doctoral Dissertation. Faculty of Information and Informatics. Croatia: University of Zagreb.

Venkatraman, N. and V. Ramanujam. 1986. 'Measurement of Business Performance in Strategy Research: A Comparison of Approaches.' *Academy of Management Review* 11(4): 801–14.

Wan, Chun-Cheong. 1998. 'International diversification, industrial diversification and firm performance of Hong Kong MNCs.' *Asia Pacific Journal of Management* Special Issue: The Asian MNC. 15(2).

Wang, H. C. and Barney, J. B. 2006. 'Employee Incentives to Make Firm-Specific Investments: Implications for Resource Based Theories of Corporate Diversification.' *Academy of Management Review*. 31: 466–76.

Weinstein, D. and Yafeh, Y. 1998 'On the Costs of A Bank-Centered Financial System: Evidence from the Changing Main Bank Relations in Japan.' *Journal of Finance* 53: 635–72

Wernerfelt, Briger and Cynthia A. Montgomery. 1988. 'Tobin's Q and the importance of focus in firm performance.' *The American Economic Review* 78(1): 246–50.

Weston, J. F. and S. K. Mansinghka. 1971. 'Tests of the efficiency performance of conglomerate firms.' *Journal of Finance* 26(4): 909–14.

Weston, J. F., K. V. Smith, and R. E. Shrieves. 1972. 'Conglomerate performance and using the capital asset pricing model.' *Review of Economics and Statistics* 54: 357–63.

Whitley, Richard D. 1990. 'Eastern Asian Enterprise Structures and the Comparative Analysis of Forms of Business Organization.' *Orgnaization Studies* 11(1): 47–74.

Williamson, Oliver E. 1975. *Markets and Hierarchies: Analysis and Antitrust Implications*. New York: Free Press.

Williamson, Oliver E. 1991. 'Strategizing, Economizing and Economic Organization.' *Strategic Management Journal* 12: 75–94.

Williamson, Oliver E. 1985. *The Economic Institutions of Capitalism: Firms, Markets, Relational Contracting* New York: Free Press.

World Bank. 2000. *India: Reducing Poverty, Accelerating Development*. New Delhi: Oxford University Press.

Wrigley, L. 1970. *Divisional Autonomy and Diversification*. Doctoral Dissertation. Boston: Harvard Business School.

Yiu, D., Lu, Y., Bruton, G.D., and Hoskisson, R. 2007. 'Business Groups: An Integrated Model to Focus Future Research.' *Journal of Management Studies* 44(8)1551–79.

Yoshiro Miwa and J. Mark Ramseyer. 2002. 'The Fable of the Kieretsu.' *Journal of Economics and Management Strategy* 11 (2): 169–224.

Young, M., Peng, M., Ahlstrom, D., and Bruton, G. 2003. 'Principal-Principal Agency.' *Web Journal of Chinese Management Review* 617–44.

Index

About the Authors

Ram Kumar Kakani is professor at the Institute for Financial Management and Research (IFMR), Satyavedu, Andhra Pradesh. He is a former professor of Lal Bahadur Shastri National Academy of Administration (LBSNAA), Mussoorie, Uttarakhand and the Xavier School of Management (XLRI), Jamshedpur. Kakani has published widely in the areas of finance and strategic management.

Santosh Sangem is assistant professor of Finance at the Xavier School of Management (XLRI), Jamshedpur. He is also a fellow of the Indian Institute of Management, Calcutta. His research interests lie in the areas of trends in banking, financial analysis, monetary economics and management control.

Madhvi Sethi is associate professor at SIBM, Symbiosis University, Bengaluru. She holds a doctorate from Vikram University, Ujjain and further continued her post-doctoral research on 'Product Market and Capital Structure Interaction: Evidence from Spectrum Auctions' at the Indian School of Business, Hyderabad. Her research interests lie in the areas of corporate finance and securities analysis.